INGLÉS
IDIOMÁTICO
2

INGLÉS
IDIOMÁTICO
2

Eugene E. Long • William Buckwald

EDITORIAL TRILLAS

México, Argentina, España,
Colombia, Puerto Rico, Venezuela
®

Catalogación en la fuente

Long, Eugene E.
    Inglés idiomático 2. -- 10a ed. -- México : Trillas, 1990
(reimp. 2008).
    293 p. ; 21 cm.
    ISBN 978-968-24-4001-4

    1. Inglés - Estudio y enseñanza - Estudiantes
extranjeros. I. Buckwald, William. II. t.

D- 421'L245i   LC- PE1129.58'L6.5   51

División Administrativa
Av. Río Churubusco 385
Col. Pedro María Anaya, C. P. 03340
México, D. F.
Tel. 56884233, FAX 56041364

División Comercial
Calzada de la Viga 1132
C. P. 09439, México, D. F.
Tel. 56330995, FAX 56330870

www.trillas.com.mx

Miembro de la Cámara Nacional de
la Industria Editorial
Reg. núm. 158

Segunda edición MT
(Primera publicada por
Editorial Trillas, S. A. de C. V.)
Tercera edición ML
☥ (MA)
Cuarta edición MM
☥ (ME, MX, MO)
Quinta edición ES
Sexta edición ET
Séptima edición ER
☥ (4-9-EI, EL, EA, EM, 3-9-EE, EX)
Octava edición EO (ISBN 968-24-0733-8)
☥ (XS, XT, 4-10-XR, XL, XA, XM, XE, XX)
Novena edición XO (ISBN 968-24-3176-X)
Décima edición OS (ISBN 978-968-24-4001-4)
☥ (OT, OR, OL, OA, OM, OE, OX, OO, SS, ST,
SR, SI, SL, 3-10-SA, SM)

Reimpresión, 2008

Impreso en México
Printed in Mexico

Índice de contenido

Lección 1

Vocabulary

1. **to fly, flew** volar, voló
2. **to believe, believed** creer, creyó
3. **to correct, corrected** corregir, corrigió
4. **to sing, sang** cantar, cantó
5. **to catch, caught** atrapar, atrapó; coger, cogió
6. **since** desde que; puesto que, ya que
7. **just** solamente
8. **like** como
9. **right** correcto; cierto; derecho
10. **left** izquierdo
11. **polite** cortés
12. **pretty** bonito, lindo
13. **wide** ancho, amplio
14. **thick** espeso; grueso
15. **thin** delgado
16. **bird** pájaro
17. **cheese** queso
18. **voice** voz
19. **piece** pedazo
    a piece of candy un dulce
20. **wing** ala
21. **breast** pecho; seno
22. **feather** pluma
23. **ground** tierra, suelo
24. **horse** caballo
25. **one week** ocho días
    two weeks quince días
    three weeks veinte días

IDIOMS

1. **to steal, stole** robar, robó
   to rob, robbed robar, robó

9

(**to steal** indica que se ha llevado el objeto, mientras **to rob** implica nada más que algo se ha llevado, sin mencionar el objeto.)
He stole my book. El me robó el libro.
(*Se llevó el libro.*)
He robbed a bank. Robó un banco.
(*Se llevó el dinero, no el banco.*)

2. **to arrive in** llegar a (*país o ciudad*)
He arrived in Mexico, New York. Él llegó a México, Nueva York.
to arrive at llegar a (*cualquier lugar menos país o ciudad*)
He arrived at school, at the office. Él llegó a la escuela, a la oficina.

3. **to get married, got married** casarse, se casó
He got married. Él se casó.

4. **to marry, married** casarse con, se casó con
He married my cousin. Él se casó con mi prima.
(Se emplea **to get married** cuando no se indica con quién se casa y **to marry** cuando se indica con quién.)

5. **to be married (to)** estar casado (con)
He's married (to my sister). El está casado (con mi hermana).

6. **to rain, rained** llover, llovió
It rains. Llueve.
It rained. Llovió.
It's raining. Está lloviendo.

7. **to snow, snowed** nevar, nevó
It snows. Nieva.
It snowed. Nevó.
It's snowing. Está nevando.

8. **to be born** nacer
Where were you born? ¿Dónde nació?

9. **I'm sure.** Estoy seguro.
I was sure. Estaba seguro.
Be sure to bring it. No se te olvide traerlo.

10. **I don't believe it.** No lo creo.

11. **How long ago did you study English?**
¿Cuánto tiempo hace que estudiaste inglés?
I studied English a year ago.
Estudié inglés hace un año.
How long ago did you see him?
¿Cuánto tiempo hace que Ud. lo vio?
I saw him a little while (a short time) ago.
Lo vi hace un rato (poco tiempo).
I saw him a long time ago.
Lo vi hace mucho tiempo.

10

(**Ago** indica una acción que terminó en el pasado, y por tanto se emplea con un verbo en el pasado.)

12. **to the right** a la derecha
   to the left a la izquierda

EXERCISE I

Verb Practice

1. Hurry up.
2. Don't hurry.
3. Let's hurry.
4. Let him try.
5. Don't let him try.
6. You try, don't you?
7. You don't try, do you?
8. You're trying, aren't you?
9. You aren't trying, are you?
10. John broke the glass, didn't he?
11. John didn't break the glass, did he?
12. John is going to break the glass, isn't he?
13. John isn't going to break the glass, is he?
14. What are you killing that animal for?
15. What were you killing that animal for?
16. What was Mr. Clay killing that animal with?
17. What did Mr. Clay kill that animal for?
18. What did Mr. Clay kill that animal with?
19. What did you do that for?
20. What did you do it with?

THE FUTURE TENSE
EL TIEMPO FUTURO

Se forma el tiempo futuro (**future**) con el auxiliar **will**, seguido del infinitivo sin la partícula **to**. El auxiliar **will** corresponde a las terminaciones **é, ás, á, emos, án.**

Se forma la contracción en afirmativo juntando el pronombre y el auxiliar **will.**

Afirmativo sin contracción

   I will work   trabajaré

11

you will work	trabajarás
he will work	él trabajará
she will work	ella trabajará
it will work	trabajará
we will work	trabajaremos
you will work	Uds. trabajarán
they will work	ellos trabajarán

Afirmativo con contracción

I'll work	trabajaré
you'll work	trabajarás
he'll work	él trabajará
she'll work	ella trabajará
it'll work	trabajará
we'll work	trabajaremos
you'll work	Uds. trabajarán
they'll work	ellos trabajarán

La contracción negativa de **will not** es **won't**. Estudie las siguientes formas.

Negativo

I won't work	no trabajaré
you won't work	no trabajarás
he won't work	él no trabajará
she won't work	ella no trabajará
it won't work	no trabajará
we won't work	no trabajaremos
you won't work	Uds. no trabajarán
they won't work	ellos no trabajarán

Interrogativo

Recuerde el orden de las palabras para el interrogativo: auxiliar, sustantivo o pronombre, verbo.

will I work?	¿trabajaré?
will you work?	¿trabajarás?
will he work?	¿trabajará él?

12

will she work?	¿trabajará ella?
will it work?	¿trabajará?
will we work?	¿trabajaremos?
will you work?	¿trabajarán Uds.?
will they work?	¿trabajarán ellos?

Interrogativo Negativo

won't I work?	¿no trabajaré?
won't you work?	¿no trabajarás?
won't he work?	¿no trabajará él?
won't she work?	¿no trabajará ella?
won't it work?	¿no trabajará?
won't we work?	¿no trabajaremos?
won't you work?	¿no trabajarán Uds.?
won't they work?	¿no trabajarán ellos?

Este tiempo se tiene que emplear en inglés cuando en español se emplea el presente para expresar una idea que va a desarrollarse en el futuro inmediato.

Ejemplos:

Will you come tomorrow?
¿Vienes mañana?

Good-bye. I'll see you on Monday.
Adiós. Lo veo el lunes.

El auxiliar **shall** se usa en la forma interrogativa en la primera persona del singular (**I**) y en la primera persona del plural (**we**) para proponer o sugerir una acción futura, y se traduce con el presente en español. No se puede usar **shall** en la forma negativa. Las preguntas con **shall** se contestan en la forma imperativa.

Ejemplos:

Shall I bring all the books?
¿Traigo todos los libros?

| Yes, bring them. | No, don't bring them |
| Sí, tráelos. | No, no los traigas. |

Shall we go to the movies?
¿Vamos al cine?

Yes, let's go to the movies.   Yes, go to the movies.
Sí, vamos al cine.   Sí, vayan al cine.

No, let's not go to the movies.   No, don't go.
No, no vayamos al cine.   No, no vayan.

El auxiliar **will**, no **shall**, debe usarse en la forma interrogativa en la primera persona del singular y del plural cuando se pide mera información de una acción futura.

Ejemplos:

Will I have to work tomorrow?
¿Tendré que trabajar mañana?

Will we be late if we don't take a taxi?
¿Llegaremos tarde si no tomamos un coche?

TO THE TEACHER

The exercises in each lesson marked **Verb Practice** are to be used as a verb conjugation study. Each exercise of this type will consist of a group of short sentences that will serve as a model for all the verb tenses and constructions with which the students have become familiar.

The sentences should be 1) translated into Spanish so that the student will know exactly what he is repeating in English; 2) read in English one at a time by the teacher with emphasis placed on pronunciation and repeated in chorus by the students; 3) read in chorus by the students until they have mastered the verb tenses, construction, and word order.

EXERCISE 2

Verb Practice *Practice using the contractions in the affirmative.*

1. He'll eat at Sanborns tomorrow.
2. He won't eat at Sanborns tomorrow.
3. Will he eat at Sanborns tomorrow?
4. Won't he eat at Sanborns tomorrow?
5. What time will he eat at Sanborns tomorrow?

14

EXERCISE 3

Verb practice *Repeat exercise 2, using forms of the verbs* **take, bring, fill, change, break, steal, buy, sell, begin** *in short sentences. Use a different noun or pronoun with each verb. Use the interrogative words when it is possible. Practice using* **shall I** *and* **shall we.**

EXERCISE 4

Fill the blanks with **shall** *or* **will,** *as required, and translate. Use the contractions when it is possible.*

1. What time _____ you start home?
2. _____ I buy a loaf of bread, or do you have enough?
3. _____ you bring me my book tomorrow?
4. _____ we go to the movies, or _____ we visit John?
5. _____ he come early today?
6. Yes, he' _____ come early today, but he _____ (*negative*) come early tomorrow.
7. I know you' _____ like this house, but I don't think you' _____ want to buy it.
8. I'm sure she' _____ be here in a few minutes.
9. We' _____ go to the movies first. Then we' _____ go to eat.
10. They' _____ get up early on Saturday, but they _____ (*negative*) get up early on Sunday.
11. Are you sure he _____ (*negative*) forget to bring your book?
12. _____ (*interrogative negative*) he come on Wednesday?
13. She _____ (*negative*) see him any more.
14. He _____ (*negative*) read that book, and he _____ (*negative*) let me read it either.
15. If you lose your book, I _____ (*negative*) give you mine.

EL INFINITIVO *TO BE ABLE*

No hay infinitivo para los auxiliares **can** o **could.** Cuando se quiere traducir el infinitivo **poder** al inglés, hay que emplear el infinitivo **to be able.**

Ejemplo: I'm going to be able.
Voy a poder.

THE FUTURE OF *CAN*
EL FUTURO DE *CAN*

Puesto que el auxiliar **can** existe solamente en el presente (**can**) y en el pasado (**could**), se forma el futuro (**future**) de **can** empleando el verbo **be able**. Es decir, se tiene que emplear el auxiliar **will** seguido por el infinitivo **to be able** sin la partícula **to**.

Hay que emplear el infinitivo con la partícula **to** después de las formas del verbo **be able**.

Nunca se emplea el auxiliar **shall** con el futuro de **be able**.

Ejemplo: He'll be able to go.
         El podrá ir.

EXERCISE 5

Verb Practice

1. He'll be able to drink two glasses of milk.
2. He won't be able to drink two glasses of milk.
3. Will he be able to drink two glasses of milk?
4. Won't he be able to drink two glasses of milk?
5. Why won't he be able to drink two glasses of milk?

EXERCISE 6

Verb Practice *Repeat exercise 5, using forms of the verbs* come, go, speak, read, hear, work, become, kill, come back *in short sentences. Use a different noun or pronoun with each verb. Use the interrogative words when it is possible.*

EXERCISE 7

Change these sentences to the past tense and future tense. Translate each time.

1. I can make a dress.
2. You can go to the United States.
3. He can speak English well.
4. She can live in Mexico.
5. We can sell our house.

6. They can give me the money.
7. Mr. and Mrs. Clay can come in the afternoon.
8. Those men can put their things in that room.
9. Alice can understand Spanish.
10. We can go.

THE USE OF *HOW* AFTER *KNOW, SHOW, TEACH, LEARN*

Por regla general se emplea la palabra **how** antes de un infinitivo que sigue formas de los verbos **know, show, teach, learn.**

Ejemplo: My son knows how to read.
Mi hijo sabe leer.

EXERCISE 8

Study the following sentences and translate them into Spanish.

1. She taught them how to speak English.
2. Will you teach me how to pronounce these words?
3. She's going to show her sister how to make a cake.
4. Show him how to open that window.
5. Do you know how to read and write?
6. I don't know how to answer that question.
7. The girls are learning how to wash their dresses.
8. When are you going to learn how to fix the radio?

EXERCISE 9

Translate into English.

1. ¿Sabe este niño ponerse los zapatos?
2. Ud. no puede aprender a hablar inglés en unos pocos meses.
3. Enséñame a poner la televisión.
4. Mi mamá me enseñó a leer.
5. Si te enseño a hablar español, ¿me enseñas a hablar inglés?
6. Mi tío sabe hacer muchas cosas interesantes.
7. Aquel niño aprenderá a caminar muy pronto.
8. Te iba a enseñar cómo hacerlo.

17

TAN ... COMO – AS ... AS

El equivalente de **tan ... como** en inglés es **as ... as.**

Estudie las siguientes frases.

as big as	tan grande como
as blue as	tan azul como
as early as	tan temprano como
as late as	tan tarde como
as cold as	tan frío como
as dirty as	tan sucio como
as much as	tanto como
as much money as	tanto dinero como
as many as	tantos como
as many books as	tantos libros como

EXERCISE 10

Translate into English.

1. Acapulco es tan caliente como Veracruz.
2. Juan no es tan viejo como Roberto.
3. ¿No estás tan cansado como yo?
4. Este lápiz es tan largo como el otro.
5. Tu coche no corre (go) tan rápido como el mío.
6. Él es tan rico como el Sr. Astor.
7. Él come tanto como su papá.
8. No tengo tanto tiempo como Ud.
9. ¿Compraste tantas como Juan?
10. Ella llevará tantos libros como tú.

TO RAIN y TO SNOW

Rain (llover) y **snow** (nevar) son verbos impersonales, y por eso solamente se pueden conjugar en la tercera persona singular. Puesto que en inglés siempre se tiene que expresar un sujeto, se usa el pronombre **it** con los verbos impersonales.

18

EXERCISE 11

Verb Practice

1. It rains.
2. It doesn't rain.
3. Does it rain?
4. Doesn't it rain?
5. When does it rain?
6. It rained.
7. It didn't rain.
8. Did it rain?
9. Didn't it rain?
10. When did it rain?
11. It's raining.
12. It isn't raining.
13. Is it raining?
14. Isn't it raining?
15. It was raining.
16. It wasn't raining.
17. Was it raining?
18. Wasn't it raining?
19. When was it raining?
20. It's going to rain.
21. It isn't going to rain.
22. Is it going to rain?
23. Isn't it going to rain?
24. When is it going to rain?
25. It was going to rain.
26. It wasn't going to rain.
27. Was it going to rain?
28. Wasn't it going to rain?
29. When was it going to rain?
30. It'll rain.
31. It won't rain.
32. Will it rain?
33. Won't it rain?
34. When will it rain?
35. Let it rain.

EXERCISE 12

Verb Practice *Repeat exercise 11, using forms of the verb* **snow**.

TO BE BORN — *NACER*

Por regla general el verbo **be born** se usa solamente en tiempo pasado. Se conjuga el verbo **be**, agregando **born**. Estudie estas oraciones.

I was born in Mexico.	Nací en México.
Where were you born?	¿Dónde naciste?
When were you born?	¿Cuándo naciste?
He was born in the United States.	El nació en los Estados Unidos.
He was born in 1920.	El nació en 1920.

EXERCISE 13

Translate into Spanish.

19

1. I wanted to buy some curtains for the bedroom, but there weren't any left when I got to the store.
2. If I can't see Mr. Lake tomorrow, I'm going to give up.
3. It was raining very hard when I came home.
4. Does it ever snow in Mexico?
5. His wife is as pretty as his sister.
6. If you have a lot of time, why don't you study?
7. There was plenty of rain last year, but there wasn't enough this year.
8. There's a great deal of time left before the movie starts.
9. He said there wasn't any more room in the bus, but I don't believe it.
10. That old man was born in Texas eighty-five years ago.
11. He was here a little while ago, but I didn't see him.
12. A long time ago, when I was a little boy, we lived in New York.
13. Be sure to bring your book on Friday.
14. It was raining a short time ago, but it isn't raining now.
15. Since there was no room in the car, we had to walk.

EXERCISE 14

Verb Practice

1. Why doesn't Miss Davis get married?
2. Miss Davis got married in New York.
3. Miss Davis didn't get married in New York.
4. Did Miss Davis get married in New York?
5. Didn't Miss Davis get married in New York?
6. Why didn't Miss Davis get married in New York?
7. Miss Davis is going to get married tomorrow.
8. Miss Davis isn't going to get married tomorrow.
9. Is Miss Davis going to get married tomorrow?
10. Isn't Miss Davis going to get married tomorrow?
11. Why isn't Miss Davis going to get married tomorrow?
12. Miss Davis wanted to get married a week ago.
13. Miss Davis didn't want to get married a week ago.
14. Did Miss Davis want to get married a week ago?
15. Didn't Miss Davis want to get married a week ago?
16. Why didn't Miss Davis want to get married a week ago?
17. Miss Davis can marry him the day after tomorrow.
18. Miss Davis can't marry him the day after tomorrow.

19. Can Miss Davis marry him the day after tomorrow?
20. Can't Miss Davis marry him the day after tomorrow?
21. Why can't Miss Davis marry him the day after tomorrow?
22. Miss Davis will be able to marry him soon.
23. Miss Davis won't be able to marry him soon.
24. Will Miss Davis be able to marry him soon?
25. Won't Miss Davis be able to marry him soon?
26. Why won't Miss Davis be able to marry hin soon?
27. Miss Davis will marry him in June.
28. Miss Davis won't marry him in June.
29. Will Miss Davis marry him in June?
30. Won't Miss Davis Marry him in June?
31. Why won't Miss Davis marry him in June?

EXERCISE 15

Verb Practice . *Repeat exercise 14, using forms of the verbs* steal, rob, fly, believe, sing, catch, arrive (in, at), correct *in short sentences. Use a different noun or pronoun with each verb. Use the interrogative words when it is possible. Practice using* shall I *and* shall we.

EXERCISE 16

Read and translate.

THE FOX AND THE CROW

One day a crow stole a piece of cheese from a farmer's table and flew with it to the top of a tall tree, where he was going to eat it.

A fox saw the crow steal the cheese and fly away (volar) with it. "If I can think of a way," said the fox, "I'll have cheese for supper."

So, as the fox sat under the tree, he began to speak to the crow in a very polite way. "Good morning, Mr. Crow," he said. "The feathers on your wings and on your breast are very black and very pretty today. I didn't hear your voice when all the birds were singing, but I'm sure that you have a very beautiful voice."

The crow was very happy to hear the fox say these words, and he believed everything he heard. He liked what the fox said about his voice because the other birds sometimes told him that he couldn't sing very well.

"I'll try to sing again," thought the crow, "because I'm sure that what the fox says is right. I believe that my voice is very beautiful."

So the crow opened his mouth very wide (mucho) and started to sing. The piece of cheese dropped out of the crow's mouth, and the fox caught it before it reached the ground. In a minute there was nothing left of the cheese.

As the fox walked away (se fue), he said to the crow, "The next time someone tells you how beatifully you sing, don't believe everything you hear."

EXERCISE 17

Write in English.

1. ¿Vienes mañana o paso por tu casa?
2. ¿Naciste en Veracruz?
3. Puesto que mi mamá no puede venir a México este año, creo que la visitaré el próximo año.
4. Él se fue a Acapulco tan pronto como se casó.
5. ¿Estaba lloviendo cuando llegaste?
6. Mire Ud. a la derecha y a la izquierda.
7. Puesto que estaré en Acapulco quince días, sólo voy a llevar (a) poco dinero.
8. Estoy seguro que Ud. va a ser muy feliz en Estados Unidos.
9. Mi mamá no creerá que me casé hasta que vea (sees) a mi mujer.
10. Ellos no podrán comprar un coche tan grande como el nuestro.
11. ¿Vamos a la casa de Juan? (*sugiriendo*) Sí, vamos (vayamos) en la tarde.
12. ¿Llevo el dinero conmigo? (*sugiriendo*) No, no lo lleves.

EXERCISE 18

Dictation

1. Don't eat that bread because I dropped it on the ground.
2. I visited Veracruz a long time ago.
3. Your suit is like mine.
4. He was born in California, but he lives in Texas now.
5. I saw that movie about three months ago.
6. If you bring the meat and cheese, we'll be able to eat by twelve o'clock.

7. We're sure that you'll like Mexico a lot.
8. Why won't they believe you?
9. Shall we go to the movies now or wait until tomorrow?
10. We won't be able to go on Wednesday if it's raining.

EXERCISE 19

Conversation *Answer the following questions.*

1. Where were you born?
2. When were you born?
3. How long ago did it rain?
4. How long ago did she leave?

Answer the following questions in the affirmative and in the negative. Questions beginning with **shall** *are answered in the imperative.*

5. Is it raining?
6. Was it raining?
7. Is it going to rain?
8. Are you sure?
9. Were you born in June?
10. Were you born in Mexico?
11. Did he leave an hour ago?
12. Did you see him a little while ago?
13. Did you meet him a long time ago?
14. Will you go with me?
15. Will you do me a favor?
16. Will we eat soon?
17. Will I see you before you leave?
18. Will you be able to help me next week?
19. Will he be able to go to school?
20. Shall I begin now?
21. Shall we go to the movies?
22. Did he get married?
23. Did he marry her?
24. Do you know how to read?
25. Do you have any money left?
26. Do they have any left?
27. Do you have a lot of money left?
28. Did they steal a piece of candy?

29. Will he steal the books?
30. Are they going to steal everything?
31. Did she rob you?
32. Will they rob me?

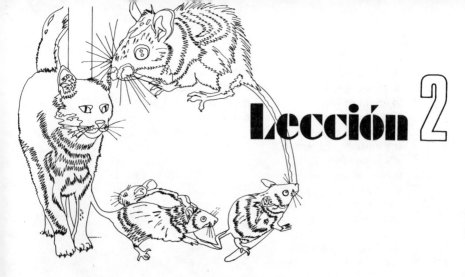

Lección 2

Vocabulary

1. **to hang, hung, hung,** colgar
2. **to play, played, played** jugar
3. **to escape, escaped, escaped** escaparse
4. **to swim, swam, swum** nadar
5. **to dress, dressed, dressed** vestir (se)
6. **to clap, clapped, clapped** aplaudir
7. **during** durante
8. **simple** sencillo
9. **important** importante
10. **difficult** difícil
11. **safe** seguro; a salvo
12. **dangerous** peligroso
    danger peligro
13. **mouse** ratón
    mice ratones
14. **cat** gato
15. **enemy** enemigo
16. **meeting** junta, mitin; encuentro
17. **plan** plan
18. **bell** campana; cascabel
19. **downtown** en el (al) centro
20. **block** cuadra, manzana
21. **neck** cuello; pescuezo
22. **hair** pelo; vello
23. **face** cara
24. **nose** nariz
25. **hand** mano
26. **great** gran

IDIOMS

1. **to get away, got away, got away** escaparse
2. **to look** (*with an adjective*) verse, parecer (*con adjetivo*)

25

He looks sad. Él se ve triste. Lo veo triste.
She looks good in blue. Ella se ve bien de azul.
3. **to look like** (*with a noun*) parecer, parecerse a (*con sustantivo*)
   He looks like a teacher. Parece profesor.
   He looks like his father. Él se parece a su papá.
4. **It's possible.** Es posible.
5. **It's impossible.** Es imposible.
6. **finally, at last** por fin
7. **all of us** todos nosotros
   all of them todos ellos
   all of you todos Uds.
8. **what else?** ¿qué más?
   who else? ¿quién más?
9. **just then** en ese momento
10. **There'll be cheese.** Habrá queso.

EXERCISE 1

Translate the following sentences and practice reading them.

1. It rains, doesn't it?
2. It doesn't rain, does it?
3. It rained, didn't it?
4. It didn't rain, did it?
5. It'll rain, won't it?
6. It won't rain, will it?
7. It's raining, isn't it?
8. It isn't raining, is it?
9. It was raining, wasn't it?
10. It wasn't raining, was it?
11. It was going to rain, wasn't it?
12. It wasn't going to rain, was it?
13. John will get married, won't he?
14. John won't get married, will he?
15. John will be able to get married, won't he?
16. John won't be able to get married, will he?
17. What's John getting married for?
18. What was John getting married for?
19. What did John get married for?
20. Let's get married.
21. Marry her.
22. Don't marry her.

THE PAST PARTICIPLE OF REGULAR VERBS
EL PARTICIPIO DE LOS VERBOS REGULARES

El participio de los verbos regulares es igual al tiempo pasado. Estudie lo siguiente.

Verb	Past Tense	Past Participle
ask	asked	asked
answer	answered	answered
arrive (in, at)	arrived (in, at)	arrived (in, at)
believe	believed	believed
call	called	called
clean	cleaned	cleaned
close	closed	closed
clap	clapped	clapped
complete	completed	completed
change	changed	changed
correct	corrected	corrected
drop	dropped	dropped
dictate	dictated	dictated
dress	dressed	dressed
escape	escaped	escaped
fix	fixed	fixed
finish	finished	finished
fill	filled	filled
form	formed	formed
help	helped	helped
hurry	hurried	hurried
invite	invited	invited
jump	jumped	jumped
kill	killed	killed
live	lived	lived
like	liked	liked
learn	learned	learned
look (at)	looked (at)	looked (at)
look (for)	looked (for)	looked (for)
laugh (at)	laughed (at)	laughed (at)

THE PAST PARTICIPLE OF IRREGULAR VERBS
EL PARTICIPIO DE LOS VERBOS IRREGULARES

Verb	Past Tense	Past Participle
be	was, were	been
bring	brought	brought
buy	bought	bought
begin	began	begun
become	became	become
break	broke	broken
catch	caught	caught
come	came	come
come back	came back	come back
cut	cut	cut
do	did	done
drink	drank	drunk
eat	ate	eaten
feel	felt	felt
fly	flew	flown
forget	forgot	forgotten
find	found	found
go	went	gone
go back	went back	gone back
go to bed	went to bed	gone to bed
go to sleep	went to sleep	gone to sleep
give	gave	given
give up	gave up	given up

Learn these words.

SUPPLEMENTARY VOCABULARY

1. **arrival** llegada
2. **completion** terminación
3. **complete** completo
4. **completely** completamente
5. **change** cambio
6. **correction** corrección
7. **correct** correcto
8. **correctly** correctamente
9. **dictator** dictador
10. **dictation** dictado
11. **full** lleno; satisfecho
12. **feeling** sentimiento

28

13. **form** forma, esqueleto
14. **formation** formación
15. **help** ayuda
16. **helper** ayudante
17. **helpful** útil; comedido
18. **invitation** invitación
19. **knowledge** conocimiento (s)
20. **killer** asesino
21. **life** vida
22. **loss** pérdida
23. **loser** (*noun*) perdedor
24. **losing** (*adj.*) perdedor
25. **love** amor
26. **lover** amante; galán
27. **lovely** encantador, hermoso
28. **listener** el que escucha, oyente
29. **necessity** necesidad
30. **necessary** necesario
31. **necessarily** necesariamente
32. **player** jugador
33. **playful** juguetón
34. **pronunciation** pronunciación
35. **runner** corredor
36. **seat** asiento
37. **sitting** sentando
38. **speaker** orador
39. **speech** discurso
40. **sale** venta; barata
41. **salesman** vendedor
42. **saleslady** vendedora
43. **singer** cantante
44. **song** canción
45. **swimmer** nadador
46. **swimming** natación
47. **talk** plática
48. **talkative** locuaz, parlanchín
49. **teacher** maestro
50. **thought** pensamiento
51. **thoughtful** considerado; atento
52. **thoughtless** desatento, desconsiderado
53. **translation** traducción
54. **use** uso
55. **useful** útil
56. **useless** inútil
57. **visitor** visitante, visita
58. **visit** visita
59. **worker** trabajador; obrero
60. **writer** escritor
61. **winner** (*noun*) ganador
62. **winning** (*adj.*) ganador

EXERCISE 2

Translate the following questions. Answer them in the affirmative and in the negative.

1. Will you visit your cousin after your arrival?
2. Are crows completely black?
3. Do you have change for five pesos?
4. Is that sentence correct?
5. Do you like to take dictation?
6. Is that glass full of water?
7. Can you give all the forms of the verb be?

8. Do you need any help?
9. Is he the teacher's helper?
10. Did you get an invitation?
11. Do they have a good knowledge of English?
12. Is that man a killer?
13. Is your life interesting?
14. Is her husband thoughtful?
15. Are their children thoughtless?
16. Was Clark Gable a great lover in the movies?
17. Are you a good listener?
18. Is money a necessity?
19. Is he a good football player?
20. Is English pronunciation hard?
21. Is he a fast runner?
22. Did you have a good seat at the movies?
23. Is your teacher a good speaker?
24. Do you like to make speeches?
25. Is that store having a sale?
26. Do you like that song?
27. Is he a good swimmer?
28. Is he a good teacher?
29. Was my translation correct?
30. Is English useful?
31. Are women very talkative?
32. Did you have a visitor last night?
33. Is that man a good worker?
34. Is that man a writer?
35. Is that girl the winner?

EXERCISE 3

Translate the following sentences and practice reading them.

1. There'll be four children.
2. There won't be four children.
3. Will there be four children?
4. Won't there be four children?
5. How many children will there be?
6. There'll be a cake.
7. There won't be a cake.
8. Will there be a cake?

9. Won't there be a cake?
10. How many cakes will there be?
11. I'll be hungry.
12. I won't be hungry.
13. You'll be sleepy.
14. You won't be sleepy.
15. She'll be afraid.
16. She won't be afraid.
17. It'll be cold.
18. It won't be cold.
19. It'll be hot.
20. It won't be hot.
21. I'll have to work.
22. I won't have to work.
23. You'll have to speak.
24. You won't have to speak.
25. She'll have to go.
26. She won't have to go.

EXERCISE 4

Translate the following sentences into Spanish, using forms of the verb verse, parecer. *Change them to the negative, interrogative, and interrogative negative.*

1. She looks good in green.
2. The water looks very black.
3. Her husband looks very young.
4. The sick child looks weak.
5. Your brother looks nice in brown.
6. That cake looks good.
7. That woman looks sad.
8. Those children look happy.
9. That car looks new.
10. That man looks sick.

EXERCISE 5

Translate the following sentences into English, using forms of the verb look (*verse*).

1. Tu casa se ve muy limpia.

2. Sus cortinas se ven muy blancas.
3. Él se vio muy enojado.
4. La escuela se ve muy grande, ¿verdad?
5. Ud. se verá cansada si no duerme esta noche.
6. Ella dijo que su vestido era azul, pero se ve verde.
7. Sus manos se ven rojas.
8. Su pelo se veía muy negro ayer.
9. ¿Se vio cansado el maestro?
10. ¿Por qué no se ve bien su hermana de verde?

EXERCISE 6

Translate the following sentences into Spanish, using forms of the verb **parecer, parecerse a.** *Change them to the negative, interrogative, and interrogative negative.*

1. John looks like his father.
2. These boys look like Mexicans.
3. My little dog looks like a cat.
4. You look like your mother.
5. It looks like it's going to rain.
6. That dress looks like mine.
7. That house looks like a barn.
8. He looks like his cousin.
9. They look like people from the country.
10. We look like farmers.

EXERCISE 7

Translate the following sentences into English, using forms of the verb **look like** *(parecer, parecerse a).*

1. Si eres doctor, ¿por qué no lo (one) pareces?
2. Él no parece profesor, ¿verdad?
3. Sé que ese hombre es americano, pero él parece mexicano.
4. Ellos parecían agricultores.
5. ¿Crees que ella se parece a mí?
6. Esa niñita se parecerá a su mamá dentro de diez años.
7. Ese libro se parece al mío.
8. Ayer parecía que (like) iba a llover, pero no llovió.
9. Este café parece agua sucia.
10. Tu abuelito no se parece a tu papá.

32

EXERCISE 8

Translate into Spanish.

1. The woman that looks like your aunt doesn't live on this street any more.
2. If you don't have any money left, what are you going to do?
3. We're going to live in a city far from here.
4. We have a lot of things to do before six o'clock.
5. John is here, but Bill can't come until eight-fifteen.
6. Don't look out of the window because everybody will see you.
7. He went out of town on Monday and came back on Tuesday.
8. I lived above him on the third floor for ten years.
9. We washed the wall below that window, but it's dirty again.
10. He robbed my house. He stole all my money.
11. Do you know how to swim?
12. Take that chair out of the bedroom, and take that rug out of the living room.
13. I won't be able to hear from here.
14. Will you be able to put that table behind the sofa?
15. I didn't go out yesterday because I didn't feel well.

EXERCISE 9

Verb Practice

1. She hangs her hat in the closet every day.
2. She doesn't hang her hat in the closet every day.
3. Does she hang her hat in the closet every day?
4. Doesn't she hang her hat in the closet every day?
5. Why does she hang her hat in the closet every day?
6. She hung her dress in the closet yesterday.
7. She didn't hang her dress in the closet yesterday.
8. Did she hang her dress in the closet yesterday?
9. Didn't she hang her dress in the closet yesterday?
10. Why did she hang her dress in the closet yesterday?
11. She's hanging it in the kitchen.
12. She isn't hanging it in the kitchen.
13. Is she hanging it in the kitchen?
14. Isn't she hanging it in the kitchen?
15. What's she hanging it in the kitchen for?
16. She'll hang them here tomorrow.

17. She won't hang them here tomorrow.
18. Will she hang them here tomorrow?
19. Won't she hang them here tomorrow?
20. How many will she hang here tomorrow?
21. She likes to hang her dress there.
22. She doesn't like to hang her dress there.
23. Does she like to hang her dress there?
24. Doesn't she like to hang her dress there?
25. Why doesn't she like to hang her dress there?
26. She had to hang his suit in the closet.
27. She didn't have to hang his suit in the closet.
28. Did she have to hang his suit in the closet?
29. Didn't she have to hang his suit in the closet?
30. Why did she have to hang his suit in the closet?
31. She'll be able to hang it over the bed.
32. She won't be able to hang it over the bed.
33. Will she be able to hang it over the bed?
34. Won't she be able to hang it over the bed?
35. Why won't she be able to hang it over the bed?

EXERCISE 10

Verb Practice *Repeat exercise 9, using forms of the verbs* **dress, clap, swim, play, escape, get away, look, look like** *in short sentences. Use a different noun or pronoun with each verb. Use the interrogative words when it is possible.*

EXERCISE 11

Read and translate.

THE MICE AT A MEETING

The mice were afraid of their enemy, the cat; and for many years they lived near him, knowing that their lives were in danger.

"Let's have a meeting," said one of the mice, "and try to form some plan that will help us get away from the cat. It's possible that one of the mice has a good idea that will help us."

During the meeting they thought and talked about many plans. Finally, a young mouse got up and began to speak. "I think," he said, feeling very important, "that it's a good idea to hang a bell around the cat's neck. Then, when the cat comes, we'll hear the bell; and we'll all be able to escape."

"I think that's a very good idea," said one mouse to another; and as these words went around the room, all the mice began to clap for the young mouse that gave them the idea for this good plan.

Just then an old mouse stood up and said, "My friends, we're very happy to have a young mouse among us that can think of a plan so good and so simple as putting a bell around the cat's neck so all of us will be safe. Like all of you, I think it's a very good idea; but there's just one little thing that I don't understand—who is going to put the bell around the cat's neck?"

EXERCISE 12

Write in English.

1. Habrá toda clase de vestidos y sombreros en (at) esta barata.
2. Atrapé a ese gato, pero se escapó.
3. El se casó el 30 de junio de 1949.
4. ¿Qué más podrá Ud. contarme de México?
5. Era imposible ir al centro el 16 de septiembre.
6. Llovió todos los días durante el mes de julio.
7. Estoy seguro de que tendrás mucha hambre antes de las nueve.
8. Todos nosotros lo podremos visitar a Ud. en diciembre.
9. Aquel animal se ve muy peligroso.
10. Por fin encontramos un sombrero como el suyo (de Ud.).
11. ¿Te ayudamos? (*sugiriendo*). No, no me ayuden.

EXERCISE 13

Dictation

1. All of them look like Americans.
2. Will you be able to catch that mouse that's in the kitchen?
3. My house is four blocks from the store.
4. We had to walk four blocks in the rain before we got to the store.
5. When I looked out of the window, it wasn't raining.
6. I was out of town for three days and didn't know about your arrival.
7. Besides working all day, I have to work two hours at night.
8. I sat beside him yesterday at the meeting, but he didn't say anything to me.

9. You'll have to take the seat out of the car if you want to clean it.
10. There'll be twenty visitors in the city tomorrow.

EXERCISE 14

Conversation *Answer the following questions.*

1. Where were you born?
2. When were you born?
3. Where are you from?
4. Where are your parents from?
5. Who did you come with?
6. Who did you go with?
7. What are you thinking about?
8. What was the movie about?
9. What are you talking about?

Answer the following questions in the negative.

10. Don't you play football any more?
11. Don't you play basketball any more?
12. Don't you live in Mexico any more?
13. Don't they go to school any longer?

Answer the following questions in the affirmative and in the negative.

14. Is the car full of people?
15. Will they eat downtown?
16. Will he come on Monday?
17. Shall I come tomorrow?
18. Shall we study the new vocabulary?
19. Will she be able to finish by three o'clock?
20. Will the children be able to hear from here?
21. Will there be school on Tuesday?
22. Will there be enough bread for dinner?
23. Will you have to work on Sunday?
24. Will they have to leave in July?
25. Do you look like your mother?
26. Do you look good in red?
27. Are you as tall as your father?
28. Did you come as soon as possible?
29. Do we have any bread left?
30. Does Robert know how to swim?

Lección 3

Vocabulary

1. **to get off, got off, got off** bajarse (de)
2. **to shout (at), shouted (at), shouted (at)** gritar
3. **to cry, cried, cried** llorar
4. **to pay, paid, paid** pagar
5. **to take off, took off, taken off** quitarse
6. **to rest, rested, rested** descansar
7. **even though** aunque
8. **large** grande (*de tamaño*)
9. **sharp** agudo, filoso
10. **kind** amable, bondadoso; clase
    kindness amabilidad, bondad
11. **quick** rápido
    quickly rápidamente
12. **different (from)** diferente, distinto (a, de)
13. **crooked** torcido, chueco
14. **lion** león
15. **cave** cueva
16. **paw** pata (*de animal*)
17. **net** red
18. **hole** agujero
19. **tooth** diente
    teeth dientes
20. **newspaper** periódico
21. **paper** papel; periódico
22. **box** caja
23. **party** fiesta
24. **corner** rincón; esquina
25. **bus** camión
26. **instead of** en vez de
27. **cheap** barato; corriente
28. **expensive** caro; costoso

IDIOMS

1. **to make money** ganar dinero

37

How much do you make a month? ¿Cuánto ganas al mes?
2. **to be over** acabarse, terminarse (*de tiempo*)
   The movie is over. Ya se acabó la película.
   The movie was over at ten. La película se acabó a las diez.
3. **a dollar an hour** un dólar la hora
   ten dollars a day diez dólares por día
   three times a week tres veces por semana
   twice a month dos veces al mes
   once a year una vez al año
4. **You're right.** Ud. tiene razón.
   You were right. Ud. tenía razón.
5. **What did you do on the week end?** ¿Qué hiciste el fin de semana?

EXERCISE 1

Translate the following sentences and practice reading them.

1. Swim.
2. Don't swim.
3. Let him swim.
4. Don't let him swim.
5. He played in the yard yesterday, didn't he?
6. He didn't play in the yard yesterday, did he?
7. He wants to play in the yard, doesn't he?
8. He doesn't want to play in the yard, does he?
9. He wanted to play in the yard, didn't he?
10. He didn't want to play in the yard, did he?
11. They swam, didn't they?
12. They didn't swim, did they?
13. They'll be able to swim, won't they?
14. They won't be able to swim, will they?
15. They'll have to swim, won't they?
16. They won't have to swim, will they?
17. There'll be a party at my house tomorrow night.
18. There won't be a party at my house tomorrow night.
19. There'll be a newspaper on your desk in the morning.
20. There won't be a newspaper on your desk in the morning.
21. There'll be a lot of people here, won't there?
22. There won't be a lot of people here, will there?

THE PRESENT PERFECT
EL ANTEPRESENTE

Se forma el antepresente (**present perfect**) en inglés igual que en castellano. Se forma usando el presente del verbo **have** (haber) como auxiliar y el participio del verbo empleado. La contracción negativa de **have not** es **haven't** y de **has not** es **hasn't**.

Se forma la contracción en afirmativo juntando el pronombre y el auxiliar **have** o **has**. Esta contracción no se emplea en la forma afirmativa más que acompañada del participio.

Afirmativo sin contracción

I have lived	he vivido
you have lived	Ud. ha vivido
he has lived	él ha vivido
she has lived	ella ha vivido
it has lived	ha vivido
we have lived	hemos vivido
you have lived	Uds. han vivido
they have lived	ellos han vivido

Afirmativo con contracción

I've lived	he vivido
you've lived	Ud. ha vivido
he's lived	él ha vivido
she's lived	ella ha vivido
it's lived	ha vivido
we've lived	hemos vivido
you've lived	Uds. han vivido
they've lived	ellos han vivido

Negativo

I haven't lived	no he vivido
she hasn't lived	ella no ha vivido
they haven't lived	ellos no han vivido

Interrogativo

Recuerde el orden de las palabras para el interrogativo: auxiliar, sustantivo o pronombre, verbo.

have I lived?	¿he vivido?
has John lived?	¿ha vivido Juan?
have you lived?	¿has vivido?

Interrogativo Negativo

haven't we lived?	¿no hemos vivido?
hasn't John lived?	¿no ha vivido Juan?
haven't you lived?	¿no has vivido?

Este tiempo se emplea en inglés para indicar una acción que comienza en el pasado y continúa hasta el momento actual.

Se emplea la palabra **for** (hace, desde hace) para especificar el plazo de tiempo y **since** (desde, desde que) para indicar cuándo comenzó la acción. Compare el inglés con el castellano.

How long have you been in Mexico?
¿Cuánto tiempo hace que estás en México?
¿Cuánto tiempo llevas en México?
¿Cuánto tiempo tienes (de estar) en México?

I've been here for a week.
Estoy (aquí) desde hace una semana.
Llevo una semana (aquí).
Hace una semana.
Tengo una semana.

I've been here since last Tuesday.
Estoy (aquí) desde el martes pasado.
Tengo (aquí) desde el martes pasado.

I've lived here since I got married.
Vivo aquí desde que me casé.
Llevo aquí desde que me casé.
Estoy aquí desde que me casé.
Tengo aquí desde que me casé.

EXERCISE 2

Verb Practice

1. We've bought everything.
2. We haven't bought everything.

3. Have we bought everything?
4. Haven't we bought everything?
5. How many things have we bought?

EXERCISE 3

Verb Practice *Repeat exercise 2, using forms of the verbs* **come back, shout (at), forget, come, begin, eat, catch, drink, feel** *in short sentences. Use a different noun or pronoun with each verb. Use the interrogative words when it is possible.*

Study the past tense and past participle of these regular verbs.

Verb	Past Tense	Past Participle
cry	cried	cried
listen (to)	listened (to)	listened (to)
love	loved	loved
marry	married	married
need	needed	needed
open	opened	opened
pass	passed	passed
pick out	picked out	picked out
pick up	picked up	picked up
place	placed	placed
pronounce	pronounced	pronounced
play	played	played
practice	practiced	practiced
reply	replied	replied
reach	reached	reached
rest	rested	rested
rain	rained	rained
shout (at)	shouted (at)	shouted (at)
study	studied	studied
start	started	started
stop	stopped	stopped
show	showed	showed
snow	snowed	snowed
talk	talked	talked
turn off	turned off	turned off
turn on	turned on	turned on

try	tried	tried
translate	translated	translated
use	used	used
visit	visited	visited
work	worked	worked
wash	washed	washed
wait (for)	waited (for)	waited (for)
walk	walked	walked
want	wanted	wanted

Study the past tense and past participle of these irregular verbs.

Verb	Past Tense	Past Participle
get	got	got
get angry (at)	got angry (at)	got angry (at)
get mad (at)	got mad (at)	got mad (at)
get away	got away	got away
get married	got married	got married
get off	got off	got off
get rich	got rich	got rich
get sleepy	got sleepy	got sleepy
get to	got to	got to
get here, there	got here, there	got here, there
get thirsty	got thirsty	got thirsty
get up	got up	got up
hang	hung	hung
have	had	had
hear	heard	heard
know	knew	known
leave	left	left
lie down	lay down	lain down
lose	lost	lost
make	made	made
meet	met	met
pay	paid	paid
put	put	put
put on	put on	put on
read	read	read
run	ran	run

LA POSICIÓN DE *ALREADY* (YA)

Generalmente la posición de **already** (ya) en las oraciones es igual a la de los adverbios de frecuencia—antes de todos los verbos principales menos en las formas del verbo **be** donde se colocan después. **Already** no debe emplearse con el pretérito en inglés sino con el antepresente, pero sí se empleará con el pasado del verbo **be (was, were)**. Ejemplo: **He was already here.**

Ejemplos:

> **They've already come.**
> Ya han llegado.
> Ya llegaron.
>
> **It's already late.**
> Ya es tarde.

EXERCISE 4

Place **already** *in the correct position in each sentence and translate.*

1. He's here.
2. They can speak English.
3. He has eaten.
4. They're working in the garden.
5. It's six o'clock.
6. He was there when we came.
7. Helen was making my birthday cake when I arrived.
8. Have the children gone to bed?
9. I've given him three hundred dollars.
10. Has it rained today?
11. It was time to go to bed when we got there.
12. We have had our breakfast.
13. Has John been here?
14. My mother has read everything.
15. Do you have four children?

EXERCISE 5

Answer the following questions in the affirmative, using **already**.

1. Is he here?

2. Have they eaten?
3. Have the children got up?
4. Do you have one hundred chickens?
5. Can you speak English?
6. Have they eaten supper?
7. Has she bought what she needs?
8. Is she living in her new house?
9. Have they been here?
10. Have they opened the windows?

THE PRESENT PERFECT OF *CAN*
EL ANTEPRESENTE DE *CAN*

Puesto que el auxiliar **can** existe solamente en el presente (**can**) y en el pasado (**could**), se forma el antepresente (**present perfect**) de can empleando el verbo **be able**. Es decir, se tiene que emplear el presente del verbo **have** (**have, has**) y el participio del verbo **be able** (**been able**).

Hay que emplear el infinitivo con la partícula **to** después de las formas del verbo **be able**.

Ejemplo: He's been able to go.
El ha podido ir.

EXERCISE 6

Verb Practice

1. You've been able to understand everything.
2. You haven't been able to understand everything.
3. Have you been able to understand everything?
4. Haven't you been able to understand everything?
5. How much have you been able to understand?

EXERCISE 7

Verb Practice *Repeat exercise 6, using forms of the verbs* **pick out, break, get, pick up, read, hear, lie down, lose, make** *in short sentences. Use a different noun or pronoun with each verb. Use the interrogative words when it is possible.*

44

EXERCISE 8

Change these sentences to the past tense, future tense, and present perfect tense. Translate each time.

1. I can answer all the questions.
2. He can speak English.
3. That man can escape.
4. She can fill the glass with water
5. We can help them.
6. Mrs. Clay can invite us.
7. Mary can make a dress.
8. Jack can translate those sentences.
9. We can make more money.
10. We can change these sentences to the negative.

EL USO DE LA PALABRA *ONE* O *ONES*
DESPUÉS DE LOS ADJETIVOS

Se emplea la palabra **one** o **ones** (plural) con un adjetivo en vez de repetir un sustantivo ya mencionado. Estudie los ejemplos:

This book is mine. **The blue one** is yours.
Este libro es mío. **El azul** es tuyo.

Do you want the big plates or the **little ones**?
¿Quieres los platos grandes o **los chicos**?

Did you study the first lesson or the **second one**?
¿Estudió Ud. la primera lección o **la segunda**?

EXERCISE 9

Fill the blanks with **one** *or* **ones,** *as required, and translate.*

1. I have a brown suit and a black _____ .
2. I like to sing new songs, but not old _____ .
3. There was no room on the first class buses, so we had to take a second class _____ .
4. This chair is old, but it's a good _____ .
5. Shall I wear my blue dress or my red _____ ?
6. The first five lessons are easy, but the sixth _____ is hard.

45

7. Here are five big chairs and two little _____ .
8. What kind of girls do you like – short _____ or tall _____ ?
9. I don't want that _____ . Give me the other _____ .
10. Do you want these? No, I want the other _____ .

EXERCISE 10

Translate the following sentences. Change them to the negative, interrogative, and interrogative negative.

1. He made a lot of money last year.
2. I make $4.00 (dollars) a day.
3. They make a lot.
4. That teacher makes $300.00 (dollars) a month.
5. We've made a lot of money this year.
6. We'll be able to make $100.00 (dollars) a week next year.
7. She'll make $10.000 (dollars) a year.
8. I'll have to make more money next year.
9. John is making a lot of money now.
10. He could make much more.

EXERCISE 11

Translate into Spanish.

1. Mr. Nash knows how to make money, doesn't he?
2. He doesn't look like the man who came yesterday.
3. This street looks very crooked.
4. I'll be able to make as much money as my brother next year.
5. How long has she studied English? She's studied English since last year.
6. Has it already snowed this year?
7. He won't have to go out of town on Monday, will he?
8. After you hang the new curtains, I won't be able to look out of the window.
9. It's rained every day this week, so we haven't been able to do anything.
10. Helen won't be able to go out this afternoon because she doesn't feel well.
11. Those flowers look beautiful between those two tall trees.

12. Joe called that man and asked him the way to Cuernavaca.
13. It's dangerous to walk through the woods.
14. If you ever live among American people, you'll soon learn how to speak English.
15. The horses and cows are behind the barn.

EXERCISE 12

Verb Practice

1. The teacher gets off the bus.
2. The teacher doesn't get off the bus.
3. Does the teacher get off the bus?
4. Doesn't the teacher get off the bus?
5. Where does the teacher get off the bus?
6. The teacher got off the bus.
7. The teacher didn't get off the bus.
8. Did the teacher get off the bus?
9. Didn't the teacher get off the bus?
10. Where did the teacher get off the bus?
11. The teacher was going to get off the bus.
12. The teacher wasn't going to get off the bus.
13. Was the teacher going to get off the bus?
14. Wasn't the teacher going to get off the bus?
15. Where was the teacher going to get off the bus?
16. The teacher will get off the bus.
17. The teacher won't get off the bus.
18. Will the teacher get off the bus?
19. Won't the teacher get off the bus?
20. Where will the teacher get off the bus?
21. The teacher will be able to get off the bus.
22. The teacher won't be able to get off the bus.
23. Will the teacher be able to get off the bus?
24. Won't the teacher be able to get off the bus?
25. Where will the teacher be able to get off the bus?
26. The teacher has got off the bus.
27. The teacher hasn't got off the bus.
28. Has the teacher got off the bus?
29. Hasn't the teacher got off the bus?
30. Where has the teacher got off the bus?
31. The teacher has been able to get off the bus.

32. The teacher hasn't been able to get off the bus.
33. Has the teacher been able to get off the bus?
34. Hasn't the teacher been able to get off the bus?
35. Where has the teacher been able to get off the bus?

EXERCISE 13

Verb Practice *Repeat exercise 12, using forms of the verbs* **pay, shout (at), cry, take off, make money, be over, rest** *in short sentences. Use a different noun or pronoun with each verb. Use the interrogative words when it is possible.*

EXERCISE 14

Read and translate.

THE LION AND THE MOUSE

One day a lion was asleep in a cave in the woods when a mouse ran across his face. The lion woke up and caught the mouse between his paws.

"Please don't kill me," said the mouse. "Let me live, and some day I'll do you a favor."

The lion didn't believe that a little animal like a mouse could ever help him, but the mouse looked so small and so weak that the lion said to him, "Even though I'm a very large and important animal, I'm very kind. I won't kill you. I'm going to let you go."

Then the lion put the mouse down on the ground, and the mouse ran away.

Many weeks after that, the mouse saw some men putting nets in different places in the woods to catch lions. The next morning the mouse thought he heard someone calling for help. When he stopped his work to listen, he knew that it was the lion's voice.

"I'll go to him at once," thought the mouse. "Now I can do him a favor."

The mouse ran through the woods looking for the lion. Finally he found him caught in one of the men's nets.

"Help me!" shouted the lion. "These men have caught me, and they'll kill me if you don't do something quick."

"I've come to help you," said the mouse.

48

"But what can an animal as small as you are do?" asked the lion.

"Just wait a minute and you'll see," answered the mouse. "I'll be able to help you."

Then the mouse began to cut the net with his sharp teeth. Soon there was a hole big enough for the lion to walk through.

When the lion was out of the net, the mouse said to him, "Now I've paid you for the favor you did for me."

EXERCISE 15

Write in English.

1. ¿Se terminará la película a las diez?
2. Tenías razón acerca del periódico. Es difícil de leer.
3. ¿Has podido ganar veinte dólares al día todo el año?
4. No podremos salir de la ciudad este fin de semana.
5. Ellos se fueron a casa cuando se acabó la fiesta.
6. El dijo que tenía razón, pero no lo creí.
7. Los amigos de Juan no podrán venir a las diez.
8. ¿Cuánto tiempo hace que estudia Ud. inglés? Hace un año que estudio inglés.
9. Habrá una fiesta en la casa de Alicia el primero de julio.
10. ¿Ya comiste? Sí, ya comí.

EXERCISE 16

Dictation

1. I got so sleepy before the party was over that I went to bed.
2. Have you already been to California?
3. I'll have to work on Saturday, but I won't have to work on Sunday.
4. Take off your black hat and put on this one.
5. We haven't been able to see Mr. Miller for three days.
6. A lot of people left before the movie was over.
7. We'll see if you're right.
8. There won't be any school next week.
9. The children will get cold if it begins to rain.
10. I'll meet you in front of the park at nine-thirty.

EXERCISE 17

Conversation *Answer the following questions.*

1. When were you born?
2. Where were you born?
3. Where do you get off the bus?

Answer the following questions, using **for** *and* **since**.

4. How long have you lived in Mexico?
5. How long has he lived in the United States?
6. How long have you studied English?
7. How long has Henry studied English?
8. How long have you worked at Ford?
9. How long have you been here?

Answer the following questions in the negative.

10. Don't you live there any more?
11. Don't you go out of town on week ends any more?
12. Doesn't he study English any longer?

Answer the following questions in the affirmative.

13. Has it already rained today?
14. Has he already come?
15. Have you already visited the United States?

Answer the following questions in the affirmative and in the negative.

16. Do you know how to read?
17. Is the movie over?
18. Was the movie over early?
19. Do you make a lot of money?
20. Is this knife as sharp as that one?
21. Is this box as big as that one?
22. Is it raining?
23. Shall I open the window?
24. Shall I read?
25. Shall I translate?

Lección 4

Vocabulary

1. **to fall (down), fell (down), fallen (down)** caer(se)
2. **to shake, shook, shaken** sacudir; moverse; temblar; agitar
3. **to spill, spilled, spilled** derramarse, tirar (*líquido*)
4. **to carry, carried, carried** cargar, llevar (*cargando*)
5. **to disappear, disappeared, disappeared** desaparecer
6. **to dance, danced, danced** bailar
7. **even** a mano; hasta
   even if aunque, aun cuando
   not even ni siquiera
8. **against** contra
9. **along** a lo largo, por
10. **empty** vacío
11. **careful** cuidadoso
    carefully con cuidado
12. **market** mercado
13. **bucket** cubeta
14. **neighbor** vecino
15. **head** cabeza
16. **favorite** favorito, predilecto
17. **ribbon** listón
18. **dream** sueño
19. **happiness** felicidad
20. **road** camino
21. **highway** carretera
22. **spring** primavera
23. **summer** verano
24. **fall** otoño
25. **winter** invierno
26. **far** lejos
27. **increasing scale** escala ascendente
28. **degree** grado

IDIOMS

1. **to have a good time** divertirse, pasarlo bien

51

to have fun divertirse, pasarlo bien
2. **Have a nice week end.** Que pase un buen fin de semana.
Have a nice vacation. Que pase felices vacaciones.
3. **to get sick** enfermarse
4. **Be careful.** Tenga cuidado.
5. **like this, this way** así, de esta manera
like that, that way así, de esa manera
6. **good luck** buena suerte
bad luck mala suerte
7. **You're lucky.** Ud. tiene suerte, Ud. es afortunado.
8. **You're unlucky.** Ud. tiene mala suerte.
9. **the one that** el que, la que
the ones that los que, las que
The one that doesn't study won't pass. El que no estudie no pasará.
10. **He didn't even tell me.** Ni siquiera me dijo.
11. **Have you ever been to Taxco?** ¿Conoce Ud. Taxco?
Yes, I've been there. Sí, lo conozco.

EXERCISE 1

Translate the following sentences and practice reading them.

1. Shout.
2. Don't shout at me.
3. Let them shout.
4. Don't let them shout at you.
5. They've been able to rest, haven't they?
6. They haven't been able to rest, have they?
7. Have they been able to rest?
8. Haven't they been able to rest?
9. They'll rest, won't they?
10. They won't rest, will they?
11. They'll be able to pay you, won't they?
12. They won't be able to pay you, will they?
13. They've been able to pay you, haven't they?
14. They haven't been able to pay you, have they?
15. Have they been able to pay you?
16. Haven't they been able to pay you?
17. What are they getting off here for?
18. What did they get off here for?

52

19. There'll be a party tonight.
20. There won't be a party tonight.

COMPARACIÓN DE ADJETIVOS y ADVERBIOS MONOSÍLABOS EL GRADO COMPARATIVO DE SUPERIORIDAD

Se usa el grado comparativo cuando se comparan dos personas u objetos o dos grupos de personas u objetos. Los adjetivos y los adverbios de una sola sílaba (y los de dos sílabas que terminan en y y en w) forman el grado comparativo de superioridad agregando **er**. La partícula **er** en este caso equivale a **más** en castellano. Si la palabra termina en **e**, solamente se agrega **r**.

Generalmente se usa la palabra **than** después del comparativo cuando se exprese la palabra **que** en castellano. Estudie los siguientes ejemplos.

Adjective or Adverb	Comparative Degree Increasing Scale	
blue	bluer than	más azul que
young	younger than	más joven que
big	bigger than	más grande que
easy	easier than	más facil que

EL GRADO SUPERLATIVO DE SUPERIORIDAD

Se usa el grado superlativo cuando se comparan una o más personas u objetos con otros o uno o más grupos de personas u objetos con otros. Los adjetivos y los adverbios de una sola sílaba (y los de dos sílabas que terminan en y en w) forman el grado superlativo de superioridad agregando **est**. La partícula **est** en este caso equivale a **más** en castellano. Si la palabra termina en **e**, solamente se agrega **st**.

Generalmente el superlativo se usa precedido de la palabra **the**.

Cuando se expresa la palabra **de** en castellano, el superlativo va seguido de la palabra **of** o **in**, según el caso.

(Véase la página siguiente.)

Adjective or Adverb	Comparative Degree Increasing Scale		Superlative Degree Increasing Scale	
blue	bluer than	más azul que	the bluest	el más azul
young	younger than	más joven que	the youngest	el más joven
big	bigger than	más grande que	the biggest	el más grande
easy	easier than	más fácil que	the easiest	el más fácil

Estudie el grado comparativo y superlativo de superioridad.

angry	angrier than	más enojado que	the angriest	el más enojado
big	bigger than	más grande que	the biggest	el más grande
blue	bluer than	más azul que	the bluest	el más azul
busy	busier than	más ocupado que	the busiest	el más ocupado
black	blacker than	más negro que	the blackest	el más negro
clean	cleaner than	más limpio que	the cleanest	el más limpio
cold	colder than	más frío que	the coldest	el más frío
dirty	dirtier than	más sucio que	the dirtiest	el más sucio
early	earlier than	más temprano que	the earliest	el que más temprano
easy	easier than	más fácil que	the easiest	el más fácil
fast	faster than	más rápido que	the fastest	el más rápido
fine	finer than	más fino que	the finest	el más fino
full	fuller than	más lleno que	the fullest	el más lleno
green	greener than	más verde que	the greenest	el más verde
happy	happier than	más feliz que	the happiest	el más feliz
hard	harder than	más duro que	the hardest	el más duro

Adjective or Adverb	Comparative Degree Increasing Scale		Superlative Degree Increasing Scale	
hot	hotter than	más caliente que	the hottest	el más caliente
kind	kinder than	más amable que	the kindest	el más amable
large	larger than	más grande que	the largest	el más grande
late	later than	más tarde que	the latest	el que más tarde
little	littler than	más pequeño que	the littlest	el más pequeño
long	longer than	más largo que	the longest	el más largo
mad	madder than	más enojado que	the maddest	el más enojado
narrow	narrower than	más estrecho que	the narrowest	el más estrecho
near	nearer than	más cerca que	the nearest	el que más cerca
nice	nicer than	más bonito que	the nicest	el más bonito
simple	simpler than	más sencillo que	the simplest	el más sencillo

Aprenda estas comparaciones irregulares.

good	better than	mejor que	the best	el mejor
well	better than	mejor que	the best	el mejor
bad	worse than	peor que	the worst	el peor
far	farther than	más lejos que	the farthest	el que más lejos
a lot, much, many	more than	más que	the most	el que más
little	less than	menos que	the least	el que menos
few	less than	menos que	the least	el que menos

55

Study the following sentences.

1. The living room is clean.
   The dining room is cleaner
   than the living room.   (comparative degree)

   The kitchen is the cleanest
   room in the house.   (superlative degree)

2. John is happy.
   John is happier than Robert.   (comparative degree)
   John is the happiest boy in
   school.   (superlative degree)

3. Mexico City is warm.
   Cuernavaca is warmer than
   Mexico City.   (comparative degree)

   Acapulco is the warmest of
   the three.   (superlative degree)

4. John was late.
   (Juan llegó tarde.)
   Robert was later than John.
   (Roberto llegó más tarde que
   Juan.)   (comparative degree)

   Mary was the latest of all.
   (María fue la que más tarde
   llegó de todos.)   (superlative degree)

EXERCISE 2

Fill the blanks with the comparative degree of the adjective or adverb indicated (increasing scale) and translate.

(young)   1. Mary is _____ than her sister, isn't she?
(cold)   2. Is the United States _____ than Mexico?
(easy)   3. The first book isn't _____ than the second one.
(fast)   4. Did the rabbit run _____ than the turtle?
(hard)   5. The first lesson is _____ than the second one.
(large)   6. The table in the dining room is _____ than
             the one in the kitchen.

56

(long)	7. The movies we saw today were _____ than the ones we saw yesterday.
(late)	8. I arrived _____ than you, didn't I?
(happy)	9. These children are _____ than those.
(full)	10. Is your glass _____ than mine?

EXERCISE 3

Fill the blanks with the superlative degree of the adjective or adverb indicated (increasing scale) and translate.

(big)	1. What city in Mexico is the _____ ?
(hot)	2. Is Acapulco the _____ place in Mexico?
(good)	3. The fifth lesson is the _____ one in the book.
(dirty)	4. You have the _____ hands of all the children.
(nice)	5. I think this dress is the _____ of all of them.
(little)	6. Paul is the _____ child in the family.
(long)	7. The Pan American Highway is the _____ highway in Mexico.
(early)	8. Who arrived the _____ ?
(far)	9. John lives the _____ from school.
(well)	10. This store pays the _____ .

EXERCISE 4

Fill the blanks with the comparative or the superlative degree, as required, of the adjective or adverb indicated (increasing scale) and translate.

(warm)	1. Summer is _____ than winter.
(narrow)	2. I live on the _____ street in the city.
(hard)	3. This chair is _____ than the sofa.
(fast)	4. Can a lion run _____ than a horse?
(cold)	5. The bedroom is the _____ room in the house.
(full)	6. This box is the _____ of all.
(kind)	7. My grandmother is the _____ woman I know.
(bad)	8. I had to sleep in the _____ room in the hotel.
(green)	9. The grass looks _____ than the trees, doesn't it?
(good)	10. This book is _____ than that one.

EXERCISE 5

Place **already** *in the correct position in each sentence and translate.*

1. Has he gone?
2. Have they eaten?
3. Have you gone to bed?
4. She's put on her dress.
5. Mr. Clay has opened the store.
6. We've read that book.
7. Has Miss Clay picked out her new hat?
8. The boys have picked up the papers on the floor.
9. Has it snowed in Chicago?
10. Have the girls turned off the radio?

EXERCISE 6

Answer the following questions in the affirmative, using **already**.

1. Has he already come?
2. Have you already translated these sentences?
3. Have they already arrived?
4. Has she already finished her work?
5. Have we already learned the lesson?
6. Have the girls already met my cousin?
7. Has Mary already put on her new dress?
8. Have Robert and Paul already had their English lesson?
9. Has Mrs. Clay already drunk that water?
10. Have the boys already come back?

Study the past tense and past participle of these irregular verbs.

Verb	Past Tense	Past Participle
be able	could	been able
fall (down)	fell (down)	fallen (down)
say	said	said
see	saw	seen
shake	shook	shaken
sit (down)	sat (down)	sat (down)
speak	spoke	spoken
sleep	slept	slept
sell	sold	sold

stand up	stood up	stood up
swim	swam	swum
steal	stole	stolen
take	took	taken
take off	took off	taken off
teach	taught	taught
think	thought	thought
understand	understood	understood
write	wrote	written
wake up	woke up	woke up
wear	wore	worn
win	won	won

LA POSICIÓN DE *STILL* (TODAVÍA) y *YET* (YA)

La palabra **still** (todavía) se coloca generalmente en la posición igual a la palabra **already** (ya) —antes del verbo principal y después de las formas del verbo **be**.

La palabra **yet** (ya) se coloca generalmente al final de la oración, y se puede emplear en el interrogativo. En el afirmativo no se emplea la palabra **yet**, sino **already**.

YA *ALREADY*

¿Ya comiste?   Sí, ya comí.
¿Ya has comido?   Sí, ya he comido.
Have you already eaten?   Yes, I've already eaten.
Have you eaten yet?   Yes, I've already eaten.

TODAVÍA... NO *NOT ... YET*

No, todavía no como.
No, todavía no he comido.
No, I haven't eaten yet.

TODAVÍA *STILL*

¿Todavía estás comiendo?   Sí, todavía estoy comiendo.

59

¿Sigues comiendo?	Sí, sigo comiendo.
Are you still eating?	**Yes, I'm still eating.**

YA ... NO *NOT ... ANY MORE*

No, ya no estoy comiendo.
No, I'm not eating any more.

EXERCISE 7

Fill the blanks with **still** *or* **yet,** *as required, and translate.*

1. Do you _____ have to go to the doctor every week?
2. Hasn't my new suit come _____ ? No, not _____ .
3. Is your son _____ playing football?
4. Yes, he's _____ playing football.
5. Do you _____ love me?
6. Have they eaten breakfast _____ ? No, not _____ .
7. They haven't gone to work _____ , and it's already ten-thirty.
8. I _____ have all my knives and forks.
9. Do you _____ like coffee and cake?

EXERCISE 8

Fill the blanks with **one** *or* **ones,** *as required, and translate.*

1. I studied all the lessons except the last _____ .
2. Don't take this bus. Take the next _____ .
3. He ate all the apples, even the bad _____ .
4. The first class buses go faster than the second class _____ .
5. I'll give you a book. Which _____ do you want?
6. Shall I buy this suit or the other _____ ?
7. There are all kinds of newspapers in the United States—good _____
   _____ and bad _____ .
8. I want a piece of candy, but not a large _____ .
9. It's a small car, but it's a good _____ .
10. These cups are bigger than the other _____ .

EXERCISE 9

Translate the following sentences and practice reading them.

1. There've been many parties.

2. There haven't been many parties.
3. Have there been many parties?
4. Haven't there been many parties?
5. There's been a lot of rain this month.
6. There hasn't been much rain this month.
7. Has there been a lot of rain this month?
8. Hasn't there been a lot of rain this month?
9. I've been sleepy.
10. I haven't been sleepy.
11. He's been thirsty.
12. He hasn't been thirsty.
13. We've been afraid.
14. We haven't been afraid.
15. You've been hungry.
16. I haven't had to work this week.
17. They've had to study every day.
18. They haven't had to study every day.
19. Have they had to study every day?
20. Haven't they had to study every day?

EXERCISE 10

Translate the following sentences. Change them to the negative, interrogative, and interrogative negative. Repeat the exercise, using forms of the verb have fun *instead of* have a good time.

1. I'm going to have a good time this week end.
2. He had a good time on his vacation.
3. We'll have a good time next summer.
4. You'll be able to have a good time in Cuernavaca.
5. We can have a good time tomorrow night.
6. She has a good time every spring.
7. They're having a good time with their friends.
8. The children have had a good time today.
9. I'm having a good time with my family.
10. John had a good time at Mary's party.

EXERCISE 11

Answer the following questions in the affirmative and in the negative.

1. Did you have a good time on the 16th of September?

2. Did you have fun at the party yesterday?
3. Do you have a good time when you go to the United States?
4. Do you have fun when you don't have to work?
5. Will you have a good time at school tomorrow?
6. Will you have fun when you visit your grandmother?
7. Can you have a good time in Acapulco if it rains?
8. Can you have fun if your friends aren't here?
9. Have you had a good time all week?
10. Have you had fun with the neighbor's children?

EXERCISE 12

Translate into Spanish.

1. Will you teach me how to dance?
2. I didn't make any money last week.
3. He knows that I'm right.
4. We'll be able to come as soon as we finish, won't we?
5. There's been a lot of rain this summer, hasn't there?
6. Do you think there'll be a lot of snow this winter?
7. I've already seen that movie.
8. Haven't you read that book yet? No, not yet.
9. They still believe that she can learn how to walk.
10. I still think you'll have a better time in Acapulco than in Veracruz.
11. Did you have a good time while you were in New York?
12. Spring is the best time of the year, and winter is the worst.
13. She doesn't look good in green, and I don't know why she wears it.
14. That man says he's a writer, but he doesn't look like one.
15. I'm sorry that you have had to work every day and that there's been so much work.

EXERCISE 13

Verb Practice

1. It always falls, doesn't it?
2. It never falls, does it?
3. Does it always fall?
4. Doesn't it always fall?
5. Why doesn't it ever fall?
6. It fell down, didn't it?
7. It didn't fall down, did it?
8. Did it fall down?

9. Didn't it fall down?
10. Why didn't it fall down?
11. It was falling down, wasn't it?
12. It wasn't falling down, was it?
13. Was it falling down?
14. Wasn't it falling down?
15. Why was it falling down?
16. It could fall down, couldn't it?
17. It couldn't fall down, could it?
18. Could it fall down?
19. Couldn't it fall down?
20. Why couldn't it fall down?
21. It's fallen down, hasn't it?
22. It hasn't fallen down, has it?
23. Has it fallen down?
24. Hasn't it fallen down?
25. Why hasn't it fallen down?
26. It'll be able to fall down, won't it?
27. It won't be able to fall down, will it?
28. Will it be able to fall down?
29. Won't it be able to fall down?
30. Why won't it be able to fall down?
31. It's been able to fall down, hasn't it?
32. It hasn't been able to fall down, has it?
33. Has it been able to fall down?
34. Hasn't it been able to fall down?
35. Why hasn't it been able to fall down?

EXERCISE 14

Verb Practice *Repeat exercise 13, using forms of the verbs* **disappear, dance, shake, spill, carry, get sick, have a good time, have fun** *in short sentences. Use a different noun or pronoun with each verb. Use the interrogative words when it is possible.*

EXERCISE 15

Read and translate.

THE GIRL AND THE MILK

The girl was singing as she walked along the road one summer morning. On the top of her head she carried a bucket of milk that she was taking to the market to sell.

When she stopped to rest for a few minutes under a tree, she began to think of all the things she was going to do with the money she received for the milk.

"I'll buy some chickens from a neighbor," she said, "and when they lay eggs, I'll be able to sell the eggs to the doctor's wife. With the money I receive for the eggs I can buy a new dress and a new ribbon for my hair. I want a green dress and a green ribbon because I look good in green, and I'll dress very carefully in my beautiful new dress and wear it to a dance. All the boys will ask me to dance, but I won't even look at them. Then, when they ask me again, I'll shake my head —like this."

As the girl spoke, she shook her head. The bucket fell off (se cayó) her head, and the milk spilled on the ground.

So all of her dreams of happiness disappeared, and she had nothing left but the empty bucket and the thought (idea) of listening to an angry mother when she got home.

EXERCISE 16

Write in English.

1. Estoy seguro que no nos divertiremos en la fiesta si llevamos a los niños con nosotros.
2. Adiós. Le veo el lunes. Que tenga un buen fin de semana.
3. Hágalo así. No lo haga de esa manera.
4. Este es el mejor libro que puedes encontrar, pero no creo que sea (it's) mejor que el que tienes.
5. Es Ud. muy afortunado de poder bailar con una chica tan bonita como María, ¿verdad?
6. El tiene muy mala suerte. Se enfermó la primavera pasada y todavía está en cama.
7. Ayer me sentí muy mal, pero hoy me siento peor.
8. ¿Cuánto tiempo hace que Ud. trabaja aquí? Hace seis meses que trabajo aquí.
9. ¿Van a jugar este año los Yankees contra los Giants?
10. ¿Todavía no se han levantado los niños? No, todavía no.

EXERCISE 17

Dictation

1. We're going to have a good time when we get married even if we don't have any money.
2. Those flowers you bought today are much bigger and redder than those I bought yesterday.
3. Be careful with those glasses. I paid a lot of money for them.
4. I got so sick while I was downtown that I had to go home at once.
5. There won't be enough time to finish all this work.
6. There've been plenty of potatoes in the market all fall.
7. I don't think we'll be able to visit you until winter.
8. Have you ever been to the United States?
9. Be careful or you'll spill the milk on the floor.
10. There'll be a dance on Thursday night, but there won't be one on Friday night.

EXERCISE 18

Conversation *Answer the following questions in the affirmative and in the negative.*

1. Do you still live on Madison Street?
2. Do you still work in Chicago?
3. Are you still studying English?
4. Is he still in Mexico?
5. Have you bought a new car yet?
6. Haven't you finished yet?
7. Hasn't she got married yet?
8. Hasn't he learned how to speak Spanish yet?
9. Is English easier than Spanish?
10. Is Acapulco hotter than Veracruz?
11. Is the United States colder than Mexico?
12. Is John the biggest boy in school?
13. Is winter the coldest time of the year?
14. Did you have a good time at the party?
15. Will you have a good time this week end?
16. Did you have fun in Taxco?
17. Will you have fun during your vacation?
18. Have you ever been in New York?
19. Have you always lived in Chicago?

20. Have you studied your lesson?
21. Have you danced with Mary?
22. Have you been able to sleep?
23. Have you been able to practice your English?
24. Will you be able to work tomorrow?
25. Will you be able to go to the movies tonight?

Answer the following questions.

26. How long have you lived in Cuernavaca?
27. How long have they lived in Mexico?
28. How long have you worked here?
29. How long has he studied English?
30. How long has he been there?

Lección 5

Vocabulary

1. **to blow, blew, blown** soplar
2. **to die, died, died** morirse, secarse (*plantas*)
3. **to turn over, turned over, turned over** voltear(se), volcar(se); remover
4. **to shine, shone, shone** brillar
5. **to dig, dug, dug** excavar, cavar
6. **to lend, lent, lent** prestar
7. **soft** suave, blando **softly** suavemente; quedo
8. **orchard** huerto
9. **fruit** fruta
10. **treasure** tesoro
11. **land** tierra, terreno **soil** tierra (*para sembrar*)
12. **sun** sol
13. **moon** luna
14. **star** estrella
15. **sky** cielo, firmamento
16. **sea** mar
17. **river** río
18. **mountain** montaña
19. **wind** viento
20. **world** mundo
21. **class** clase
22. **north** norte
23. **south** sur
24. **east** este
25. **west** oeste

IDIOMS

1. **to make a living** ganarse la vida, sostenerse
2. **to get old** envejecerse

3. **I can't help it.** Ni modo, No puedo remediarlo.
   I couldn't help it. Ni modo, No pude remediarlo.
4. **Let me know.** Avíseme.
5. **It's cheap.** Es barato; Es corriente.
6. **It's expensive.** Es caro; Es costoso.
7. **I think so.** Creo que sí.
   I don't think so. Creo que no.
8. **so (that)** para que
   Give me money so (that) I can buy it. Dame dinero para que lo compre.
9. **It's windy.** Hace viento, Hace aire.
   It's cloudy. Está nublado.
   It's sunny. Hace sol, Hay sol.
10. **The sun is shining.** Hace sol, Hay sol.
11. **This is the best book I've ever read.** Este es el mejor libro que he leído.

EXERCISE 1

Translate the following sentences ana practice reading them.

1. Will they be able to dance this evening?
2. Won't they be able to dance this evening? .
3. Have they been able to dance this evening?
4. Haven't they been able to dance this evening?
5. There'll be a dance tonight, won't there?
6. There won't be a dance tonight, will there?
7. Will there be a dance tonight?
8. Won't there be a dance tonight?
9. Will they be hungry after the movie?
10. Won't they be hungry after the movie?
11. There've been a lot of dances this year, haven't there?
12. There haven't been a lot of dances this year, have there?
13. Have there been a lot of dances this year?
14. Haven't there been a lot of dances this year?
15. Have they been sleepy?
16. Haven't they been sleepy?
17. Will they have to dance?
18. Won't they have to dance?
19. Have they had to dance?
20. Haven't they had to dance?

THE PAST PERFECT
EL ANTECOPRETÉRITO

Se forma el antecopréterito (**past perfect**) en inglés igual que en castellano. Se forma usando el pasado del verbo **have** (**had**, había) como auxiliar y el participio del verbo empleado. La contracción negativa de **had not** es **hadn't**.

Se forma la contracción en afirmativo con la partícula **d** agregada al pronombre.

Esta contracción no se emplea más que en la forma afirmativa, acompañada del participio. Estudie los siguientes ejemplos.

Afirmativo sin contracción

I had worked	yo había trabajado
you had worked	Ud. había trabajado
he had worked	él había trabajado
she had worked	ella había trabajado
it had worked	había trabajado
we had worked	habíamos trabajado
you had worked	Uds. habían trabajado
they had worked	ellos habían trabajado

Afirmativo con contracción

I'd worked	yo había trabajado
you'd worked	Ud. había trabajado
he'd worked	él había trabajado
she'd worked	ella había trabajado
it'd worked	había trabajado
we'd worked	habíamos trabajado
you'd worked	Uds. habían trabajado
they'd worked	ellos habían trabajado

Negativo

I hadn't worked	yo no había trabajado
he hadn't worked	él no había trabajado
they hadn't worked	ellos no habían trabajado

Interrogativo

Recuerde el orden de las palabras para el interrogativo: auxiliar, sustantivo o pronombre, verbo.

had he worked?	¿había él trabajado?
had John worked?	¿había Juan trabajado?
had they worked?	¿habían ellos trabajado?

Interrogativo Negativo

hadn't we worked?	¿no habíamos trabajado?
hadn't you worked?	¿no habías trabajado?
hadn't John worked?	¿no había Juan trabajado?

EXERCISE 2

Verb Practice

1. They'd forgotten to tell him.
2. They hadn't forgotten to tell him.
3. Had they forgotten to tell him?
4. Hadn't they forgotten to tell him?
5. Why had they forgotten to tell him?

EXERCISE 3

Verb Practice *Repeat exercise 2, using forms of the verbs* **feel, go, invite, get off, fix, live, learn, finish** *in short sentences. Use a different noun or pronoun with each verb. Use the interrogative words when it is possible.*

Study the comparative and superlative degree of the following adjectives and adverbs (increasing scale).

	Comparative	Superlative
cheap	cheaper than	the cheapest
hungry	hungrier than	the hungriest
old	older than	the oldest
poor	poorer than	the poorest
pure	purer than	the purest

pretty	prettier than	the prettiest
quick	quicker than	the quickest
red	redder than	the reddest
rich	richer than	the richest
small	smaller than	the smallest
sick	sicker than	the sickest
sad	sadder than	the saddest
slow	slower than	the slowest
soft	softer than	the softest
soon	sooner than	the soonest
strong	stronger than	the strongest
short	shorter than	the shortest
safe	safer than	the safest
sleepy	sleepier than	the sleepiest
thirsty	thirstier than	the thirstiest
tired	tireder than	the tiredest
tall	taller than	the tallest
thick	thicker than	the thickest
thin	thinner than	the thinnest
white	whiter than	the whitest
warm	warmer than	the warmest
weak	weaker than	the weakest
wide	wider than	the widest
young	younger than	the youngest

EXERCISE 4

Fill the blanks with the comparative degree of the adjective or adverb indicated (increasing scale).

(blue)   1. The sea looks _____ than the sky.

(pretty) 2. Your dress is _____ than mine.

(soft)   3. My bed is _____ than the sofa.

(short)   4. Robert is much _____ than John.

(wide)   5. The river is _____ than the highway.

(white)   6. Snow is _____ than milk.

(sleepy) 7. I'm _____ than he.

(slow)   8. A turtle is _____ than a rabbit.

(bad)   9. Her English is _____ than mine.

(warm)   10. Acapulco is _____ than Mexico City.

71

EXERCISE 5

Fill the blanks with the superlative degree of the adjective or adverb indicated (increasing scale).

(young)	1. Paul is the _____ boy in my class.
(pretty)	2. Mary is the _____ girl in school.
(rich)	3. Who is the _____ man in the world?
(safe)	4. Which road is the _____ ?
(white)	5. You'll find the _____ snow in the mountains.
(tall)	6. I'll need the _____ boy in the class.
(slow)	7. What animal is the _____ ?
(thick)	8. This book is the _____ of all of them.
(warm)	9. Is Acapulco the _____ place in the world?
(good)	10. Who is the _____ student in the class?

EXERCISE 6

Fill the blanks with the comparative or superlative degree, as required, of the adjective or adverb indicated (increasing scale).

(hungry)	1. His horse is _____ than yours.
(late)	2. Who came the _____ ?
(early)	3. Did John get up _____ than you?
(busy)	4. My father is the _____ man in the office.
(long)	5. What is the _____ river in the world?
(hot)	6. This soup is _____ than the coffee.
(small)	7. My dogs are _____ than that one.
(good)	8. This cake is _____ than that one.
(good)	9. This cake is the _____ of all the cakes.
(bad)	10. This cake is the _____ of all.

THE PAST PERFECT OF *CAN*
EL ANTECOPRETÉRITO DE *CAN*

Puesto que el auxiliar can existe solamente en el presente (**can**) y en el pasado (**could**), se forma el antecopretérito (**past perfect**) de **can** empleando el verbo **be able**. Es decir, se tiene que emplear el pasado del verbo **have** (**had**) y el participio del verbo **be able** (**been able**).

Hay que emplear el infinitivo con la partícula **to después** de las formas del verbo **be able.**

Ejemplo: He'd been able to go.
El había podido ir.

EXERCISE 7

Verb Practice

1. They'd been able to pick up everything.
2. They hadn't been able to pick up everything.
3. Had they been able to pick up everything?
4. Hadn't they been able to pick up everything?
5. Why hadn't they been able to pick up everything?

EXERCISE 8

Verb Practice *Repeat exercise 7, using forms of the verbs* practice, sleep, hear, lose, meet, leave, lend, let *in short sentences. Use a different noun or pronoun with each verb. Use the interrogative words when it is possible.*

EXERCISE 9

Change the following sentences to the past, future, present perfect, past perfect. Translate each time.

1. I can use that book.
2. We can't start early.
3. They can bring everything.
4. Can they hear anything from here?
5. Can't he teach English?
6. The boys can show you how to swim.
7. Can the children rest under that tree?
8. The girls can't sing that song.
9. John can invite Alice to the party.
10. Can't Mr. Clark see snow on the mountain?

EXERCISE 10

Fill the blanks with still *or* yet, *as required, and translate.*

1. Are you _____ trying to learn English?
2. Do you _____ have a horse?
3. I haven't gone _____ . I'm _____ waiting for Bill.
4. Hasn't Bill come _____ ? No, not _____ .
5. He hasn't been able to finish his work _____ . That's why he's _____ at the office.
6. They're _____ here, but they haven't eaten _____ .
7. I haven't read that book _____ , but I _____ have it.
8. Isn't she here _____ ? No, not _____ .
9. Can you _____ see the snow on the mountain from here?
10. Has anyone been able to do any work _____ ?

VERBOS COMPUESTOS DE DOS PALABRAS

to wake up despertar	**to turn off** apagar
to get up levantar	**to take out** sacar
to put on ponerse	**to pick out** escoger
to take off quitarse	**to pick up** recoger
to turn on prender	**to turn over** voltear

En algunos casos, al emplear un pronombre personal como complemento de un verbo que va acompañado de una partícula tal como **up**, **on**, **off**, **out**, etc., se colocará el pronombre personal entre el verbo y la partícula.

En otros casos, al emplear un sustantivo o cualquier pronombre, que no sea personal, como complemento de un verbo que va acompañado de una partícula tal como **up**, **on**, **off**, **out**, etc., se puede colocar el complemento antes o después de la partícula. Estudie las siguientes oraciones.

1. **We woke up the boys.** (*or*) We woke **the boys** up.
   We woke **them** up.
2. Mary put on **her hat**. (*or*) Mary put **her hat** on.
   Mary put **it** on.
3. I took off **my hat**. (*or*) I took **my hat** off.
   I took **it** off.
4. They turned on **the radio**. (*or*) They turned **the radio** on.
   They turned **it** on.
5. He turned off **the water**. (*or*) He turned **the water** off.
   He turned **it** off.
6. We took **the chairs** out. (*or*) We took out **the chairs**.
   We took **them** out.
7. Pick out a **suit**. (*or*) Pick a **suit** out.

Pick out **one**. (*or*) Pick **one** out.
(*pronombre indefinido, no personal*)
8. He picked up **his book**. (*or*) He picked **his book** up.
He picked up **his**. (*or*) He picked **his** up.
(*pronombre posesivo, no personal*)
9. He turned over **the page**. (*or*) He turned **the page** over.
He turned **it** over.

EXERCISE 11

Translate into English. Give two ways when possible.

1. Enciende la luz.
2. No la enciendas.
3. Apaguemos el radio.
4. Quiero apagarlo.
5. Voy a ponerme los zapatos.
6. No me los puedo poner.
7. No pudimos despertar a Carlos.
8. ¿A qué hora los vas a despertar?
9. ¿Quién puso el radio?
10. Ponte el tuyo y yo me pongo el mío.
11. Por favor saque la silla.
12. Por favor sáquela Ud.
13. Tengo que recoger los papeles.
14. Recógelos.
15. Abre la llave del agua.
16. Ábrela.
17. Ella va a escoger un vestido.
18. Ella va a escoger uno.
19. Voltee Ud. la página.
20. Voltéela.

EXERCISE 12

Translate the following sentences. Change them to the negative, interrogative, and interrogative negative.

1. She makes a living cleaning houses.
2. He made a living while he was in New York.
3. You can make a living if you try.
4. They've made a living for many years.
5. We'll be able to make a living working for Mr. Jones.
6. Henry has been able to make a living since he finished school.
7. Paul was making a living selling cars.
8. You can make a living as well as I.
9. They can make a living if they work harder.
10. I'll be able to make a better living next year.

EXERCISE 13

Answer the following questions.

1. How do you make a living?
2. Do you make a good living?
3. Do you make a living teaching school?
4. Did you make a living in the United States?
5. Can you make a living working in an office?
6. Are you going to make a living playing baseball?
7. Are you making a living now?
8. Can't you make a living?
9. Will you be able to make a living?
10. Have you been able to make a living?

EXERCISE 14

Translate into Spanish.

1. You won't be able to make a good living when you get old.
2. I'm going to work hard all week so that I can go out of town this week end.
3. Haven't you made any money yet?
4. You were still eating when I got there.
5. I always have a good time with the Clark family.
6. It doesn't make any difference what he says. I'm sure you're right.
7. The bed looked so soft that I wanted to lie down on it.
8. I'm not going to wear a dress to the party that looks like Mary's.
9. Let me know if you find a small house that's cheap.
10. If he doesn't come, I can't help it.
11. If you look out of the window now, you can see the mountains from here.
12. He walked up to me (se me acercó) and asked me the way to the market.
13. I think that small table will look nice between the chair and the sofa.
14. Will you be able to hang that picture above the dining room table?
15. He said that he'd been so sick that he hadn't been able to do anything.

EXERCISE 15

Give the past tense and past participle of the following verbs.

ask	close	cry	dress
answer	complete	carry	disappear
believe	change	die	dance
call	correct	drop	escape
clean	clap	dictate	

EXERCISE 16

Give the past tense and past participle of the following verbs.

be able	break	catch	feel
bring	be born	cut	forget
buy	blow	drink	fly
begin	come	do	find
become	come back	eat	fall (down)

EXERCISE 17

Verb Practice

1. The wind blows, doesn't it?
2. The wind doesn't blow, does it?
3. Does the wind blow?
4. Doesn't the wind blow?
5. When does the wind blow?
6. The wind blew, didn't it?
7. The wind didn't blow, did it?
8. Did the wind blow?
9. Didn't the wind blow?
10. When did the wind blow?
11. The wind is blowing, isn't it?
12. The wind isn't blowing, is it?
13. Is the wind blowing?
14. Isn't the wind blowing?
15. Why isn't the wind blowing?
16. The wind is going to blow, isn't it?
17. The wind isn't going to blow, is it?
18. Is the wind going to blow?
19. Isn't the wind going to blow?
20. When is the wind going to blow?
21. The wind will blow, won't it?

22. The wind won't blow, will it?
23. Will the wind blow?
24. Won't the wind blow?
25. When will the wind blow?
26. The wind has blown, hasn't it?
27. The wind hasn't blown, has it?
28. Has the wind blown?
29. Hasn't the wind blown?
30. When has the wind blown?
31. The wind had blown, hadn't it?
32. The wind hadn't blown, had it?
33. Had the wind blown?
34. Hadn't the wind blown?
35. When had the wind blown?

EXERCISE 18

Verb Practice *Repeat exercise 17, using forms of the verbs* **dig, lend, shine, die, turn over, get old, make a living** *in short sentences. Use a different noun or pronoun with each verb. Use the interrogative words when it is possible.*

EXERCISE 19

Read and translate.

THE FARMER AND HIS SONS

The old farmer had worked hard in his orchard all his life so that he could make a living for his wife and sons. Every spring the old man turned over the soil in the orchard so that the rain could go into the ground when it fell, and every summer he sold the fruit in the market.

One day the old farmer called his sons to him and said to them, "I'm getting old, and I don't have much time left in this world. It'll soon be time for me to die. As you boys know, I've worked hard all my life; and everything I have to leave you is in the orchard."

"He's left us a treasure in the orchard," thought the boys. We'll have to find it."

So after the old man died, the boys began to work very hard in the orchard. They got up very early every morning to dig in the soil. They dug and dug around each tree, turning over the soil again and again.

The rain fell in the spring, and the water ran into the soft ground, and the boys still dug in the orchard every day, looking for the treasure.

The warm summer sun shone down on the fruit trees as the boys worked among them, until one day they saw that it was time to take the fruit to the market.

After they'd dug in the soil for a year, they still hadn't found a treasure; but there was a lot of fruit, and after they'd sold it in the market, they had more money than they'd ever had before.

EXERCISE 20

Write in English.

1. Hace rato hacía sol, pero ahora está lloviendo.
2. Me estoy envejeciendo, pero ni modo.
3. Avísame si podrás ir conmigo el lunes.
4. Estamos estudiando inglés para que ganemos mejor.
5. Ya nos habíamos ido cuando vino él.
6. Apague Ud. el radio, por favor. Lo apagué hace un rato.
7. Él me dijo que creía que las casas en México no estaban caras.
8. Que yo sepa, ellos no habían podido comprar ese terreno.
9. Se ve más azul el cielo que el mar esta mañana.
10. Esta semana no ha habido clases porque ha estado enfermo el maestro.

EXERCISE 21

Dictation

1. The sun is much larger than the moon.
2. Are you still trying to make a living teaching school?
3. The wind from the north is colder than the wind from the south, isn't it?
4. That's the tallest man I've ever seen.
5. I don't want to go out of the room when the class is over.
6. Haven't you been able to go out of town during your vacation?
7. If it's windy or cloudy, we won't go.
8. The boys caught two rabbits, but one of them got away.
9. Do you like scrambled eggs better than fried eggs?
10. You were in a hurry when I saw you yesterday. What happened?

EXERCISE 22

Conversation *Answer the following questions.*

1. When were you born?
2. When did he die?
3. When did it rain?
4. When did it snow?
5. How long have you lived in Mexico?
6. How long have you studied English?
7. How long had you studied English before going to the United States?
8. How long had you been there when John came?
9. How long had you lived in Mexico when your father died?
10. How long had you worked at Ford when you left?

Answer the following questions in the affirmative and in the negative.

11. Is the sun still shining?
12. Is the moon still shining?
13. Is it still raining?
14. Is it still cloudy?
15. Was it sunny yesterday?
16. Have you already finished?
17. Has she already eaten?
18. Haven't you finished yet?
19. Hasn't he come yet?
20. Hasn't it rained yet?
21. Are you younger than your brother?
22. Is Acapulco warmer than Veracruz?
23. Is Acapulco the warmest place in Mexico?
24. Are you taller than your father?
25. Are you the tallest one in the family?
26. Are you shorter than your father?
27. Are you the shortest one in the family?
28. Are you older than your brother?
29. Are you the oldest one in the family?
30. Will there be classes on Monday?
31. Will you be able to lend me the money?
32. Will you be able to study tonight?
33. Has it been cold all day?
34. Have you been hungry all day?
35. Was it windy yesterday?

Lección 6

Vocabulary

1. **to knock (on), knocked (on), knocked (on)** tocar (*la puerta*)
2. **to save, saved, saved** salvar; ahorrar; guardar
3. **to watch, watched, watched** observar; vigilar
4. **to kiss, kissed, kissed** besar
5. **to cover, covered, covered** cubrir, tapar
6. **to last, lasted, lasted** durar
7. **forever** para siempre
8. **foolish** (*adj.*) tonto
9. **lazy** perezoso, flojo
10. **noise** ruido
    noisy ruidoso; escandaloso
11. **ant** hormiga
12. **pasture** campos para pastar
13. **grain** grano
14. **corn** maíz; elote
15. **wheat** trigo
16. **shade** sombra
17. **cloud** nube
18. **arm** brazo
19. **leg** pierna
20. **foot** pie
    feet pies
21. **clothes** (*plural*) ropa
22. **coat** abrigo
23. **overcoat** abrigo de invierno
24. **raincoat** impermeable
25. **address** dirección
26. **leaf** hoja (*de árbol*)
    leaves hojas

IDIOMS

1. **to try hard** hacer lo posible por, esforzarse por

81

2. **to get ready** alistarse, prepararse
3. **day after day** día tras día
4. **as usual** como de costumbre
5. **as if** como si
6. **no wonder** con razón
7. **at noon** al mediodía
8. **by car** en coche
   by bus en camión
   by plane en avión
   by train en tren
   by ship en barco
9. **There'd been work.** Había habido trabajo.
   There'd been children. Había habido niños.

EXERCISE 1

Translate the following sentences and practice reading them.

1. Don't fall.
2. Don't let them fall.
3. They'd fallen.
4. They hadn't fallen.
5. They'd been able to rest.
6. They hadn't been able to rest.
7. Had they been able to rest?
8. Hadn't they been able to rest?
9. There'll be classes tomorrow.
10. There won't be any classes tomorrow.
11. There've been classes all week.
12. There haven't been classes all week.
13. I've been hungry all morning.
14. I haven't been hungry all morning.
15. It's been cold all day.
16. It hasn't been cold all day.
17. It's been hot all afternoon.
18. It hasn't been hot all afternoon.
19. It'll be cold next week.
20. It won't be cold next week.

COMPARACIÓN DE ADJETIVOS y ADVERBIOS DE MÁS DE UNA SÍLABA EL GRADO COMPARATIVO DE SUPERIORIDAD

Los adjetivos y adverbios de más de una sílaba forman el comparativo de superioridad usando la palabra **more** antes del adjetivo o adverbio. Cuando se usa la palabra **que** en español, el adjetivo o el adverbio irá seguido de la palabra **than** en inglés.

EL GRADO SUPERLATIVO DE SUPERIORIDAD

Los adjetivos y adverbios de más de una sílaba forman el superlativo de superioridad usando las palabras **the most** antes del adjetivo o adverbio.

En esta regla se incluyen también los adverbios terminados en **ly**, que equivale a **mente** en español, ejemplos: **slowly, more slowly than, the most slowly, quickly, more quickly than, the most quickly** *pero:* **early, earlier than, the earliest** (aunque la palabra **early** consta de dos sílabas, la terminación **ly** no equivale a mente.) Estudie los siguientes ejemplos:

	Comparative Degree Increasing Scale	Superlative Degree Increasing Scale
softly	more softly than	the most softly
beautiful	more beautiful than	the most beautiful
comfortable	more comfortable than	the most comfortable
complete	more complete than	the most complete

Estudie el grado comparativo y superlativo de superioridad de los siguientes adjetivos y adverbios de más de una sílaba.

	Comparative Degree Increasing Scale	Superlative Degree Increasing Scale
beautiful	more beautiful than	the most beautiful
comfortable	more comfortable than	the most comfortable
complete	more complete than	the most complete
correct	more correct than	the most correct
careful	more careful than	the most careful

carefully	more carefully than	the most carefully
difficult	more difficult than	the most difficult
dangerous	more dangerous than	the most dangerous
expensive	more expensive than	the most expensive
interesting	more interesting than	the most interesting
important	more important than	the most important
impossible	more impossible than	the most impossible
possible	more possible than	the most possible
quickly	more quickly than	the most quickly
slowly	more slowly than	the most slowly
selfish	more selfish than	the most selfish
softly	more softly than	the most softly
useful	more useful than	the most useful

EXERCISE 2

Fill the blanks with the comparative degree of the adjective or adverb indicated and translate (increasing scale).

(beautiful)   1. Helen's dress is _____ _____ than Mary's.

(comfortable)   2. That chair is _____ _____ than the sofa.

(complete)   3. This exercise is _____ _____ than the other one.

(difficult)   4. Do you think the second lesson is _____ _____ than the first one?

(dangerous)   5. Is the road to Acapulco _____ _____ than the one to Veracruz?

(expensive)   6. Clothes are _____ _____ every year.

(interesting)   7. This book is _____ _____ than that one.

(important)   8. The verbs are much _____ _____ than the adjectives.

(slowly)   9. Time passes much _____ _____ when we aren't working.

(quickly)   10. I'm sure he'll learn how to speak English much _____ _____ than his brother.

EXERCISE 3

Fill the blanks with the superlative degree of the adjective or adverb indicated and translate (increasing scale).

84

(selfish)	1. He's the _____ _____ man that I've ever known.
(useful)	2. This is the _____ _____ thing that I have.
(dangerous)	3. Is the lion the _____ _____ animal in Africa?
(correct)	4. Bill has written the _____ _____ sentence.
(important)	5. This lesson is the _____ _____ one in the book.
(expensive)	6. This is the _____ _____ coat we have in the store.
(interesting)	7. This is the _____ _____ movie I've seen this year.
(difficult)	8. Of Spanish, English, and French which is the _____ _____ to learn?
(expensive)	9. Which of these cars is the _____ _____ ?
(difficult)	10. The first book is the _____ _____ one we have.

EXERCISE 4

Fill the blanks with the comparative or superlative degree, as required, of the adjective or adverb indicated and translate (increasing scale).

(beautiful)	1. I think summer is the _____ _____ time of the year.
(useful)	2. Why do you think that English is much _____ _____ than French?
(dangerous)	3. Are planes _____ _____ than trains?
(correct)	4. She said that my pronunciation was the _____ _____ .
(complete)	5. I want to find a book a little _____ _____ than this one.
(difficult)	6. This kind of cake is the _____ _____ to make.
(beautiful)	7. They have the _____ _____ clothes in that store.
(softly)	8. She speaks _____ _____ than the other children.
(possible)	9. It's _____ _____ to reach the moon now than it was twenty years ago.
(selfish)	10. Do you think that girls are _____ _____ than boys?

EXERCISE 5

Give the comparative and superlative degree of the following adjectives and adverbs (increasing scale).

angry	black	dirty	full
big	clean	early	green
blue	cold	easy	good
bad	close (to)	empty	happy
busy	cheap	fine	hungry

EXERCISE 6

Fill the blanks with the comparative or superlative degree, as required, of the adjective or adverb indicated and translate (increasing scale).

(noisy)   1. I live on the _____ street in Mexico City.
(thirsty)   2. Are you _____ than your brother?
(cheap)   3. Are Ford cars _____ than Buicks?
(large)   4. Which of these animals is the _____ ?
(good)   5. Is this your _____ dress?
(good)   6. I like Mexico City _____ than Veracruz
(bad)   7. That sick child is _____ today.
(bad)   8. I have the _____ class in school.
(happy)   9. My parents are much _____ in Mexico City than they were in the United States.
(busy)   10. We are much _____ now than we were last year.

EXERCISE 7

Translate into English. Give two ways when possible.

1. Ponte el vestido.
2. Póntelo.
3. Ponte los tuyos y yo me pongo el mío.
4. Juan va a poner la televisión.
5. Ibamos a apagarla.
6. Él no quiso encenderla.
7. A él le gusta despertarme.
8. Despiérteme Ud. temprano.
9. Apaguémosla.
10. No la apaguemos.
11. Abre la llave de la cocina.
12. No la abras.
13. Quisimos sacar la mesa.
14. No la saqué.

EXERCISE 8

Translate the following sentences and practice reading them.

1. There'd been a lot of parties.
2. There hadn't been a lot of parties.
3. Had there been a lot of parties?
4. Hadn't there been a lot of parties?
5. There's been a lot of rain this month.
6. There hasn't been much rain this month.
7. Has there been a lot of rain this month?
8. Hasn't there been a lot of rain this month?
9. They'd been sleepy all morning.
10. They hadn't been sleepy all morning.
11. Had they been sleepy all morning?
12. Hadn't they been sleepy all morning?
13. It'd been very hot.
14. It hadn't been very hot.
15. Had it been very hot?
16. Hadn't it been very hot?
17. I'd had to study very hard.
18. I hadn't had to study very hard.
19. You'd had to work every day.
20. You hadn't had to work every day.
21. Had you had to work every day?
22. Hadn't you had to work every day?

EXERCISE 9

Translate the following sentences. Change them to the negative, interrogative, and interrogative negative.

1. He tried hard to speak English.
2. We'll try hard to finish by five o'clock.
3. They've tried hard to make more money.
4. She's going to try hard to visit the United States next year.
5. Helen and Martha were trying hard to swim across the river.
6. Richard tried hard to learn Spanish.
7. Her little daughter tried hard to make a cake.
8. He tried hard to drink all the milk.
9. He tried hard to leave at noon.
10. The children try hard to practice their English every day.

EXERCISE 10

Answer the following questions in the affirmative and in the negative.

1. Did you try hard to read that book?
2. Do they try hard to answer in English?
3. Have you tried hard to visit Acapulco?
4. Have they tried hard to find a house that's warm?
5. Will he try hard to buy a new car next year?
6. Does your father try hard to go to the office every day?
7. Will she try hard to go out of town this week end?
8. Did he try hard to drink all the milk?
9. Will you try hard to get work?
10. Are you going to try hard to come to my birthday party?

EXERCISE 11

Translate into Spanish.

1. No wonder he makes so much money if he works from eight o'clock in the morning until nine at night.
2. It's already noon, and they haven't come yet.
3. Are you studying English as usual?
4. This soup looks like dirty water.
5. Mrs. Nelson is getting old.
6. We tried hard to put all the things in the car, but there wasn't enough room.
7. I don't think you'll have a good time if you go out of town during your vacation.
8. It's hard to make a living teaching English.
9. You were right. We visited this place two years ago.
10. We've had to get up early every day this week so that we can get to the office before eight o'clock.
11. He caught two chickens, but both of them got away.
12. They'd already gone to bed before I got sleepy.
13. There've been many Americans in Mexico this summer.
14. Will there be enough time for us to get to the market before it closes?
15. There's been so much rain this summer that we haven't been able to go out a great deal.

EXERCISE 12

Give the past tense and past participle of the following verbs.

fix	hurry	like	laugh (at)
finish	invite	learn	love
fill	jump	look like	need
form	kill	look (at)	open
help	live	look (for)	pass

EXERCISE 13

Give the past tense and past participle of the following verbs.

go	give up	get sleepy	get off
go back	get	get thirsty	get married
go to bed	get up	get old	get away
go to sleep	get angry	get ready	get rich
go out	(at)	get to (here,	have
give	get mad	there)	
	(at)		

EXERCISE 14

Verb Practice

1. She usually knocks on the door.
2. She doesn't usually knock on the door.
3. Does she usually knock on the door?
4. Doesn't she usually knock on the door?
5. Why doesn't she usually knock on the door?
6. She knocked on the window.
7. She didn't knock on the window.
8. Did she knock on the window?
9. Didn't she knock on the window?
10. Why didn't she knock on the window?
11. She wants to knock on the door.
12. She doesn't want to knock on the door.
13. Does she want to knock on the door?
14. Doesn't she want to knock on the door?
15. Why doesn't she want to knock on the door?
16. She has to knock on the window.

17. She doesn't have to knock on the window.
18. Does she have to knock on the window?
19. Doesn't she have to knock on the window?
20. Why does she have to knock on the window?
21. She'd knocked on the door.
22. She hadn't knocked on the door.
23. Had she knocked on the door?
24. Hadn't she knocked on the door?
25. Why hadn't she knocked on the door?
26. She's been able to knock on the window.
27. She hasn't been able to knock on the window.
28. Has she been able to knock on the window?
29. Hasn't she been able to knock on the window?
30. Why hasn't she been able to knock on the window?
31. She'd been able to knock on the door.
32. She hadn't been able to knock on the door.
33. Had she been able to knock on the door?
34. Hadn't she been able to knock on the door?
35. Why hadn't she been able to knock on the door?

EXERCISE 15

Verb Practice *Repeat exercise 14, using forms of the verbs* **save, watch, kiss, cover, last, get ready, try hard** *in short sentences. Use a different noun or pronoun with each verb. Use the interrogative words when it is possible.*

EXERCISE 16

Read and translate.

THE ANT AND THE GRASSHOPPER
(CHAPULÍN)

It was summer, and the warm sun shone down on the pasture where the ant and the grasshopper had lived since spring.

The ant, as usual, was working. She was always working. Day after day she carried grains of wheat and corn to her house so she could have plenty of food for the winter.

The grasshopper was always flying around (dando vueltas) in the soft wind, singing and playing. He sang and played all day. "Why work and save food for the winter when there's enough to eat lying on the ground?" he asked.

One day as the grasshopper sat in the shade watching the ant carry a very large grain of wheat, the grasshopper said to the ant. "Why are you so foolish? You work all day and never have any fun. Don't you know that summer is a time to be happy?"

"Summer won't last forever," replied the ant. "What will you do when winter comes and there's snow on the ground? You won't have anything to eat, and you won't be able to find any food. Why are you so lazy?"

"I'm not hungry yet," answered the grasshopper, as he flew away singing (voló cantando).

The ant went back to her work, carrying grains of wheat and corn. Soon her house was full of food, so she closed the door and began to get ready for winter.

The next morning the wind blew from the north, bringing rain and snow with it. The flowers in the field died, the leaves fell off the trees, and clouds covered the sun.

The poor grasshopper had no place to go. He was tired and hungry, and his wings were so cold that he couldn't fly. Then he began to think of the ant, warm and safe in her house full of food; so he knocked on the door of the ant's house.

"Please give me something to eat," the grasshopper said when the ant opened the door. "I'm cold and hungry and there's no food."

"What were you doing all summer while I was working?" asked the ant.

"I was singing," answered the grasshopper.

"Well, dance now," said the ant as she closed the door in the grasshopper's face.

EXERCISE 17

Write in English.

1. Dame tu dirección para que te escriba.
2. Con razón nunca has podido aprender inglés. Nunca vas a clase.
3. Ya nos habíamos ido cuando vino mi tío, ¿verdad?
4. Cuando salí, estaba lloviendo muy fuerte, así es que me tapé la cabeza con un periódico.
5. No habrá clases mañana, así es que no me despiertes temprano.

6. No ha habido suficiente lluvia este verano, y se está secando (dying) todo el pasto.
7. No sé por qué he tenido tanta hambre toda la mañana. Comí bastante en (for) el desayuno.
8. ¿Va su tío (de Ud.) por avión o por tren?
9. ¿A qué hora cree Ud. que podrá acabar mi vestido?
10. Estas son las flores más hermosas que jamás (ever) he visto.

EXERCISE 18

Dictation

1. Her dress looks more expensive than mine, doesn't it?
2. I had a very good time while I was in Monterrey.
3. If your cousin comes by plane, she'll arrive at ten o'clock.
4. No wonder your flowers died. You haven't given them any water for a month, have you?
5. My mother writes the most interesting letters that I've ever read.
6. He said that he hadn't been able to study since he lost his books.
7. Will they be able to see if they sit behind us?
8. It's been so cold all winter that we haven't been able to work in the garden.
9. Was it hot in Chicago when you were there?
10. If it looks like rain, take your raincoat.

EXERCISE 19

Conversation *Answer the following questions.*

1. What did you take your raincoat for?
2. Where did your parents come from?
3. Who did you talk to?
4. Who did you go with?
5. What's that movie about?
6. What are you talking about?
7. How long have you lived on Madison Street?
8. How long has he been there?
9. How long had you been there when it began to rain?
10. How long had he lived in Mexico before he left?

Answer the following questions in the affirmative and in the negative.

11. Is Alice more beautiful than Mary?
12. Is English more difficult than Spanish?
13. Are planes more dangerous than trains?
14. Is television more interesting than the movies?
15. Is English more useful than Spanish?
16. Is Jane the most beautiful girl in the office?
17. Is this the most comfortable chair in the house?
18. Is this the most interesting book you have?
19. Is Mexico City the most important city in Mexico?
20. Are raincoats cheaper than overcoats?
21. Is English easier than Spanish?
22. Is Spanish harder than English?
23. Do you get up earlier than Henry?
24. Are you bigger than your brother?
25. Is this the noisiest street in the city?
26. Is this the best one you could buy?
27. Is he the richest man in the world?
28. Is February the shortest month of the year?
29. Did you get tired?
30. Did you get sleepy?
31. Did you get thirsty?
32. Did you get married?
33. Did you get mad?
34. Is it windy today?
35. Was it cloudy this morning?

Lección 7

Vocabulary

1. **to stay, stayed, stayed** quedarse; alojarse
2. **to feed, fed, fed** dar de comer
3. **to hide, hid, hidden** esconder(se), ocultar(se)
4. **to spend, spent, spent** gastar (dinero); pasar (*tiempo*)
5. **to travel, traveled, traveled** viajar
6. **to worry (about), worried (about), worried (about)** preocuparse (por)
7. **dark** oscuro
8. **heavy** pesado
9. **loud** fuerte, recio (*de sonido*); chillante (*de color*)
10. **huge** gigantesco, enorme
11. **own** propio
    owner dueño
12. **excitement** emoción; excitación
13. **remains** restos
14. **building** edificio
15. **fortune** fortuna
16. **peace** paz
17. **music** música
18. **meal** comida
19. **news** (*sing.*) noticias
20. **trip** viaje
21. **God** Dios
22. **town** pueblo
23. **beans** frijoles
24. **nut** nuez
25. **station** estación (*de ferrocarril*)
26. **light** claro; liviano, ligero

IDIOMS

1. **to wear out** acabarse

it'd work	trabajaría
we'd work	trabajaríamos
you'd work	Uds. trabajarían
they'd work	ellos trabajarían

Negativo

you wouldn't eat	tú no comerías
John wouldn't eat	Juan no comería
they wouldn't eat	ellos no comerían

Interrogativo

Recuerde el orden de las palabras para el interrogativo: auxiliar, sustantivo o pronombre, verbo.

would they study?	¿estudiarían ellos?
would the boys study?	¿estudiarían los muchachos?
would he study?	¿estudiaría él?

Interrogativo Negativo

wouldn't you speak?	¿no hablarías tú?
wouldn't Mr. Cox speak?	¿no hablaría el Sr. Cox?
wouldn't we speak?	¿no hablaríamos nosotros?

EXERCISE 2

Verb Practice

1. He'd play football.
2. He wouldn't play football.
3. Would he play football?
4. Wouldn't he play football?
5. What would he play?

EXERCISE 3

Verb Practice *Repeat exercise 2, using forms of the verbs* dance, understand, die, blow, shine, rest, stop, win, kill *in short sentences. Use a different noun or pronoun with each verb. Use the interrogative words when it is possible.*

97

EXERCISE 4

Give the comparative and superlative degree of the following adjectives and adverbs (increasing scale).

hot	light	near	pure
hard	long	narrow	pretty
kind	large	noisy	quick
little	lazy	old	red
late	nice	poor	rich

EXERCISE 5

Give the comparative and superlative degree of the following adjectives and adverbs (increasing scale).

beautiful	difficult	impossible	useful
comfortable	dangerous	polite	useless
complete	expensive	possible	
correct	foolish	**selfish**	
careful	interesting	usual	

EXERCISE 6

Fill the blanks with the comparative or superlative degree, as required, of the adjective or adverb indicated and translate (increasing scale).

(difficult)   1. The _____ _____ lessons are in the second book.

(lazy)   2. Those are the _____ people in the world.

(useful)   3. Is English _____ _____ than Spanish?

(polite)   4. Are Mexicans _____ _____ than Americans?

(hungry)   5. I'm always _____ than you.

(light)   6. Your books are _____ than mine.

(rich)   7. Who is the _____ man in Mexico?

(old)   8. This is the _____ building in the city.

(comfortable)   9. Planes are _____ _____ than trains.

(beautiful)   10. The _____ _____ girl in school is in my class.

(noisy)   11. The boys in my class are _____ than the girls.

(pretty)   12. The _____ girls will dance tonight.

(red)   13. Your curtains are _____ than your rug.

(interesting)   14. We saw the _____ _____ movie last night.

(poor)   15. He is _____ than I was when I was young.

98

THE CONDITIONAL OF *CAN*
EL POSPRETÉRITO DE *CAN*

Puesto que el auxiliar **can** existe solamente en el presente (**can**) y en el pasado (**could**), se forma el pospretérito (**conditional**) empleando el verbo **be able**. Es decir, se tiene que emplear el auxiliar **would** seguido por el infinitivo **to be able** sin la partícula **to**.

Hay que usar el infinitivo con la partícula **to** después de las formas del verbo **be able**.

Could también equivale al pospretérito de **poder** (podría), así es que existen dos maneras de traducir **podría** en inglés.

Ejemplos:

They could go. (*or*) They would be able to go.
Ellos podrían ir.

They couldn't go. (*or*) They wouldn't be able to go.
Ellos no podrían ir.

EXERCISE 7

Verb Practice

1. They'd be able to do everything.
2. They wouldn't be able to do everything.
3. Would they be able to do everything?
4. Wouldn't they be able to do everything?
5. How much would they be able to do?

EXERCISE 8

Verb Practice *Repeat exercise 7, using forms of the verbs* ask, answer, give, cut, cry, break, become, begin, drop *in short sentences. Use a different noun or pronoun with each verb. Use the interrogative words when it is possible.*

EXERCISE 9

Change these sentences to the past, future, present perfect, past perfect, and conditional. Translate each time.

1. They can escape from that building.
2. He can drink all the milk.
3. They can come back.
4. We can close the store at nine o'clock.
5. You can come back.
6. I can catch those mice.
7. She can sing that song.
8. That bird can fly out of the house.
9. John can put on his new shoes.
10. My mother can pick out a new dress.

EXERCISE 10

Translate the following sentences. Change them to the negative, interrogative, and interrogative negative.

1. His shoes wore out.
2. My raincoat is wearing out.
3. All their clothes have worn out.
4. Those suits wear out easily.
5. It can wear out.
6. He'll wear out his shoes.
7. She wore out her coat.
8. I'm going to wear it out.
9. John wore out his suit.
10. The children have worn them out.

EXERCISE 11

Answer the following questions in the affirmative and in the negative.

1. Did John's hat wear out?
2. Is your sister's raincoat wearing out?
3. Have the children's shoes worn out?
4. Can it wear out?
5. Were their shoes wearing out?
6. Would that suit wear out?
7. Did you wear out your sweater?
8. Has he worn it out?
9. Do you want to wear your new shoes out?
10. Will they wear them out soon?

100

EXERCISE 12

Translate into Spanish.

1. You're right. The child looks like his father.
2. They tried hard to make a lot of money, but they died poor.
3. I won't be able to buy a new suit when this one wears out.
4. He has to work so hard to make a living that he doesn't have any time to have fun.
5. I still think that John is right.
6. We haven't visited his mother yet.
7. This hat doesn't fit me. It's too big.
8. If your shoes don't fit you, they'll soon wear out.
9. Don't worry about us if we aren't at home at three-thirty.
10. How long will a new dress last?
11. Does it make you sick to fly?
12. How long is your hair?
13. How long is the English class?
14. Your new raincoat has already started to wear out.
15. Those green apples are going to make you sick.

EXERCISE 13

Give the past tense and past participle of the following verbs.

open	practice	rain	stop
pass	pronounce	rest	show
pick out	play	study	snow
pick up	reply	stay	shout (at)
place	reach	start	spill

EXERCISE 14

Give the past tense and past participle of the following verbs.

hear	lie down	make	read
hang	let	meet	run
hide	lay eggs	put	say
know	lend	put on	see
leave	lose	pay	speak

EXERCISE 15

Verb Practice

101

1. The President stays in that hotel, doesn't he?
2. The President doesn't stay in that hotel, does he?
3. The President stayed in that hotel, didn't he?
4. The President didn't stay in that hotel, did he?
5. The President is staying in that hotel, isn't he?
6. The President isn't staying in that hotel, is he?
7. The President was staying in that hotel, wasn't he?
8. The President wasn't staying in that hotel, was he?
9. The President is going to stay in that hotel, isn't he?
10. The President isn't going to stay in that hotel, is he?
11. The President was going to stay in that hotel, wasn't he?
12. The President wasn't going to stay in that hotel, was he?
13. The President liked to stay in that hotel, didn't he?
14. The President didn't like to stay in that hotel, did he?
15. The President wanted to stay in that hotel, didn't he?
16. The President didn't want to stay in that hotel, did he?
17. The President had to stay in that hotel, didn't he?
18. The President didn't have to stay in that hotel, did he?
19. The President can stay in that hotel, can't he?
20. The President can't stay in that hotel, can he?
21. The President could stay in that hotel, couldn't he?
22. The President couldn't stay in that hotel, could he?
23. The President will be able to stay in that hotel, won't he?
24. The President won't be able to stay in that hotel, will he?
25. The President has stayed in that hotel, hasn't he?
26. The President hasn't stayed in that hotel, has he?
27. The President had stayed in that hotel, hadn't he?
28. The President hadn't stayed in that hotel, had he?
29. The President has been able to stay in that hotel, hasn't he?
30. The President hasn't been able to stay in that hotel, has he?
31. The President had been able to stay in that hotel, hadn't he?
32. The President hadn't been able to stay in that hotel, had he?
33. The President would stay in that hotel, wouldn't he?
34. The President wouldn't stay in that hotel, would he?
35. The President would be able to stay in that hotel, wouldn't he?
36. The President wouldn't be able to stay in that hotel, would he?

EXERCISE 16

Verb Practice *Repeat exercise 15, using forms of the verbs* travel, worry, spend, feed, hide, get wet, get your hair (feet, etc.) wet, wear out, wear (something) out, feel at home *in short sentences. Use a different noun or pronoun with each verb. Use the interrogative words when it is possible.*

EXERCISE 17

Read and translate.

THE COUNTRY MOUSE AND THE TOWN MOUSE

A country mouse, who had a friend in town, invited his city friend to spend some time with him in the country. The country mouse tried hard to make his visitor from the city as comfortable as possible; so he fed him all kinds of simple country food such as beans, cheese, nuts, apples, wheat, and corn.

But the town mouse wasn't happy in the country. He liked the noise and excitement of the city and the different kinds of food that he could have there.

"Aren't you tired of living in the country?" the town mouse asked his friend. "Why do you stay here day after day doing nothing? Come to the city with me, and I'll show you how to live. A mouse, you know, doesn't live forever; and I'll show you what life is like (cómo es la vida) in town."

"I'd like to visit the city someday," answered the country mouse.

So, at last, the two mice started for the city. It was dark when they reached the big house where the city mouse lived. On the table were the remains of a huge meal. They were both tired and hungry, and the town mouse gave the country mouse all kinds of rich and expensive food to eat.

The country mouse began to feel at home in this new place, and he thanked God for his good fortune and such a nice change in his way of life. He had never thought that he'd be able to live in such comfort.

Just then he heard a loud noise outside the door.

"What's that?" asked the country mouse.

"Oh, that's only the owner's dog," replied the town mouse.

"Only!" said the visitor. "I don't like that kind of music with my meals."

At that moment some people came into the room with two huge dogs. The two mice jumped off the table and hid in a corner of the room.

After the people and the dogs had gone, the country mouse said to his friend, "This fine way of living is all right for those who like it, but it's better to eat simple food in peace than to eat fine food when you're afraid. Good-bye."

EXERCISE 18

Write in English.

1. ¿Cuánto tiempo te durarán los nuevos zapatos?
2. Quítate ese sombrero y ponte el verde.
3. La semana pasada me mojé todos los días.
4. ¿Le gustaría a Ud. vivir en Chicago durante el invierno?
5. Si te mojas el cabello, te hará daño.
6. Mi papá dijo que no podríamos ir en avión.
7. ¿Por qué no has podido encontrar un sombrero que te venga?
8. No podremos esperarte (meet you) en la estación, pero no te preocupes.
9. Ellos han tenido que viajar mucho durante este año.
10. No hemos podido quedarnos mucho tiempo (very long) en un lugar.

EXERCISE 19

Dictation

1. I told him that he'd have a good time if he spent his vacation with you.
2. The trip was very long, but we weren't tired when we got there.
3. I told you those shoes weren't very good. I knew they'd soon wear out.
4. Would you like to have dinner with me on Sunday?
5. She turned over that bucket of water and got her dress wet.
6. Don't walk in that water, or you'll get your feet wet.
7. A man such as John will feel at home in my country.
8. This is the most beautiful dress that I've ever seen, but it doesn't fit me.
9. It's easier to go by car than by train.
10. The nights are very dark when the moon isn't shining.

EXERCISE 20

Conversation *Answer the following questions.*

1. How long is your English class?

104

2. How long was the movie?
3. How long is your hair?
4. How long have you lived in Mexico?
5. How long have you been in Acapulco?
6. Where did you spend your vacation?
7. Where did you spend your money?

Answer the following questions in the affirmative and in the negative.

8. Do you feel at home at your cousin's house?
9. Did you feel at home among so many Americans?
10. Does that suit fit you?
11. Does that hat fit you?
12. Has your suit worn out?
13. Did you get wet yesterday?
14. Do you get wet when it rains?
15. Do you worry about your family?
16. Did you worry about me?
17. Did you spend your vacation in Acapulco?
18. Did you spend any time in Chicago?
19. Do you like to travel by car?
20. Do you like to travel by plane?
21. Would you like to live in Mexico?
22. Would you like to visit the United States?
23. Would you like to go with us?
24. Wouldn't he come?
25. Wouldn't she study?

Lección 8

1. **to build, built, built** construir
2. **to mean, meant, meant** querer decir, significar
3. **to tie, tied, tied** amarrar
4. **to keep, kept, kept** conservar; guardar; quedarse con
5. **to fight, fought, fought** pelear, luchar
6. **to prefer, preferred, preferred** preferir
7. **hardly** apenas
8. **exact** exacto, preciso **exactly** exactamente, precisamente
9. **together** junto(s)
10. **bright** brillante
11. **tight** apretado, ajustado
12. **fat** gordo; gordura
13. **ugly** feo
14. **free** libre; gratis **freedom** libertad
15. **wolf** lobo **wolves** lobos
16. **thief** ladrón **thieves** ladrones
17. **skin** piel; cutis
18. **bone** hueso
19. **finger** dedo
20. **mark** marca
21. **chain** cadena
22. **watch** reloj (*de pulso*)
23. **roof** techo; azotea
24. **surprise** sorpresa
25. **bathing suit** traje de baño
26. **elevator** elevador
27. **decreasing scale** escala descendente

IDIOMS

1. **to shake hands (with)** dar la mano (a), saludar (a)
2. **to get drunk** emborracharse
3. **to get sick** enfermarse
4. **to tie (someone or something) up** amarrar (a alguien o algo)
5. **one by one** uno por uno, uno a uno
6. **side by side** uno al lado del otro
7. **It's out of order.** Está descompuesto. No funciona.
   It doesn't work. Está descompuesto. No funciona.
8. **What a pity.** Qué lástima.
9. **Would you like … ?** ¿Le gustaría (Quiere) … ? (*para invitar*)
   Would you like to go to the movies? ¿Le gustaría (Quiere) ir al cine?
10. **There'd be work.** Habría trabajo.
    There'd be children. Habría niños.

EXERCISE 1

Translate the following sentences and practice reading them.

1. Hide in the bedroom.
2. Don't hide in the bedroom.
3. Let's hide in the bedroom.
4. Let's not hide in the bedroom.
5. What are you hiding behind the sofa for?
6. Who are you hiding from?
7. What are you hiding from?
8. What have you hidden behind the sofa for?
9. Who have you hidden from?
10. What have you hidden from?
11. You'd hide under the bed.
12. You wouldn't hide under the bed.
13. Would you hide under the bed?
14. Wouldn't you hide under the bed?
15. You'd be able to hide under the table.
16. You wouldn't be able to hide under the table.
17. Would you be able to hide under the table?
18. Wouldn't you be able to hide under the table?
19. He'll have to get off at the next corner.
20. He won't have to get off at the next corner.

EL GRADO COMPARATIVO DE INFERIORIDAD

Se forma el grado comparativo de inferioridad de los adjetivos y adverbios colocando la palabra **less** (menos) antes del adjetivo o adverbio, cualquiera que sea el número de sílabas de éstos. Cuando se usa la palabra **que** en castellano equivale a **than** en inglés. Estudie los siguientes ejemplos:

less cold than	menos frío que
less easily than	menos fácilmente que
less beautiful than	menos hermoso que
less ugly than	menos feo que
less carefully than	con menos cuidado que
less difficult than	menos difícil que

EL GRADO SUPERLATIVO DE INFERIORIDAD

Se forma el grado superlativo de inferioridad de los adjetivos y adverbios colocando las palabras **the least** (el menos) antes del adjetivo o adverbio. Estudie los siguientes ejemplos:

the least cold	el menos frío
the least easily	con menos facilidad
the least beautiful	el menos hermoso
the least ugly	el menos feo
the least carefully	con menos cuidado
the least difficult	lo menos difícil

EXERCISE 2

Give the comparative and superlative degree of the following adjectives and adverbs (decreasing scale).

bright	pretty	green	wide
tight	clean	kind	far
fat	correct	noisy	bad
ugly	easy	warm	young
free	difficult	weak	loud

EXERCISE 3

Fill the blanks with the comparative degree of the adjective or adverb indicated and translate (decreasing scale).

(heavy)   1. My books are _____ _____ than yours.

(light)   2. This stone is _____ _____ than the other one.

(dark)   3. Are the nights _____ _____ than before?

(hard)   4. English is _____ _____ than Spanish.

(noisy)   5. The street that we live on now is _____ _____ than the one that we lived on before.

(polite)   6. Why are these children _____ _____ than those?

(poor)   7. The people in our city are _____ _____ than those in the country.

(rich)   8. My husband is _____ _____ than yours.

(busy)   9. I am _____ _____ today than yesterday.

(full)   10. The glass is _____ _____ than the bucket.

EXERCISE 4

Fill the blanks with the superlative degree of the adjective or adverb indicated and translate (decreasing scale).

(wide)   1. This street is the _____ _____ of all of them.

(beautiful)   2. Mary is the _____ _____ of the three girls.

(clean)   3. The bedroom is the _____ _____ of all the rooms in the house.

(interesting)   4. Of Cuernavaca, Toluca, and Taxco, Toluca is the _____ _____ .

(red)   5. Those flowers are the _____ _____ **of all** the ones in the garden.

(pretty)   6. Does this little bird sing the _____ _____ of all of them?

(comfortable)   7. Of all the chairs in the house, this one is the _____ _____ .

(warm)   8. Is this room the _____ _____ in the house?

(easy)   9. This book is the _____ _____ to read.

(kind)   10. Of all the teachers in the school Mr. Simons is the _____ _____ .

EXERCISE 5

Fill the blanks with the comparative or superlative degree, as required, of the adjective or adverb indicated and translate (decreasing scale).

(tight)   1. My overcoat is _____ _____ than my rain-coat.

(bright)   2. The moon is _____ _____ than the sun.

(expensive)   3. Are Ford cars the _____ _____ of all the cars?

(cheap)   4. Are Buicks _____ _____ than Fords?

(loud)   5. The children from that school sing _____ _____ than those.

(warm)   6. This suit is the _____ _____ of all my suits.

(hot)   7. Of all the cities in Mexico this one is the _____ _____.

(cold)   8. It's _____ _____ today than it was yester-day.

(tall)   9. Are Mexican women _____ _____ than American women?

(near)   10. Of the house, the school, and the market, the school is the _____ _____ .

EXERCISE 6

Give the comparative and superlative degree of the following adjectives and adverbs (increasing scale).

small	strong	tired	ugly
sick	short	tall	weak
sad	safe	thick	wide
slow	sharp	thin	warm
soon	soft	tight	white

EXERCISE 7

Give the comparative and superlative degree of the following adjectives and adverbs (increasing scale).

slowly	complete	dangerous	usual
softly	correct	expensive	important

110

useful	careful	exact	impossible
beautiful	carefully	interesting	quickly
comfortable	difficult	foolish	polite

EXERCISE 8

Fill the blanks with the comparative or superlative degree, as required, of the adjective or adverb indicated and translate (increasing scale).

(foolish) 1. She's _____ _____ than her husband.

(slowly) 2. We'll walk _____ _____ when we go out today.

(soon) 3. I can get there _____ than you.

(safe) 4. This is the _____ place to hide the money.

(white) 5. The _____ clouds are the big ones.

(thick) 6. The green rug is _____ than the blue one.

(interesting) 7. I had the _____ _____ conversation with my teacher.

(quickly) 8. We can do the work _____ _____ than they.

(tired) 9. My husband is _____ today than he was last week.

(strong) 10. Is this the _____ chain you could find?

EXERCISE 9

Translate the following sentences and practice reading them.

1. There'll be a party on the 10th of June.
2. There won't be a party on the 1st of March.
3. Will there be a party on the 3rd of July?
4. There'll be time to eat before two o'clock.
5. There won't be time to eat before two o'clock.
6. Will there be time to eat before two o'clock?
7. I'd be hungry.
8. I wouldn't be hungry.
9. He'd be afraid.
10. He wouldn't be afraid.
11. It'd be cold.
12. It wouldn't be cold.
13. You'd have to go early.

111

14. You wouldn't have to go early.
15. Would you have to go early?
16. Wouldn't you have to go early?
17. It's raining today.
18. It isn't raining today.
19. It rained yesterday.
20. It didn't rain yesterday.

EL USO DEL GERUNDIO DESPUÉS DE LAS PREPOSICIONES

En inglés se emplea el gerundio después de las preposiciones, mientras que en castellano se usa el infinitivo.

Aprenda las siguientes preposiciones y estudie los ejemplos que siguen.

before	antes de
after	después de
without	sin
besides	además de
on	al
instead of	en lugar de
in spite of	a pesar de

1. I'm going to rest before eating.
   Voy a descansar antes de comer.
2. After swimming we're going to rest.
   Después de nadar vamos a descansar.
3. He went out without saying good-bye to me.
   Él salió sin despedirse de mí.
4. Besides working in the office all day, I have to help my husband in the evening.
   Además de trabajar en la oficina todo el día, tengo que ayudar a mi esposo en la tarde.
5. On turning on the light, I saw that there was a mouse in my room.
   Al prender la luz, vi que había un ratón en mi cuarto.
6. Instead of studying English, I'm going to study Spanish.
   En lugar de estudiar inglés, voy a estudiar español.
7. In spite of being sick, he's going to the office.
   A pesar de estar enfermo, él va a ir a la oficina.

112

EXERCISE 10

Translate the following phrases and practice reading them.

1. before working
2. after looking for
3. without going
4. on speaking
5. besides playing
6. instead of reading
7. in spite of having
8. before dying
9. without saying
10. besides taking off
11. instead of spending
12. after singing
13. in spite of being
14. before doing
15. after buying
16. on thinking
17. without picking out
18. in spite of winning
19. besides getting up
20. instead of sleeping

EXERCISE 11

Translate the following sentences. Change them to the negative, interrogative, and interrogative negative.

1. You shook hands with Mr. Cox.
2. They'll shake hands with my father.
3. He's shaken hands with all the boys.
4. She'd shake hands with them.
5. They shake hands with men.
6. We've been able to shake hands with all of them.
7. My father would be able to shake hands with my uncle.
8. The teachers are going to shake hands with me.
9. Henry wants to shake hands with you.
10. Mary had to shake hands with the president.

EXERCISE 12

Answer the following questions in the affirmative and in the negative.

1. Was he going to shake hands with us?
2. Did they want to shake hands with the girls?
3. Would you like to shake hands with my wife?
4. Would they have to shake hands with the doctor?
5. Will you be able to shake hands with all those people?
6. Will you have to shake hands with the children?
7. Did she shake hands with you?

8. Did Henry shake hands with my mother?
9. Do you always shake hands with your friends?
10. Have you shaken hands with me?

EXERCISE 13

Translate into Spanish.

1. Why did he say he wouldn't try hard to learn English?
2. It looks very dark outside.
3. He looks like a thief.
4. My raincoat wore out before the summer was over.
5. Before shaking hands with her father, I shook hands with her mother.
6. You can always make a living if you work hard.
7. I was about forty years old when I began to make a lot of money.
8. He makes a lot of money without working.
9. How long will the movie last?
10. You're the luckiest man in the world.
11. What a pity that you had such bad luck.
12. He knows that I'm right.
13. We had very bad luck on our last trip.
14. Those boys are very foolish to get drunk.
15. That man was so fat that he could hardly walk.

EXERCISE 14

Give the past tense and past participle of the following verbs.

save	turn over	use	walk
stay	translate	visit	want
talk	try	work	watch
turn off	travel	wash	worry (about)
turn on	tie	wait (for)	ask

EXERCISE 15

Give the past tense and past participle of the following verbs.

sit (down)	sing	take	understand
sleep	swim	teach	write

114

sell	shake	tell	wake up
stand up	shine	think	wear
set	spend	take off	win

EXERCISE 16

Verb Practice

1. They build houses, don't they?
2. They don't build houses, do they?
3. Where do they build houses?
4. They built a factory, didn't they?
5. They didn't build a factory, did they?
6. Where did they build a factory?
7. They were building a factory, weren't they?
8. They weren't building a factory, were they?
9. Where were they building a factory?
10. They were going to build a house, weren't they?
11. They weren't going to build a house, were they?
12. Where were they going to build a house?
13. They'll build a store, won't they?
14. They won't build a store, will they?
15. Where will they build a store?
16. They've built an office building, haven't they?
17. They haven't built an office building, have they?
18. Where have they built an office building?
19. They'd built a school, hadn't they?
20. They hadn't built a school, had they?
21. Where had they built a school?
22. They'd build a movie theater, wouldn't they?
23. They wouldn't build a movie theater, would they?
24. Where would they build a movie theater?
25. They'll be able to build downtown, won't they?
26. They won't be able to build downtown, will they?
27. Where will they be able to build downtown?
28. They've been able to build a house, haven't they?
29. They haven't been able to build a house, have they?
30. Where have they been able to build a house?
31. They'd been able to build a store, hadn't they?
32. They hadn't been able to build a store, had they?
33. Where had they been able to build a store?

34. They'd be able to build a movie theater, wouldn't they?
35. They wouldn't be able to build a movie theater, would they?
36. Would they be able to build a movie theater?

EXERCISE 17

Verb Practice *Repeat exercise 16, using forms of the verbs* **mean, tie (someone or something) up, keep, fight, prefer, get sick, get drunk, shake hands with** *in short sentences. Use a different noun or pronoun with each verb. Use the interrogative words when it is possible.*

EXERCISE 18

Read and translate.

THE DOG AND THE WOLF

The moon was very bright one night when a very poor wolf met a fat dog on the road.

"How is it that you're so fat and happy?" asked the wolf. "I can hardly find enough food to eat."

"Why don't you work as I do," answered the dog, "so that you can have three meals a day?"

"I'd work, but I can't find a place to work," said the wolf.

"Come with me to my owner's house and help me watch for thieves at night," said the dog.

"All right," said the wolf. "Since I live in the woods, I'm often hungry. There's nothing like having a roof to sleep under and food all the time."

While they were walking along the road together, the wolf saw a mark on the dog's neck.

"What made that mark on your neck?" asked the wolf.

"Oh, That's nothing," replied the dog. "I think the chain that my owner puts around my neck is a little too tight."

"Chain!" cried the wolf in surprise. "Do you mean that you aren't free to go where you want?"

"No, not exactly," said the dog. "You see, my owner ties me up during the day, but he lets me run free at night. I sleep during the day so that I can watch the house better at night. My owner feeds me very well. He's always giving me food from the kitchen. Wait. Where are you going?"

As the wolf ran back into the forest, he said, "You can keep your fine food and your chains. As for me, I prefer my freedom to your fat."

116

EXERCISE 19

Write in English.

1. ¿Por qué no le darías la mano a él?
2. El teléfono está descompuesto, ¿verdad?
3. ¿Cuál vestido les gusta más—el rojo o el verde?
4. Los niños vinieron uno por uno al frente de la sala para darle la mano al presidente.
5. ¿Para qué te vas a emborrachar el 16 de septiembre?
6. ¿Qué quiere decir esta palabra?
7. Apáguela. Ya no quiero leer más.
8. Iremos al cine juntos el domingo, ¿verdad?
9. Los muchachos americanos y las muchachas mexicanas están parados unos al lado de las otras.
10. Qué lástima que tengas miedo de viajar en avión.

EXERCISE 20

Dictation

1. Those boys want to fight when they get drunk.
2. My watch chain is pure gold.
3. What are you keeping these old papers for?
4. That thief stole your bathing suit, didn't he?
5. The boys and the girls were standing side by side in the living room.
6. He cut his finger while he was cutting the meat.
7. We'll be able to see the mountains from the roof, won't we?
8. The road to Puebla is less dangerous than the highway to Acapulco.
9. We picked out the least expensive bathing suit.
10. The stove won't work. It's out of order.

EXERCISE 21

Conversation *Answer the following questions in the affirmative and in the negative.*

1. Is the elevator out of order?
2. Does the elevator work?
3. Is the telephone out of order?
4. Does the telephone work?
5. Did you get sick?

6. Did you get sleepy?
7. Did you get ready?
8. Did you get married last year?
9. Did you get drunk on Saturday night?
10. Did you get mad at your wife?
11. Did you get rich in the United States?
12. Did you get wet this afternoon?
13. Did you get your hair wet this afternoon?
14. Did you get up early?
15. Did you get there on time?
16. Did you give up?
17. Is it less dangerous to travel by train than by plane?
18. Is the moon less bright than the sun?
19. Are you shorter than your brother?
20. Are you taller than your cousin?

Answer the following questions.

21. What's the table made of?
22. What are you building a house for?
23. What did you build a house for?
24. What color is your sweater?
25. What color is your bathing suit?

Lección 9

Vocabulary

1. **to ride, rode, ridden** montar; andar o ir (*en vehículo*)
2. **to drown, drowned drowned** ahogar(se)
3. **to grow, grew, grown** crecer; cultivar
4. **to drive, drove, driven** manejar; arrear; ir en coche
5. **to remember, remembered, remembered** recordar, acordarse (de)
6. **to turn, turned, turned** doblar, dar vuelta, voltear
7. **brown** color café
8. **yellow** amarillo
9. **pink** color de rosa
10. **ashamed** apenado, avergonzado
11. **funny** chistoso, divertido; raro
12. **crazy** loco, demente
13. **sweet** dulce
14. **sour** agrio, ácido
15. **donkey** burro
16. **fish** pez, peces; pescado(s)
17. **fool** (*sust.*) tonto
18. **respect** respeto
19. **age** edad
20. **edge** orilla; borde
21. **pole** poste; pértiga
22. **bridge** puente
23. **shoulder** hombro
24. **business** (*sing.*) negocio(s)
25. **pupil** alumno
26. **student** alumno
27. **alone** solo

IDIOMS

1. **to have just + (past part.)** acabar de + (inf.)

I've just eaten. Acabo de comer.

I'd just eaten. Acababa de comer.

2. **to get scared** asustarse
3. **to get on** subirse (a); montar (a, en)
4. **I don't remember.** No recuerdo.

   Do you remember me? ¿Te acuerdas de mí?
5. **Aren't you ashamed?** ¿No te da pena? ¿No te da vergüenza?
6. **Turn around.** Dése vuelta, Voltee.
7. **more or less** más o menos
8. **It's none of your business.** No te importa. No te incumbe.

EXERCISE 1

Translate the following phrases and sentences and practice reading them.

1. before fighting
2. after fighting
3. besides fighting
4. instead of fighting
5. in spite of fighting
6. Let them fight.
7. Don't let them fight.
8. Let's fight.
9. He's had to travel a lot this year.
10. He hasn't had to travel a lot this year.
11. He'd had to travel all the time.
12. He hadn't had to travel all the time.
13. You'd be sleepy in the morning.
14. You wouldn't be sleepy in the morning.
15. It'd be cold in January.
16. It wouldn't be cold in January.
17. It'd be hot in Acapulco.
18. It wouldn't be hot in Acapulco.
19. Would they have to spend the money?
20. Wouldn't they have to spend the money?

AUXILIARES DE OBLIGACIÓN
SHOULD, OUGHT TO, MUST

Se expresa obligación usando los auxiliares **should, ought to** y **must** seguidos del infinitivo sin la partícula **to**. **Should** y **ought to** significan la misma cosa, pero **must** es más fuerte, puesto que éste indica necesidad absoluta y los otros dos auxiliares no. **Should** y **ought to** equivalen a **debería**. **Must** equivale a **tener que**.

Se usan todos estos auxiliares en afirmativo; pero generalmente, se usa **should** en negativo e interrogativo en vez de ought to. La contracción de **should not** es **shouldn't**.

Tanto **must** como **have to** equivalen a **tener que**, pero para negar e interrogar se usa **have to**, y no **must**. Estudie los siguientes ejemplos:

Afirmativo

I should study English	debería estudiar inglés
he ought to study English	él debería estudiar inglés
they must study English	ellos tienen que estudiar inglés

Negativo

I shouldn't study English	no debería estudiar inglés
he shouldn't study English	él no debería estudiar inglés
they don't have to study English	ellos no tienen que estudiar inglés

Interrogativo

Recuerde el orden de las palabras para el interrogativo: auxiliar, sustantivo o pronombre, verbo.

should I study English?	¿debería estudiar inglés?
should he study English?	¿debería él estudiar inglés?
do they have to study English?	¿tienen ellos que estudiar inglés?

Interrogativo Negativo

shouldn't I study English?	¿no debería estudiar inglés?
shouldn't he study English?	¿no debería él estudiar inglés?
don't they have to study English?	¿no tienen ellos que estudiar inglés?

EXERCISE 2

Verb Practice

1. He should keep his books.
2. He shouldn't keep his books.
3. Should he keep his books?
4. Shouldn't he keep his books?
5. How many books should he keep?

EXERCISE 3

Verb Practice *Repeat exercise 2, using forms of the verbs* **build, knock (on), hide, dig, fight, lend, pay, rest, save** *in short sentences. Use a different noun or pronoun with each verb. Use the interrogative words when it is possible.*

SHOULD HAVE + *PARTICIPIO*

El uso de **should have** más un participio en inglés equivale en español a **debió** más un infinitivo; o **debió (debería)** más un participio; o **hubiera** más un participio. La contracción negativa es **shouldn't have**. Fíjese en el ejemplo:

You should have eaten earlier.
Debiste comer más temprano.
Debiste (deberías) haber comido más temprano.
Hubieras comido más temprano.

EXERCISE 4

Verb Practice

1. She should have gone to the party.
2. She shouldn't have gone to the party.
3. Should she have gone to the party?
4. Shouldn't she have gone to the party?
5. When should she have gone to the party?

EXERCISE 5

Verb Practice *Repeat exercise 4, using past participles of the verbs* **eat, come, fill, escape, cut, break, become, cover, hide** *in short sentences. Use a different noun or pronoun with each verb. Use the interrogative words when it is possible.*

122

MUST *PARA EXPRESAR PROBABILIDAD*

Se expresa probabilidad en el presente con el auxiliar **must**, seguido del infinitivo sin la partícula **to**. Aprenda las expresiones de abajo. Recuerde que **ha de (debe) tener, ha de (debe) hacer** se traducen con una forma del verbo **be** cuando se emplean como modismos.

> **must be** ha de (debe) ser
> **must be** ha de (debe) estar
> **must be** ha de (debe) tener
> **must be** ha de (debe) hacer

Para expresar probabilidad en el negativo se emplea la palabra **probably** (que sigue al sujeto) con el verbo en negativo. Aprenda las expresiones de abajo.

I'm probably not no he de (debo) ser
he probably isn't él no ha de (debe) estar
they probably aren't ellos no han de (deben) tener
it probably isn't no ha de (debe) hacer

Estudie las siguientes oraciones y compárelas con el español.

1. It must be very hot in Acapulco.
   Ha de (debe) hacer mucho calor en Acapulco.

2. He probably isn't the English teacher.
   No ha de (debe) ser el profesor de inglés.

3. She must be about thirty years old now.
   Ella tendrá ahora unos treinta años.

4. They probably aren't hungry.
   Ellos no han de (deben) tener hambre.

5. He must eat a lot. He's very fat.
   Ha de (debe) comer mucho. Está muy gordo.

6. He probably doesn't eat a lot. He's very thin.
   No ha de (debe) comer mucho. Está muy delgado.

MUST HAVE + *PARTICIPIO*

Se expresa probabilidad en el pasado con los auxiliares **must have**, seguido de un participio. Aprenda las expresiones de abajo. Recuerde que **ha de (debe) haber tenido**, **ha de (debe) haber hecho** se traducen con una forma del verbo be cuando se emplean como modismos.

> **must have been** ha de (debe) haber sido
> **must have been** ha de (debe) haber estado
> **must have been** ha de (debe) haber tenido
> **must have been** ha de (debe) haber hecho

Para expresar probabilidad en el negativo se emplea la palabra **probably** (que sigue al sujeto) con el tiempo **pasado** (no antepresente) del verbo empleado. Aprenda las expresiones de abajo. Recuerde que **no ha de (debe) tener**, **no ha de (debe) hacer** se traducen con una forma del verbo be cuando se emplean como modismos.

> **I probably wasn't** no he de (debo) haber sido
> **he probably wasn't** él no ha de (debe) haber estado
> **they probably weren't** ellos no han de (deben) haber tenido
> **it probably wasn't** no ha de (debe) haber hecho

1. It must have been very hot in Acapulco.
   Ha de (debe) haber hecho mucho calor en Acapulco.
   Haría mucho calor en Acapulco.

   It probably wasn't very hot in Acapulco.
   No ha de (debe) haber hecho mucho calor en Acapulco.
   No haría mucho calor en Acapulco.

2. He must have been very rich.
   Ha de (debe) haber sido muy rico.
   Sería muy rico.

   He probably wasn't very rich.
   No ha de (debe) haber sido muy rico.
   No sería muy rico.

3. He must have eaten a lot. He got sick.
   Ha de (debe) haber comido mucho. Se enfermó.
   Comería mucho. Se enfermó.

   He probably didn't eat a lot. He's still hungry.
   No ha de (debe) haber comido mucho. Todavía tiene hambre.
   No comería mucho. Todavía tiene hambre.

EXERCISE 6

Verb Practice

1. He must be very hungry.
2. He probably isn't very hungry.
3. He must have been very hungry.
4. He probably wasn't very hungry.

EXERCISE 7

Verb Practice *Repeat exercise 6, using forms of the verbs* be thirsty, be (*tener*) cold, be (*tener*) warm, be (*tener*) hot, be sleepy, be afraid, be (*hacer*) cold, be (*hacer*) warm, be (*hacer*) hot, be a doctor, have money, eat a lot, work hard, study English, get up early, work late. *Use a different noun or pronoun with each verb when possible.*

EXERCISE 8

Verb Practice

1. He should drive tomorrow, shouldn't he?
2. He shouldn't drive tomorrow, should he?
3. Should he drive tomorrow?
4. Shouldn't he drive tomorrow?
5. Why shouldn't he drive tomorrow?
6. He should have driven yesterday, shouldn't he?
7. He shouldn't have driven yesterday, should he?
8. Should he have driven yesterday?
9. Shouldn't he have driven yesterday?
10. Why shouldn't he have driven yesterday?
11. He must drive every day.
12. He probably doesn't drive every day.
13. He must have driven every day.
14. He probably didn't drive every day.
15. The children should be hungry, shouldn't they?
16. The children shouldn't be hungry, should they?
17. Should the children be hungry?
18. Shouldn't the children be hungry?
19. Why should the children be hungry?
20. The children should have been hungry, shouldn't they?
21. The children shouldn't have been hungry, should they?

22. Should the children have been hungry?
23. Shouldn't the children have been hungry?
24. Why should the children have been hungry?
25. The children must be hungry.
26. The children probably aren't hungry.
27. The children must have been hungry.
28. The children probably weren't hungry.
29. There must be a bridge here.
30. There probably isn't a bridge here.
31. There must have been a bridge here.
32. There probably wasn't a bridge here.

EXERCISE 9

Give the comparative and superlative degree of the following adjectives and adverbs (increasing and decreasing scale).

angry	beautiful	comfortable	dirty
big	black	complete	difficult
blue	bright	correct	dangerous
bad	clean	carefully	dark
busy	cold	cheap	early

EXERCISE 10

Fill the blanks with the comparative or superlative degree, as required, of the adjective or adverb indicated and translate (increasing scale).

(young)   1. Are you _____ than your cousin?
(wide)   2. What is the _____ river in Mexico?
(weak)   3. Women are _____ than men.
(white)   4. Her dress is _____ than mine.
(useful)   5. This is the _____ _____ book I have.
(warm)   6. It's _____ today than it was yesterday.
(warm)   7. Is this the _____ coat you could find?
(comfortable)   8. It's _____ _____ to travel by plane than by bus.
(lazy)   9. My neighbor is the _____ man in the world.
(foolish)   10. I think they're _____ _____ than we.

126

EXERCISE 11

Fill the blanks with the comparative or superlative degree, as required, of the adjective or adverb indicated and translate (decreasing scale).

(sharp)   1. My knife is the _____ _____ of all the knives.

(heavy)   2. His raincoat is _____ _____ than his overcoat.

(hungry)   3. She is _____ _____ now than she was an hour ago.

(full)   4. Of all the boxes that one is the _____ _____ .

(difficult)   5. The second book is _____ _____ than the others.

(cheap)   6. Food is _____ _____ now than it was last year.

(dangerous)   7. Which of the two **roads is** _____ _____ ?

(expensive)   8. Why did you buy the _____ _____ nuts?

(good)   9. This cake is the _____ _____ .

EXERCISE 12

Change these sentences to the past, future, present perfect, past perfect, and conditional. Translate each time.

1. He can see you every day.
2. They can go back by car.
3. We can get ready in an hour.
4. She can finish on time.
5. You can wash the glasses without breaking them.
6. John can study before going to bed.
7. That man can carry two buckets of water.
8. In spite of being sick, you can do a little work.
9. They can hide the money in that box under the bed.
10. Your sister can dance very well.

EXERCISE 13

Translate the following sentences. Change them to the interrogative and interrogative negative.

1. He's just eaten.

2. They'd just gone.
3. She's just finished the work.
4. She's just closed the store.
5. You've just begun.
6. I've just cleaned the house.
7. The teacher has just read that book.
8. The girls have just set the table.
9. I'd just made a cake.
10. They had just heard the news.

EXERCISE 14

Answer the following questions in the affirmative.

1. Have you just come from the movies?
2. Had she just answered the question?
3. Have they just spoken to you?
4. Had we just broken the window?
5. Has he just caught a fish?
6. Have you just drunk the milk?
7. Had they just danced?
8. Has she just fed the chickens?
9. Have the boys just looked at the picture?
10. Have the men just put their coats on?

EXERCISE 15

Translate into Spanish.

1. We tried hard to understand them.
2. That house looks like the place where I was born.
3. She's crying. She must have fallen down.
4. I didn't shake hands with him because my hands were dirty.
5. When this suit wears out, I'll be able to buy a new one.
6. If you can't make a living when you're twenty years old, you'll never be able to make a living.
7. It must be cold outside. Everybody is wearing a coat.
8. When I sold newspapers, I made ten dollars a week, more or less.
9. If that man turns around, I can tell you if he's our neighbor.
10. We've just visited our cousins in the United States.
11. We got so scared when we saw the dogs that we started to run.

128

12. There weren't any seats left when I got on the bus.
13. Aren't you ashamed to eat that little girl's apple?
14. Shouldn't we have got to Monterrey by eight o'clock?
15. It's none of your business what I do.

EXERCISE 16

Give the past tense and past participle of the following verbs.

answer	complete	carry	disappear
arrive (in, at)	change	call	dance
believe	correct	cover	die
clean	clap	dictate	drown
close	cry	dress	drop

EXERCISE 17

Give the past tense and past participle of the following verbs.

wear out	become	come back	dig
be	break	cut	eat
bring	blow	catch	feel
buy	build	do	find
begin	come	drink	forget

EXERCISE 18

Verb Practice

1. Those men ride in the park on Sunday, don't they?
2. Those men don't ride in the park on Sunday, do they?
3. Those men rode in the park on Sunday, didn't they?
4. Those men didn't ride in the park on Sunday, did they?
5. Those men are going to ride in the park on Sunday, aren't they?
6. Those men aren't going to ride in the park on Sunday, are they?
7. Those men will ride in the park on Sunday, won't they?
8. Those men won't ride in the park on Sunday, will they?
9. Those men like to ride on Saturday afternoon, don't they?
10. Those men don't like to ride on Saturday afternoon, do they?
11. Those men want to ride on Saturday afternoon, don't they?
12. Those men don't want to ride on Saturday afternoon, do they?

13. Those men have to ride on Saturday afternoon, don't they?
14. Those men don't have to ride on Saturday afternoon, do they?
15. Those men had to ride on Saturday afternoon, didn't they?
16. Those men didn't have to ride on Saturday afternoon, did they?
17. Those men could ride very well, couldn't they?
18. Those men couldn't ride very well, could they?
19. Those men have ridden every day this week, haven't they?
20. Those men haven't ridden every day this week, have they?
21. Those men had ridden every day this week, hadn't they?
22. Those men hadn't ridden every day this week, had they?
23. Those men would ride on the first of the month, wouldn't they?
24. Those men wouldn't ride on the first of the month, would they?
25. Those men should ride on the 16th of September, shouldn't they?
26. Those men shouldn't ride on the 16th of September, should they?
27. Those men will be able to ride tomorrow, won't they?
28. Those men won't be able to ride tomorrow, will they?
29. Those men have been able to ride every day, haven't they?
30. Those men haven't been able to ride every day, have they?
31. Those men had been able to ride in the park, hadn't they?
32. Those men hadn't been able to ride in the park, had they?
33. Those men would be able to ride all day, wouldn't they?
34. Those men wouldn't be able to ride all day, would they?

EXERCISE 19

Verb Practice *Repeat exercise 19, using forms of the verbs* **remember, turn, drive, drown, grow, get on, get scared** *in short sentences. Use a different noun or pronoun with each verb. Use the interrogative words when it is possible.*

EXERCISE 20

Read and translate.

THE FARMER, HIS SON, AND THEIR DONKEY

Once there was a farmer who had a donkey that was too old to work any more.

"Let's drive the donkey to the market and sell him," said the father to his son, "and take the money and buy a younger donkey that will be able to help us in the field."

So the farmer and his son started to the market with the donkey walking in front of them. On the way they met some girls walking along the road.

"Look at those fools," said the girls laughing. "They're both walking and the donkey isn't carrying anything. They ought to ride the donkey."

"They're right," said the old man to his son. "One of us should ride. Get on the donkey, and I'll walk behind."

Later they met some old men who were standing beside the road talking.

"Look at that," said one old man to the others. "That's just exactly what I was telling you. No one has any respect for old age these days. Look at that lazy, young boy riding the donkey while his poor old father has to walk. Get off the donkey and let your father ride."

"Those old men are right," said the father to the boy, "Get off the donkey and let me ride."

So the father got on the donkey, and they started down the road again.

After a while they saw some women washing clothes near the road.

"You must be crazy," said one of the women to the farmer, "to ride the donkey and let that poor little boy walk. You should let him ride too."

"I believe you're right," answered the farmer. "The boy ought to ride too."

The farmer put the boy on the donkey behind him, and they rode on toward the city.

Just as they reached the edge of town, a man who lived there said to them, "You two big, strong men should be ashamed to ride that poor little donkey. Two young men like you should be able to carry the donkey."

"I think he's right," said the father. "We must carry the donkey for a while."

The farmer and his son got off the donkey and tied the donkey's legs together. Then they tied the donkey's legs to a pole, put the pole across their shoulders, and carried the donkey over the bridge.

They looked so funny that the people came out of their houses to laugh at them. The poor donkey got scared of all the noise and began to try to get away. In the excitement the animal jumped off the bridge into the water and drowned.

Try to please (complacer) everybody, and you please nobody, not even yourself.

EXERCISE 21

Write in English.

1. Cuando nos despertamos, estaba el suelo cubierto de nieve.
2. Has crecido mucho desde el año pasado, ¿verdad?
3. Deberías recordar todos los nombres de los niños.
4. De noche, cuando estoy solo en la casa me asusto.
5. Cuando Uds. se estaban bajando del camión, nosotros subimos.
6. ¿Va a dar vuelta el camión en la próxima esquina?
7. En vez de voltearse, ella se quedó con la cara hacia la pared.
8. Han de ser las seis de la mañana.
9. Ellos han de haberse divertido mucho porque no regresaron hasta las dos de la mañana.
10. ¿Trajo Ud. las manzanas más dulces que pudo encontrar?

EXERCISE 22

Dictation

1. My business is doing very well this year.
2. Would you like to see the fish I caught last Sunday?
3. He'd be able to make a living if he worked hard.
4. You'll never learn English without studying.
5. No one knows the age of that tree.
6. They think we're completely crazy, don't they?
7. That's the funniest movie I ever saw.
8. My flowers haven't grown very much because it's been so cold.
9. He said that I'd have to work on Saturday and Sunday.
10. I knew it'd be cold in Chicago in December.

EXERCISE 23

Conversation *Answer the following questions.*

1. How long did the meeting last?
2. How long did the class last?
3. How long did the movie last?

132

4. When was the meeting over?
5. When was the movie over?
6. When was the class over?
7. What time did you get up?
8. What time did you get there?
9. What time did you wake up?
10. What time did you get ready?
11. What did you get off the bus for?
12. What did you get on the bus for?
13. Where are you from?
14. Where did you come from?
15. What state did you come from?
16. What city did you come from?
17. Who did you come with?
18. Who did you go with?
19. Where were you born?
20. When were you born?
21. What's the movie about?
22. What's the book about?

Answer the following questions in the affirmative and in the negative.

23. Do you still live in the same place?
24. Do you still teach English?
25. Do you still like to dance?
26. Do you still like to go to the movies?
27. Do you still like to travel?
28. Have they already come?
29. Have they already gone?
30. Are they already here?

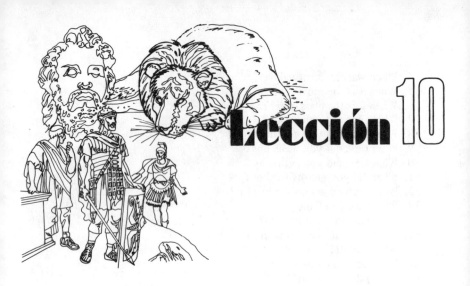

Lección 10

Vocabulary

1. **to decide, decided, decided** decidir
2. **to hunt, hunted, hunted** cazar
3. **to notice, noticed, noticed** fijarse en
4. **to send, sent, sent** mandar, enviar
5. **to bleed, bled, bled** sangrar
6. **to capture, captured, captured** capturar
7. **also** también
8. **grateful** agradecido
9. **sore** adolorido, lastimado
10. **cruel** cruel
11. **fresh** fresco
12. **unhappy** infeliz
13. **whole** entero
14. **several** varios
15. **chance** oportunidad
    opportunity oportunidad, ocasión
16. **slave** esclavo
17. **master** amo
18. **king** rey
19. **soldier** soldado
20. **toe** dedo del pie
21. **thorn** espina; púa
22. **story** cuento
23. **shelter** albergue
24. **weather** tiempo
25. **season** estación (*del año*); temporada

IDIOMS

1. **How long does it take?** ¿Cuánto tiempo tarda?
   How long will it take me (you, him, etc.)? ¿Cuánto tiempo tardaré (ás, á, etc.)?

2. **It takes a long time.** Tarda mucho.
   It took a long time. Tardó mucho.
   It'll take me (you, him, etc.) a long time. Tardaré (ás, á, etc.) mucho.
3. **It takes about two hours.** Tarda como dos horas.
   It took about a year. Tardó como un año.
   It'll take me (you, him, etc.) about three days. Tardaré (ás, á, etc.) como tres días.
4. **It doesn't take long.** No tarda mucho.
   It didn't take long. No tardó mucho.
   It won't take me (you, him, etc.) long. No me tardaré (ás, á, etcétera) mucho.
5. **Does it take long?** ¿Tarda mucho?
   Did it take long? ¿Tardó mucho?
   Will it take me (you, him, etc.) long? ¿Tardaré (ás, á, etc.) mucho?
6. **to get better** mejorarse
7. **to get worse** empeorarse
8. **at first** al principio
9. **I have a bad cold.** Tengo un fuerte catarro.
   I have a bad headache. Tengo un fuerte dolor de cabeza.
   I have a bad toothache. Tengo un fuerte dolor de muelas.
   I have a bad earache. Tengo un fuerte dolor de oído.
   I have a bad stomach-ache. Tengo un fuerte dolor de estómago.

EXERCISE 1

Translate the following phrases and sentences and practice reading them.

1. without turning around
2. besides turning around
3. instead of turning around
4. in spite of turning around
5. on turning around
6. Let her turn around.
7. Don't let her turn around.
8. We should ride during the day.
9. We shouldn't ride during the day.
10. Should we ride during the day?
11. Shouldn't we ride during the day?
12. We would be able to ride those horses.
13. Would we be able to ride those horses?
14. He would have to drive the car.

15. He wouldn't have to drive the car.
16. Would he have to drive the car?
17. There'd be a plane here.
18. There wouldn't be a plane there.
19. They'd be hungry all morning.

SUPPLEMENTARY VOCABULARY

1. **birth** nacimiento
2. **belief** creencia
3. **blood** sangre
4. **bloody** sangriento
5. **cover** tapa, tapadera
6. **capture** captura
7. **captive** cautivo
8. **disappearance** desaparición
9. **dance** baile
10. **dancer** bailarín
11. **death** muerte
12. **dead** (*adj.*) muerto
13. **dying** (*adj.*) moribundo
14. **decision** decisión
15. **decisive** decisivo
16. **driver** chofer, el que maneja
17. **flier** aviador
18. **flight** vuelo
19. **flying** volador
20. **fight** pelea, pleito
21. **fighter** luchador, boxeador
22. **marriage** casamiento; matrimonio
23. **growth** crecimiento
24. **hunter** cazador
25. **kiss** beso
26. **loan** préstamo
27. **meaning** significado
28. **pay** salario, sueldo
29. **pay day** día de pago
30. **payment** pago; abono
31. **preference** preferencia
32. **snow** nieve
33. **shout** grito
34. **savings** ahorros
35. **rider** jinete
36. **traveler** viajero
37. **traveling** (*adj.*) viajero

EXERCISE 2

Translate into Spanish.

1. The baby died at birth.
2. It was a bloody fight.
3. They found blood on the seat covers of the car.
4. Did you go to the dance last night?
5. Mexicans are good dancers.
6. I think the driver was drunk.
7. Are you afraid of death?
8. Have they reached a decision yet?

9. Do you think their marriage will last?
10. The growth of trees is very slow.
11. I'm going to ask my brother for a loan.
12. Why do hunters wear red hats?
13. Do you know the meaning of this word?
14. You can pick up your money on pay day.
15. Who heard the shout on the 15th of September?
16. Where do you keep your savings?
17. My sister is a good rider.
18. I asked the bus driver for my change.
19. We have to make a payment on the stove every month.
20. Do you know anything about the disappearance of the money?

EXERCISE 3

Give the comparative and superlative degree of the following adjectives and adverbs (increasing an decreasing scale).

early	green	free
easy	good	hot
empty	happy	hard
expensive	hungry	heavy
exact	fine	important
fast	full	impossible
funny	foolish	fat

EXERCISE 4

Fill the blanks with the comparative or superlative degree, as required, of the adjective or adverb indicated and translate (increasing scale).

(far)   1. We can swim _____ than they.

(funny)   2. This is the _____ story I've ever read.

(good)   3. The movie we saw today is _____ than the one we saw yesterday.

(hungry) 4. This dog is always the _____ .

(expensive) 5. Why did you buy the _____ _____ suit?

(fat)   6. We'll eat the _____ chicken.

(important) 7. The _____ _____ lessons are the last ones.

(free)   8. I'm _____ than a bird.

(fast)   9. He can run _____ than you.

(dangerous) 10. Football is _____ _____ than basketball.

137

EXERCISE 5

Fill the blanks with the comparative or superlative degree, as required, of the adjective or adverb indicated and translate (decreasing scale).

(noisy)   1. This class is the ____ ____ of all the classes.

(polite)   2. My husband is ____ ____ now than when we got married.

(expensive)   3. Bread is ____ ____ than cake.

(softly)   4. She speaks the ____ ____ of all the girls.

(sour)   5. These apples are ____ ____ than those you bought yesterday.

(sweet)   6. I want the fruit that's the ____ ____ .

(sad)   7. She'd feel ____ ____ if she went out more.

(safe)   8. I feel ____ ____ in a plane than in a train.

(tired)   9. If you didn't work today, you should be the ____ ____ .

(wide)   10. This street is the ____ ____ of all the streets in the city.

EXERCISE 6

Translate the following sentences and practice reading them.

1. There should be a phone in the office.
2. There shouldn't be a phone in the office.
3. Should there be a phone in the office?
4. Shouldn't there be a phone in the office?
5. How many phones should there be in the office?
6. There should be a light above this table.
7. There shouldn't be a light above this table.
8. Should there be a light above this table?
9. Shouldn't there be a light above this table?
10. How many lights should there be above this table?
11. The children should be hungry before twelve o'clock.
12. The children shouldn't be hungry before twelve o'clock.
13. The children should be sleepy by six o'clock.
14. The children shouldn't be sleepy by six o'clock.
15. The children should be tired now.
16. The children shouldn't be tired now.

138

17. They should have worked every day.
18. They shouldn't have worked every day.
19. Should they have worked every day?
20. Shouldn't they have worked every day?

EXERCISE 7

Answer the following questions, using It takes about—.

Ejemplo: How long does it take to learn English?
¿Cuánto tiempo tarda en aprender inglés?

It takes about three years to learn it.
Tarda como tres años en aprenderlo.

1. How long does it take to go to Acapulco by car?
2. How long does it take to go to Veracruz by train?
3. How long does it take to go to Acapulco by plane?
4. How long does it take you to go to Acapulco by bus?
5. How long does it take him to go to New York by ship?

Answer the following questions, using It'll take about—.

6. How long will it take to make a cake?
7. How long will it take to make a dress?
8. How long will it take to make a thousand dollars?
9. How long will it take her to dress?
10. How long will it take them to finish the book?

Answer the following questions, using It took about—.

11. How long did it take to learn how to swim?
12. How long did it take to learn how to drive?
13. How long did it take to fix the radio?
14. How long did it take you to write the letter?
15. How long did it take us to go downtown?

EXERCISE 8

Answer the following questions, using It takes a long time—.

Ejemplo: How long does it take to learn English?
It takes a long time to learn it.

1. How long does it take to walk up to the hotel?
2. How long does it take to get to Chicago?
3. How long does it take to build a house?
4. How long does it take Mary to translate the lesson?
5. How long does it take the boys to walk to school?

Answer the following questions, using **It'll take a long time—.**

6. How long will it take to answer all the questions?
7. How long will it take Henry to become a doctor?
8. How long will it take to get rich?
9. How long will it take your wife to get ready?
10. How long will it take to open all the boxes?

Answer the following questions, using **It took a long time—.**

11. How long did it take to pick up all the papers?
12. How long did it take to pronounce all the words?
13. How long did it take to pay the workers?
14. How long did it take the Allens to sell their house?
15. How long did it take them to save $100.00 (dollars)?

EXERCISE 9

Answer the following questions, using **It doesn't take long—.**

Ejemplo: How long does it take to learn English?
It doesn't take long to learn it.

1. How long does it take to set the table?
2. How long does it take her to sing that song?
3. How long does it take to swim across the river?
4. How long does it take your husband to spend $500.00 (dollars)?
5. How long does it take to teach them how to speak English?

Answer the following questions, using **It won't take long—.**

6. How long will it take to turn off the water?
7. How long will it take to turn on the television?
8. How long will it take you to take off your coat?
9. How long will it take him to put on his shoes?
10. How long will it take them to clean the house?

140

Answer the following questions, using It didn't take long—.

11. How long did it take her to wash the clothes?
12. How long did it take you to wear out your shoes?
13. How long did it take to close the store?
14. How long did it take the children to eat dinner?
15. How long did it take to correct the sentences?

EXERCISE 10

Translate into Spanish.

1. Is your record player out of order?
2. I tried hard to translate the lesson before class.
3. He couldn't shake hands with me because his right hand was sore.
4. He told me it wouldn't take long to learn English, but it takes a long time.
5. Your raincoat won't wear out so soon if you're careful with it.
6. Why were you afraid to tell him that you were right?
7. I'd just got to the store when they opened the door.
8. We had such a good time in Dallas that I'd like to go back again.
9. At first it was raining so hard that we couldn't see anything.
10. They thought he was getting better, but he got worse and died.
11. You shouldn't have said such a thing to your mother.
12. They should have cleaned the whole house in an hour.
13. Since Mr. Fletcher didn't have to work last Saturday, I think he should work this Saturday.
14. They must have gone back several days ago.
15. I knocked on the door and on the window, but nobody answered. Had you just gone out?

EXERCISE 11

Give the past tense and past participle of the following verbs.

escape	help	kill	look (at)
form	hurry	kiss	look for
fill	hunt	knock (on)	laugh (at)
fix	invite	live	listen (to)
finish	jump	like	love

141

EXERCISE 12

Give the past tense and past participle of the following verbs.

fly	go back	get up	get rich
fall (down)	go out	get mad (at)	get married
feed	go to bed	get sleepy	get away
fight	go to sleep	get thirsty	get off
go	get	get to (here, there)	get old

EXERCISE 13

Verb Practice

1. They decide quickly.
2. They don't decide quickly.
3. Do they decide quickly?
4. Don't they decide quickly?
5. Why don't they decide quickly?
6. They decided yesterday.
7. They didn't decide yesterday.
8. Did they decide yesterday?
9. Didn't they decide yesterday?
10. Why didn't they decide yesterday?
11. They're deciding now.
12. They aren't deciding now.
13. Are they deciding now?
14. Aren't they deciding now?
15. Why aren't they deciding now?
16. They'd decide after dinner.
17. They wouldn't decide after dinner.
18. Would they decide after dinner?
19. Wouldn't they decide after dinner?
20. Why wouldn't they decide after dinner?
21. They should decide soon.
22. They shouldn't decide soon.
23. Should they decide soon?
24. Shouldn't they decide soon?
25. Why shouldn't they decide soon?
26. They'd be able to decide in an hour.
27. They wouldn't be able to decide in an hour.

142

28. Would they be able to decide in an hour?
29. Wouldn't they be able to decide in an hour?
30. Why wouldn't they be able to decide in an hour?
31. They'll be able to decide next week.
32. They won't be able to decide next week.
33. Will they be able to decide next week?
34. Won't they be able to decide next week?
35. Why won't they be able to decide next week?

EXERCISE 14

Verb Practice *Repeat exercise 13, using forms of the verbs* **bleed, capture, send, hunt, notice, get better, get worse** *in short sentences. Use a different noun or pronoun with each verb. Use the interrogative words when it is possible.*

EXERCISE 15

Read and translate.

ANDROCLES AND THE LION

A long time ago in Rome there lived a slave called Androcles, who had a very cruel master. Androcles was very unhappy with his life as a slave, and he often thought of freedom outside the city. One day he decided to run away; so when the opportunity came, he escaped to the forest and hid there.

Life in the forest was very hard for Androcles because he had to hunt for his food like the animals. Also he was always afraid that his master would find him and take him back to Rome.

One day when Androcles went out to look for food, he met a huge lion. At first he was very scared because he was sure that the lion would eat him. Then Androcles noticed that the lion's paw was sore and bleeding and that there was a big thorn in one of his toes.

Androcles took the thorn out of the lion's foot, and said to him, "Your foot will get better now. In a few days you'll be able to walk again."

The lion was so grateful to Androcles for what he had done that he took the slave to his cave and let him hide there. Androcles had shelter from the rain and cold wind, and every day the lion brought him fresh meat to eat.

143

Everything was all right until the king sent soldiers into the forest to look for lions for the arena in Rome. The soldiers captured both Androcles and the lion and took them back to Rome. They were going to feed Androcles to a lion that hadn't eaten anything for several days.

The king came to the arena to watch the fun. Then the soldiers put the slave and the lion in the arena in front of the king's seat; but as soon as the lion came near Androcles, he knew he had found his old friend. To (ante) the surprise of everyone, the hungry lion lay down at Androcles' feet.

The king asked Androcles why the lion wouldn't (no quiso) eat him; and after Androcles had told him the whole story, the king gave the slave his freedom and let the lion return to the forest.

EXERCISE 16

Write in English.

1. ¿Por qué tocaba Ud. a la ventana en vez de tocar a la puerta?
2. Me corté el dedo y sangró.
3. Estas son las manzanas más agrias que jamás haya comido.
4. Debiste hacer tu tarea en vez de ir al cine.
5. Además de capturar dos leones, también capturaron algunos pájaros hermosos.
6. ¿Se fijaron Uds. que María tiene un vestido nuevo?
7. Hace cien años nunca hacía frío en México.
8. Él tenía un fuerte dolor de cabeza después de tomar tanto en (at) la fiesta anoche.
9. No puede venir mi esposa porque tiene catarro.
10. ¿Cuánto tiempo se tarda en llegar a Nueva York en avión?

EXERCISE 17

Dictation

1. Did you ever have an earache?
2. The weather has been very bad for two weeks.
3. What season of the year do you like best?
4. Are you sure that these eggs are fresh?
5. We've decided to take the stove out of the kitchen.
6. I'll bring you some nice flowers if I go out of town this week end.
7. Who is your favorite movie star?

8. What do you do when you have a bad headache?
9. If you drink that dirty water, it'll make you sick.
10. We should have finished all the letters before going to bed.

EXERCISE 18

Conversation *Answer the following questions.*

1. Where were you yesterday?
2. How many books did they bring?
3. When did he become a doctor?
4. How many glasses did you break?
5. When did he get married?
6. Where did you build your house?
7. Why did they come back?
8. How many fish did you catch?
9. Did you do the homework?
10. How much milk did she drink?
11. When did he die?
12. Why did you drive your car to Mexico?
13. How many pieces of bread did you eat?
14. Should he have studied?
15. Should I have given it to her?
16. Shouldn't they have done it?
17. Where did they fall down?
18. Who did you go to the movies with?
19. What time did you get up?
20. How much money did you give them?
21. When did we go back?
22. Who got sick?
23. Why did you get mad?
24. When did he go to sleep?
25. What time did you get there?

Lección 11

Vocabulary

1. **to smile (at), smiled (at), smiled (at)** sonreír
2. **to add, added, added** agregar, sumar
3. **to agree, agreed, agreed** estar de acuerdo
4. **to find out, found out, found out** averiguar, enterarse
5. **to push, pushed, pushed** empujar
6. **to pull, pulled, pulled** jalar, tirar de
7. **however** sin embargo **nevertheless** sin embargo
8. **easily** fácilmente
9. **inside** adentro
10. **rainy** lluvioso
11. **high** (*para cosas*) alto
12. **low** (*para cosas*) bajo
13. **true** verdadero **truth** verdad
14. **camel** camello
15. **pig** cochino o cerdo pequeño **hog** cochino o cerdo grande
16. **job** empleo, trabajo
17. **hump** joroba
18. **body** cuerpo
19. **gate** reja, portal
20. **peach** durazno
21. **orange** naranja
22. **side** lado
23. **game** juego
24. **present** regalo
25. **advantage** ventaja

IDIOMS

1. **Used + (infinitive)** acostumbraba + (infinitivo)
   He used to get up early. Acostumbraba levantarse temprano.

2. **to get in** subirse (a); meterse
   He got in the car. Se subió al coche.
   The thief got in through the window. El ladrón se metió por la ventana.
3. **to get out (of)** bajarse (de), salirse (de)
   He got out of the car. Se bajó del coche.
   The door was closed and I couldn't get out. La puerta estaba cerrada y no me pude salir.
4. **to give up** renunciar; dejar; darse por vencido
5. **You're wrong.** Ud. no tiene razón. Ud. está equivocado.
6. **Don't push.** No empuje Ud.
7. **every other day** cada tercer día, un día sí y otro no
8. **He just left.** Acaba de salir.
9. **It's true.** Es verdad, Es cierto.
   It's the truth. Es la verdad.
10. **I found out about the party.** Averigüé lo de la fiesta.
    I found out about it. Lo averigüé.

EXERCISE 1

Translate the following phrases and sentences and practice reading them.

1. Let them decide.
2. Let's decide now.
3. before capturing
4. after capturing
5. without capturing
6. on capturing
7. instead of capturing
8. in spite of capturing
9. There should be flowers in the market now.
10. There shouldn't be snow on the mountains in June.
11. There should be music at the party.
12. They'll be able to hide the money in the office.
13. Will they be able to hide the money in the office?
14. Won't they be able to hide the money in the office?
15. What are they going to get married for?
16. What are they getting married for?
17. What did they get married for?
18. What are they going to play with?
19. What are they playing with?
20. What did they play with?

THE PASSIVE VOICE
LA VOZ PASIVA

La voz pasiva se forma usando la forma del verbo **be** como auxiliar junto con el participio del verbo empleado. Conjugando el auxiliar (formas del verbo **be**) se forman diferentes tiempos de la voz pasiva. Nótese que se puede traducir la voz pasiva al español literalmente, pero que la traducción con la forma **se** es más común. Estudie las siguientes oraciones.

1. Many plans are made.　　　　　　(present passive)
   Se hacen muchos planes.
   (Muchos planes son hechos.)

2. Many plans were made.　　　　　　(past passive)
   Se hicieron muchos planes.
   (Muchos planes fueron hechos.)

3. Many plans will be made.　　　　　(future passive)
   Se harán muchos planes.
   (Muchos planes serán hechos.)

4. Many plans have been made.　　　　(present perfect
   Se han hecho muchos planes.　　　　passive)
   (Muchos planes han sido
   hechos.)

5. Many plans had been made.　　　　(past perfect passive)
   Se habían hecho muchos planes.
   (Muchos planes habían sido
   hechos.)

6. Many plans would be made.　　　　(conditional passive)
   Se harían muchos planes.
   (Muchos planes serían hechos.)

7. Many plans should be made.　　　　(obligation passive)
   Se deberían hacer muchos planes
   (Muchos planes deberían ser
   hechos.)

8. Many plans are being made.　　　　(present progressive
   Se están haciendo muchos planes.　passive)
   (Muchos planes están siendo
   hechos.)

148

9. Many plans were being made.   (past progressive
   Se estaban haciendo muchos planes.   passive)
   (Muchos planes estaban siendo
   hechos.)

10. Many plans can be made.   (present passive with
    Se pueden hacer muchos planes.   can)
    (Muchos planes pueden ser
    hechos.)

11. Many plans could be made.   (past passive with
    Se pudieron hacer muchos planes.   can)
    (Muchos planes pudieron ser
    hechos.)

EXERCISE 2

Translate the following sentences. Change them to the negative, interrogative, and interrogative negative.

1. Many books are written every year.
2. English was spoken all the time.
3. Shoes will be sold in that store.
4. The money was sent every year.
5. Your dress **can** be finished in an hour.
6. Spanish has been taught in that school.
7. English had been spoken.
8. The work must be done every evening.
9. The food should be eaten.
10. Snow could be seen on the mountain.

EXERCISE 3

The following sentences are in the present passive voice. Change them to past passive, future passive, present perfect passive, past perfect passive, and conditional passive. Translate each time, using the **se** *form in Spanish.*

1. All the questions are answered in English.
2. The lesson is translated into Spanish.
3. Those things are done in the kitchen.
4. The work is finished by noon.
5. Ten lions are captured every month.
6. That window is closed every evening.
7. Many houses are built of stone.

149

8. The news is known by everyone.
9. The presents are hidden from the children.
10. Spanish is spoken in Mexico.

EXERCISE 4

The following sentences are in the present passive. Change them to the present progressive passive, past progressive passive, present passive with can, past passive with can, and obligation passive. Translate each time, using the se form in Spanish.

1. Those children are dressed in white.
2. The radio is fixed every week.
3. All the sentences are dictated in Spanish.
4. All the sentences are corrected in class.
5. The money is kept in that box.
6. Some of the animals are fed at noon.
7. Your friend is invited to parties every week.
8. The coats are hung in the closet.
9. The bucket is filled with water.
10. Games are played every Sunday.

USED + *INFINITIVO*

La palabra **used**, seguida de un infinitivo con la partícula **to**, se emplea generalmente para expresar acción habitual en el pasado. **Used** + (infinitive) equivale a **acostumbraba** + (infinitivo) y al copretérito en castellano cuando éste indica costumbre en el pasado. Fíjese en los ejemplos:

He used to sing.
Él acostumbraba cantar *o* Él cantaba.

He didn't use to sing.
Él no acostumbraba cantar *o* Él no cantaba.

Did he use to sing?
¿Acostumbraba cantar él? *o* ¿Cantaba él?

Didn't he use to sing?
¿No acostumbraba cantar? *o* ¿No cantaba él?

EXERCISE 5

Translate the following sentences. Change them to the negative, interrogative, and interrogative negative.

1. They used to speak English well.
2. He used to live in Colonia del Valle.

150

3. We used to have a car.
4. You used to go to the movies on Saturday.
5. Grandmother used to stay with us during the winter.
6. The children used to take the bus on this corner.
7. We used to get up at six-thirty.
8. Martha used to walk to school.
9. John used to receive letters from Helen.
10. Mr. Adams used to bring the milk early.

EXERCISE 6

Change the following sentences to the past tense, using **used** + *(infinitive). Translate each time.*

1. He works in that office.
2. She goes back on Tuesday.
3. They go to bed very early.
4. Henry plays baseball.
5. I stay with my sister's children.
6. Ruth dances well.
7. Mr. Adams drives the car.
8. Mr. Madison closes the store at nine o'clock.
9. The teachers dictate sentences every day.
10. We eat Mexican food.

EXERCISE 7

Translate the following questions. Answer them in the affirmative and in the negative.

1. Did he use to feed the cows at night?
2. Did she use to get on the bus in front of the hotel?
3. Did the children use to get scared at night?
4. Did the president use to hunt lions in Africa?
5. Did you use to study English?
6. Did they use to listen to the radio every night?
7. Did she use to pick her own clothes out?
8. Did your wife use to read before going to sleep?
9. Did Mr. Madison use to make money without working?
10. Did the children use to spend all their time at the movies?

EXERCISE 8

Translate into Spanish.

1. I used to be able to make a living without working very hard.
2. My raincoat wore out before the rainy season was over.

151

3. How long does it take to go downtown by bus?
4. It didn't take long to learn how to swim, did it?
5. We have English every other day.
6. He said it'd take a long time to learn English, but he was wrong, wasn't he?
7. I just saw them ten minutes ago.
8. He just left a little while ago.
9. Didn't she use to have long hair?
10. Don't push. There's enough room for everyone.
11. He said we should have slept late every other day.
12. I'm going to find out why he gave up his job.
13. There were so many people at the movies that we could hardly get in. Then after we got in, we couldn't get out.
14. I knew that it'd be very cold in Chicago this fall.
15. I've waited for him since ten o'clock, and he isn't here yet. I'm going to give up and go home.

EXERCISE 9

Give the past tense and past participle of the following verbs.

last	pick out	practice	rest
need	pick up	pronounce	smile (at)
notice	push	play	remember
open	pull	prefer	shout (at)
pass	place	reach	rain

EXERCISE 10

Give the past tense and past participle of the following verbs.

get ready	get on	have	leave
get wet	get better	hear	lie down
get drunk	get worse	hang	lose
get sick	get in	hide	let
get scared	get out (of)	keep	lend

EXERCISE 11

Verb Practice

1. The doctor finds out about everything, doesn't he?
2. The doctor doesn't find out about everything, does he?
3. How does the doctor find out about everything?
4. The doctor found out about it, didn't he?
5. The doctor didn't find out about it, did he?

152

6. How did the doctor find out about it?
7. The doctor is going to find out as soon as possible, isn't he?
8. The doctor isn't going to find out as soon as possible, is he?
9. Is the doctor going to find out as soon as possible?
10. The doctor was going to find out last night, wasn't he?
11. The doctor wasn't going to find out last night, was he?
12. How was the doctor going to find out last night?
13. The doctor will find out next week, won't he?
14. The doctor won't find out next week, will he?
15. How will the doctor find out next week?
16. The doctor wanted to find out about it yesterday, didn't he?
17. The doctor didn't want to find out about it yesterday, did he?
18. Did the doctor want to find out about it yesterday?
19. The doctor has to find out about a lot of things, doesn't he?
20. The doctor doesn't have to find out about a lot of things. does he?
21. Why does the doctor have to find out about so many things?
22. The doctor has found out about the party at the club, hasn't he?
23. The doctor hasn't found out about the party at the club, has he?
24. How has the doctor found out about the party at the club?
25. The doctor would find out about the job in the store, wouldn't he?
26. The doctor wouldn't find out about the job in the store, would he?
27. How would the doctor find out about the job in the store?
28. The doctor should find out about the movie downtown, shouldn't he?
29. The doctor shouldn't find out about the movie downtown, should he?
30. Shouldn't the doctor find out about the movie downtown?
31. The doctor would be able to find out, wouldn't he?
32. The doctor wouldn't be able to find out, would he?
33. How would the doctor be able to find out?
34. The doctor should have found out in the morning, shouldn't he have?
35. Should the doctor have found out in the morning?
36. Shouldn't the doctor have found out in the morning?

EXERCISE 12

Verb Practice *Repeat exercise 11, using forms of the verbs* **smile (at)**, **add**, **agree**, **push**, **pull**, **give up**, **get in**, **get out** *in short sentences. Use a different noun or pronoun with each verb. Use the interrogative words when it is possible.*

153

Read and translate.

THE CAMEL AND THE PIG

Once there was a camel that was always laughing at a pig because he was so short.

"It's much better to be short than tall," the pig used to say when the camel laughed at him.

"No," the camel replied, "you're wrong. Those who are tall have all the advantages. If you'll come with me, I'll show you what I mean. There are many things that I can do because I'm tall, and there are many things that you can't do because you're short."

"If it isn't better to be short," replied the pig, "I'll give up my nose."

"And if it isn't better to be tall," answered the camel, "I'll give up my hump."

As the pig and the camel walked along the road, they came to an orchard that had a high wall around it. The camel easily put his long neck over the wall and ate all he wanted of the apples, peaches, and oranges that were growing there. The pig couldn't even see the fruit from where he was standing on the ground because he was so short.

After the camel had enough, he turned to the pig and asked, "Now, do you think it's better to be tall or short?"

A little later, as the two walked down the road together, they came to another orchard that had a wall around it so high that not even the camel could reach over it with his long neck. The pig, however, saw a low gate that was only three feet high in the side of the wall. He easily ran through the low gate and began to eat the fruit that was growing inside.

"Why don't you come in?" the pig asked the camel as he went through the gate. "The fruit inside is very good."

"I can't get in," answered the camel, "because I'm too tall."

When the pig, full of fruit, came out of the garden, he asked the camel, "Now, is it better to be tall or short?"

The camel thought for a minute and then answered, "Sometimes it's better to be short."

Then the pig added, "And sometimes it's better to be tall."

Since the camel and the pig both agreed that being short sometimes has its advantages and being tall sometimes has its advantages too, the pig kept his nose, and the camel kept his hump.

EXERCISE 14

Write in English.

1. Ella me sonrió cuando se metió en el coche.
2. Jalé y empujé la puerta, pero no se abrió.
3. ¿No acostumbraba Ud. jugar al otro lado de la calle?
4. Los niños empezaron a comer tan pronto como se puso la mesa.
5. Debería haber más tiempo para estudiar.
6. ¿Está Ud. de acuerdo con él?
7. Se agregan las letras **er** al adjetivo para formar el grado comparativo.
8. Podrá trabajar en algún país donde se hable castellano.
9. Se terminará el trabajo antes de las siete y media de la noche.
10. Si tiene Ud. un buen empleo, no lo deje.

EXERCISE 15

Dictation

1. We couldn't get in because the gate was broken.
2. Instead of pulling, she was pushing.
3. The oranges were eaten before breakfast.
4. You're wrong. They used to open the market at nine o'clock.
5. It'll take a long time to play a game of football.
6. Is Popo the highest mountain in Mexico?
7. They didn't believe what he said. Nevertheless, he told the truth.
8. Were the presents given to the children at the party?
9. That story isn't true.
10. If you can speak English, you'll have an advantage over the other girls that work in the office.

EXERCISE 16

Conversation *Answer the following questions in the affirmative, using forms of the expressions* it takes a long time— *and* It takes about—.

1. How long does it take to play a game of football?
2. How long does it take to go downtown by bus?
3. How long did it take to go to Monterrey by plane?
4. How long will it take to go to Africa by ship?
5. How long does it take to go to Chicago by train?
6. How long did it take them to go to New York by car?
7. How long will it take you to finish the book?

Answer the following questions in the negative, using forms of the expression It doesn't take long—.

8. How long does it take your wife to clean the house?
9. How long does it take Helen to make a dress?
10. How long will it take to get to the market?
11. How long did it take to write that letter?
12. How long does it take to learn English?
13. How long will it take to walk to school?
14. How long did it take them to learn the vocabulary?

Answer the following questions in the affirmative and in the negative.

15. Did you use to live in Mexico City?
16. Did he use to speak English well?
17. Did they use to study together every day?
18. Did she use to go to school?
19. Did you use to buy a new car every year?
20. Did he use to help his father in the office?
21. Did she use to make a living teaching English?
22. Did we use to have a good time in Acapulco?
23. Did the boys use to try hard to speak English?
24. Did John's shoes use to wear out quickly?
25. Is it already noon?
26. Are they already here?
27. Have you already finished?
28. Have they already gone?

Answer the following questions.

29. What time did you get ready?
30. When did the children get sick?
31. Why did the boys get scared?
32. When did your mother get better?
33. When did Mr. Adams get worse?
34. How did you get in the movie?
35. How did you get out of the garden?
36. Where did you get on the bus?

156

Lección 12

Vocabulary

1. **to touch,** touched, touched
   tocar, palpar
2. **to satisfy,** satisfied,
   satisfied satisfacer,
   complacer
3. **to return,** returned,
   returned regresar
4. **to examine,** examined,
   examined examinar
5. **to appear,** appeared,
   appeared aparecer
6. **to seem,** seemed, seemed
   parecer
7. **therefore** así es que, por
   lo tanto
8. **real** verdadero
   really en serio; de veras;
   verdaderamente
9. **blind** ciego
   blindness ceguera

10. **silly** tonto, zonzo; alocado
11. **flat** plano
12. **round** redondo
13. **elephant** elefante
14. **snake** víbora, serpiente
15. **guide** guía
16. **zoo** zoológico
17. **tail** rabo, cola
18. **trunk** trompa (*de elefante*);
    baúl
19. **fan** abanico; ventilador
20. **rope** soga, reata, cuerda
21. **rest** resto; descanso
22. **impression** impresión
23. **judgment** criterio
24. **lake** lago
25. **purse** bolsa (*de mujer*)
26. **so far** hasta ahora

157

IDIOMS

1. **to make, let, help (someone) do something** hacer, dejar, ayudar
   que (alguien) haga algo
   He made me go. El me hizo ir.
   He let me come. El me dejó venir.
   He helped me study. El me ayudó a estudiar.
2. **to get lost** perderse
3. **to get tired** cansarse
4. **each other** el uno al otro, se
   They love each other. Ellos se quieren.
5. **(negation) ... at all** en absoluto
   They ate nothing at all. No comieron nada en absoluto.
6. **on time** a tiempo
7. **once in a while** de vez en cuando
8. **the house, building, car, etc. across the street**
   la casa, edificio, coche, etc. de enfrente
9. **What's (he, she) it like?** ¿Cómo es (él, ella)?
   What are they like? ¿Cómo son?

EXERCISE 1

Translate the following phrases and sentences and practice reading them.

1. Let's find out about it.
2. before pushing
3. after pushing
4. without pushing
5. besides pushing
6. What are you pushing for?
7. Who are you going to go with?
8. What were you talking about?
9. There's a zoo in the park.
10. There isn't a zoo in the park.
11. Is there a zoo in the park?
12. There was a zoo near the park.
13. There wasn't a zoo near the park.
14. Was there a zoo near the park?
15. There'll be a zoo in Mexico City.
16. There won't be a zoo in Mexico City.
17. Will there be a zoo in Mexico City?

158

18. There's always been a zoo here.
19. There hasn't always been a zoo here.
20. Has there always been a zoo here?

THE SUBJUNCTIVE
EL SUBJUNTIVO

Puesto que en inglés el subjuntivo ha sido absorbido por otros tiempos verbales, podemos decir que ya casi no existe.

Así es que el presente y el pasado del subjuntivo en español se traducirán al inglés por el presente y el pasado del indicativo respectivamente, excepto en los casos ilustrados adelante. Fíjese en los siguientes ejemplos:

He's going to eat before she comes.
Él va a comer antes de que venga ella.

When they leave, we are going to close the windows.
Cuando salgan ellos, vamos a cerrar las ventanas.

He was going to eat before she came.
Él iba a comer antes de que viniera ella.

EL USO DEL INFINITIVO EN INGLÉS EQUIVALE AL PRESENTE DEL SUBJUNTIVO EN ESPAÑOL

Cuando una forma del verbo sigue a un sustantivo o a un pronombre complemento (**me, you him, her, it, us, you, them**), ésta será el infinitivo con la partícula **to**. En español se usará el presente o el pasado del subjuntivo para la traducción correspondiente, según el tiempo del verbo que precede al sustantivo o al pronombre objetivo. Esta construcción se usa mucho después de formas del verbo **want, tell** y **ask**. Estudie las siguientes oraciones:

1. I want **him to come** early.
   Quiero que él venga temprano.

2. They want **me to go** tomorrow.
   Quieren que yo vaya mañana.

3. We want **John to speak** English.
   Queremos que Juan hable inglés.

4. They always tell **him to come** early.
   Siempre le dicen a él que venga temprano.

159

5. I'm going to tell **her to go** tomorrow.
   Le voy a decir a ella que vaya mañana.

6. Tell **them to bring** the money.
   Dígales a ellos que traigan el dinero.

7. Ask **him to explain** it.
   Pídele a él que lo explique.

8. I'll ask **him to buy** it.
   Le pediré a él que lo compre.

EXERCISE 2

Verb Practice

1. She wants him to finish before two-thirty.
2. She doesn't want him to finish before two-thirty.
3. Does she want him to finish before two-thirty?
4. Doesn't she want him to finish before two-thirty?
5. When does she want him to finish?

EXERCISE 3

Verb Practice *Make short sentences with forms of the verbs* **turn, tie, travel, remember, ride, send, stay, pull, find out.** *Expand each verb practice to include different tenses, as in the exercise above. Use a different combination of a nominative and objective noun or pronoun with each verb. Use the interrogative words when it is possible.*

EXERCISE 4

Verb Practice

1. You tell them to eat three times a day.
2. You don't tell them to eat three times a day.
3. Do you tell them to eat three times a day?
4. Don't you tell them to eat three times a day?
5. Why don't you tell them to eat three times a day?

EXERCISE 5

Verb Practice *Make short sentences with forms of the verbs* **jump, hunt, hide, get off, get on, give, decide, dance, cover.** *Expand each verb prac-*

tice to include different tenses, as in the exercise above. Use a different combination of a nominative and objective noun or pronoun with each verb. Use the interrogative words when it is possible.

EXERCISE 6

The following sentences are in the present passive voice. Translate them and change them to past passive, future passive, present perfect passive, past perfect passive, conditional passive and obligation passive. Translate each time, using the se form in Spanish.

1. The sentences are changed to the past tense.
2. Is all the money lost at the horse races?
3. All the workers aren't paid the same day.
4. Is all the work done in the morning?
5. All the money is spent at once.

EXERCISE 7

Translate the following sentences. Change them to the negative, interrogative, and interrogative negative. Notice that we use the infinitive without to after forms of the verbs make, let, help.

1. I'm going to let him help me.
2. They helped him do all the work.
3. I'll make them pay you.
4. We ought to make the children get up earlier.
5. They always help me do my homework.
6. He lets the boys put on their coats.
7. We must make the pupils pronounce the words correctly.
8. You should let your daughter speak English.
9. The teacher will help the students read the lesson.
10. He wants us to make them come to class on time.

EXERCISE 8

Translate the following sentences. Change them to the negative.

1. Make them help me.
2. Help me wash the car.
3. Make him leave me alone.

161

4. Please make them learn the verbs.
5. Please make the girls come home early.
6. Please help him get on the horse.

EXERCISE 9

Answer the following questions in the affirmative and in the negative.

1. Are they going to let him help us?
2. Did he help you answer the questions?
3. Did you let the pupils bring their books?
4. Do you let the girls read in class?
5. Are you going to let them finish before ten o'clock?
6. Did you help the workers close the doors and windows?
7. Did you make him help you?
8. Will they make Mr. Brent open the office earlier?
9. Do you make your children go to bed early?
10. Did you help the pupils learn the vocabulary?

EXERCISE 10

Translate into Spanish.

1. I want you to be able to make a living when you get married.
2. Do you want your old purse to wear out so you can buy a new one?
3. How long did it take them to build that house across the street?
4. She's going to make her husband build a closet in the bedroom.
5. We used to get lost in Mexico City every day.
6. Lucy and Henry are never on time, and I get tired of waiting for them.
7. Once in a while I go to the movies on Sunday afternoon.
8. I've just examined this book, and I don't like it at all.
9. They give presents to each other every year.
10. Make her get ready on time.
11. It didn't take her long to spend the rest of the money.
12. Don't let the dog get out of the garden because he'll get lost.
13. There should be some nice weather now that the rainy season is over.
14. The stores will be opened tomorrow on time.
15. How long does it take to swim across the lake.

162

EXERCISE 11

Give the past tense and past participle of the following verbs.

spill	try	translate	use
satisfy	turn	travel	visit
save	turn off	tie	work
stay	turn on	talk	wash
seem	turn over	touch	wait (for)

EXERCISE 12

Give the past tense and past participle of the following verbs.

make	pay	see	stand up
meet	read	speak	set
mean	run	sit	sing
put	ride	sleep	swim
put on	say	sell	shake

TO THE TEACHER

Because of the many different verb tenses and constructions studied up to this time, it will be impossible to include a model in each lesson of all the verb tenses and constructions that should be practiced in these exercises. Therefore, from now on, a model of one tense to be expanded to all the tenses with which the students are familiar will be included in each lesson.

EXERCISE 13

Verb Practice *Desarrolle la siguiente práctica verbal hasta incluir todos los tiempos estudiados hasta ahora, agregando el uso de un complemento (nombre o pronombre) seguido de un infinitivo.*

1. She touches it.
2. She doesn't touch it.
3. Does she touch it?

4. Doesn't she touch it?
5. What does she touch?

EXERCISE 14

Verb Practice *Make short sentences with forms of the verbs* satisfy, return, examine, appear, seem, get lost, get tired. *Expand each verb prac-*

tice to include different tenses, as in the exercise above. Use a different noun or pronoun with each verb. Use the interrogative words when it is possible.

NOT ANTES DE UN INFINITIVO

En inglés se coloca la partícula **not** antes de un infinitivo para negar con éste. Fíjese en los ejemplos:

1. They tell me **not** to speak English.
2. Are you going to tell him **not** to go?
3. He isn't going to tell her **not** to come.
4. She doesn't want to tell him **not** to work tomorrow.
5. We'll ask them **not** to talk.

EXERCISE 15

Verb Practice *Cuando sea posible, desarrolle la siguiente práctica verbal en las formas del presente progresivo, presente del futuro idiomático, futuro, antepresente, y presente de necesidad de los verbos* **want, tell** *y* **ask** *seguidos de un complemento (nombre o pronombre) más un infinitivo. Practique usando los infinitivos en negativo. Con cada tiempo use el afirmativo, negativo, interrogativo e interrogativo negativo. Use las palabras interrogativas cuando sea posible. Fíjese en los siguientes ejemplos.*

1. He is telling me (not) to   (present progressive)
   examine the book.
   Él me está diciendo que (no)
   examine el libro.

2. He's going to tell me (not)   (idiomatic future)
   to examine the book.
   Él va a decirme que (no)
   examine el libro.

3. He will tell me (not) to   (future)
   examine the book.
   Él me dirá que (no)
   examine el libro.

4. He has told me (not) to   (present perfect)
   examine the book.
   Él me ha dicho que (no)
   examine el libro.

5. He has to tell me (not) to
   examine the book.
   Él tiene que decirme que (no)
   examine el libro.

   (necessity)

6. He should tell me (not) to
   examine the book.
   Él debe decirme que (no)
   examine el libro.

   (obligation)

EXERCISE 16

Verb Practice

1. He tells me to examine the papers.
2. He doesn't tell me to examine the papers.
3. Does he tell me to examine the papers?
4. Doesn't he tell me to examine the papers?
5. When does he tell me to examine the papers?

EXERCISE 17

Verb Practice *Make short sentences with forms of the verbs* marry, get married, touch, return, play, dress. *Expand each verb practice to include different tenses, as in the exercise above. Use a different noun or pronoun with each verb. Use the interrogative words when it is possible.*

EXERCISE 18

Read and translate.

THE FIVE BLIND MEN AND THE ELEPHANT

Once there were five blind men who were taken on a trip to the zoo "to see" the animals.

"Since you can't see," their guide said to them, "you must touch the animals and then tell each other what you think they're like (cómo son). Here's a huge animal called an elephant. We'll start with him."

The first blind man went up to the elephant and touched his huge side with both hands. He felt the elephant's side until he was satisfied that he "had seen" the elephant. "The elephant," he told the rest of the blind men, "is exactly like a solid wall."

The second blind man walked up to the elephant and put his hand on the elephant's large ear. Then he turned to the first blind man and said to him. "You're completely wrong. The elephant isn't like a wall at all. He appears to me to be much more like a large fan."

When the third blind man reached the elephant, he touched the elephant's trunk. When he went back to the rest of the blind men, he said to the other two who "had seen" the elephant, "You're both crazy. I can't see that the elephant looks like a wall or like a fan. He seems to me to be like a long snake."

"Let me touch the elephant," said the fourth blind man, "and I'll tell you what he's really like."

So the fourth blind man very carefully took the elephant by the tail. After examining the elephant's tail, he said to his friends, "I told you that I'd be able to tell you the truth about the elephant. We can all 'see' that he is exactly like a rope."

"You're crazy," said the second blind man. "He's like a big fan."

"You're the one who is crazy," said the first. "I say he's like a wall."

"You don't know what you're talking about," said the third one. "The elephant appears to be nothing but a kind of snake."

"Wait," said the fifth blind man. "I still have a chance to examine the elephant and give you my impression. I'm sure that I'll be able to do better than the rest of you."

The fifth blind man placed his hands on the elephant's leg and studied it a long time. Satisfied, at last, that he knew exactly what the elephant was like, he returned to his friends. "Where did you get such silly ideas?" he asked them. "I've examined the elephant completely, and I find that he's too big to be a snake or a rope. And a wall is flat, not round, like the elephant. The elephant couldn't be like a fan because a fan is thin and the elephant is thick. I found that the elephant was big, round, solid, and thick; therefore, the elephant must be like a tree."

The five blind men left the zoo, each one with a different impression of what an elephant was like, because with incomplete knowledge they had formed bad judgments.

EXERCISE 19

Write in English.

1. Bajémonos aquí.

166

2. ¿Quieres que haga yo que él te ayude?
3. Estas chicas tontas se perdieron, ¿verdad?
4. No le voy a decir a él que estudie.
5. Ponga el ventilador. Hace mucho calor aquí.
6. Ha de haber algunas serpientes en el zoológico.
7. ¿Son los elefantes los animales más grandes de África?
8. Le he dicho a él cien veces que no ponga los pies en el sofá.
9. Ellos se ayudaron.
10. De vez en cuando Ud. llega a tiempo, ¿verdad?

EXERCISE 20

Dictation

1. The land here is very flat.
2. Do you want me to show you some brown purses?
3. This dress doesn't fit you, does it?
4. This room seems cold.
5. Those men aren't really blind, are they?
6. Have you ever been to the zoo?
7. How long does it take to walk to the zoo?
8. All those animals were captured in Africa.
9. They want the doctor to examine the child again.
10. There ought to be a telephone in this office.

EXERCISE 21

Conversation *Answer the following questions in the affirmative and in the negative.*

1. Did they make him bring his book?
2. Did you make them study?
3. Is he going to make you come tomorrow?
4. Is he going to make you go on Saturday?
5. Will she make us work?
6. Will she make us learn English?
7. Do you make her get up early?
8. Do you make her go to bed early?

Answer the following questions.

9. How many children did they have?

167

10. Where did you hang your overcoat?
11. Where did the children hide?
12. Where did you keep the letters?
13. When did you live in Cuernavaca?
14. Where did you lose your raincoat?
15. Why did you let him come in?
16. How much money did you lend your brother?
17. Where did you meet Mr. Brent?
18. Why did you put on your best suit?
19. How much did they pay him?
20. How many books did she read?
21. When did we ride the horses?
22. What did they say?
23. What did she see?
24. Where did you sit?
25. Where did they sleep?
26. Are you still studying English?
27. Is John still in the United States?
28. Is she still having a good time?
29. How long will it take us to walk to the market?
30. How long does it take to become a doctor?

Lección 13

IDIOMS

1. **to keep (someone) from (doing something)** impedir o no dejar que (alguien haga algo)

169

He kept me from coming. Me impidió que viniera.
2. **Explain this tense to me.** Explíqueme este tiempo.
   Explain it to me. Explíquemelo.
3. **to get dark** anochecer, oscurecer
4. **to get light** amanecer
5. **on the other hand** en cambio
6. **one at a time** uno por uno
7. **at least** por lo menos
8. **any color** cualquier color
   anyone(anybody) cualquiera
   Anyone(Anybody) can learn English. Cualquiera puede aprender inglés.
   anywhere(any place) en cualquier parte
   anything cualquier cosa

EXERCISE 1

Translate the following phrases and sentences and practice reading them.

1. before agreeing
2. after agreeing
3. instead of agreeing
4. in spite of agreeing
5. without agreeing
6. What's he pushing for?
7. What was he pushing for?
8. What did he push for?
9. What's he going to push for?
10. What was he going to push for?
11. What do you want him to push for?
12. There'd been many people downtown.
13. There hadn't been many people downtown.
14. Hadn't there been many people downtown?
15. There'd be a lot of time left.
16. There wouldn't be much time left.
17. Wouldn't there be a lot of time left?
18. There should be music at the party.
19. There shouldn't be music at the party.
20. Should there be music at the party?

170

EL USO DEL INFINITIVO EN INGLES EQUIVALE AL PASADO DEL SUBJUNTIVO EN ESPAÑOL

Cuando una forma del verbo sigue a un sustantivo o a un pronombre objetivo (me, you, him, her, it, us, you, them), ésta será el infinitivo con la partícula to. En español se usará el presente o el pasado del subjuntivo para la traducción correspondiente, según el tiempo del verbo que precede al sustantivo o al pronombre objetivo. Esta construcción se usa mucho después de formas de los verbos want, tell y ask. Estudie las siguientes oraciones:

1. I wanted **him to come** early.
   Quería que él viniera temprano.
2. They wanted **me to go** tomorrow.
   Querían que yo fuera mañana.
3. We wanted **John to speak** English.
   Queríamos que Juan hablara inglés.
4. They always told **me to come** early.
   Siempre me decían que viniera temprano.
5. I was going to tell **her to go** tomorrow.
   Le iba a decir a ella que fuera mañana.
6. He told **them to bring** the money.
   Él les dijo a ellos que trajeran el dinero.
7. The teacher asked **us to study** more.
   El profesor nos pidió que estudiáramos más.
8. I asked **him to buy** it.
   Le pedí a él que lo comprara.

EXERCISE 2

Verb Practice

1. She wanted him to finish.
2. She didn't want him to finish.
3. Did she want him to finish?
4. Didn't she want him to finish?
5. When did she want him to finish?

EXERCISE 3

Verb Practice *Make short sentences with forms of the verbs* hurry, hide, grow, fight, escape, marry, drive, drop, agree. *Expand each verb practice*

171

to include different tenses, as in the exercise above. Use a different combination of a nominative and an objective noun or pronoun with each verb. Use the interrogative words when it is possible.

EXERCISE 4

Verb Practice

1. You told them to eat.
2. You didn't tell them to eat.
3. Did you tell them to eat?
4. Didn't you tell them to eat?
5. What did you tell them to eat?

EXERCISE 5

Verb Practice *Make short sentences with forms of the verbs* get up, come, buy, drink, break, believe, help, fix, get married. *Expand each verb practice to include different tenses, as in the exercise above. Use a different combination of a nominative and an objective noun or pronoun with each verb. Use the interrogative words when it is possible.*

EXERCISE 6

The following sentences are in the present passive voice. Translate them and change them to the past passive, future passive, present perfect passive, past perfect passive, conditional passive, and obligation passive. Translate each time, using the se *form in Spanish.*

1. The money is spent for clothes.
2. Fruit is sold in the market.
3. Fish is eaten for dinner.
4. The letters are put in the box.
5. Flowers are found in the garden.

LA FORMA CONCISA CON LOS AUXILIARES

La respuesta a una pregunta en la conversación se forma empleando el pronombre correspondiente al sujeto y repitiendo el auxiliar empleado en la pregunta.

Si se emplea una forma del verbo **be** en la pregunta, también se empleará una forma del verbo **be** en la respuesta.

Si la respuesta va en afirmativo, empezará con la palabra **yes**; y si va en negativo, empezará con la palabra **no**.

Ejemplos: (*Véase la pág. siguiente.*)

EXERCISE 7

Answer the following questions in the affirmative and in the negative, using the necessary pronoun as a subject and repeating the auxiliary used in the sentence.

1. Do you sleep well at night?
2. Did your sister visit your grandmother?
3. Has John found his book yet?
4. Can Mary go to the movies tonight?
5. Could she go with her mother?
6. Is he going to come late again?
7. Will the children stay at home?
8. Would your sister like to go to New York?
9. Does he often help his brother?
10. Aren't you sleepy yet?
11. Weren't there many girls at the party?
12. Is it cold in the United States in the winter?
13. Have your parents always lived in Mexico?
14. Were you born in the United States?
15. Can you speak both English and Spanish?
16. Can't you remember her name?
17. Don't you like Mexico when it rains?
18. Are there many pupils in the class?
19. Would John's friend feel at home in Boston?
20. Did the teacher forget to pay you?
21. Can you lend me about five dollars?
22. Isn't it going to rain any more?
23. Won't you take your raincoat with you?
24. Was there time to eat?

1. Are you thirsty?   Yes, I am.   No, I'm not.

2. Does he speak English?   Yes, he does.   No, he doesn't.

3. Do you have any money?   Yes, I do.   No, I don't.

4. Does John have a book?   Yes, he does.   No, he doesn't.

5. Have you ever been to Acapulco?   Yes, I have.   No, I haven't.

6. Did my father open the door?   Yes, he did.   No, he didn't.

7. Are we going to eat?   Yes, we are.   No, we aren't.

8. Can Bill's brother speak Spanish?   Yes, he can.   No, he can't.

9. Couldn't they come earlier?   Yes, they could.   No, they couldn't.

10. Will you come tomorrow?   Yes, I will.   No, I won't.

11. Wouldn't you be happier in New York?   Yes, I would.   No, I wouldn't.

12. Should we wait until six?   Yes, we should.   No, we shouldn't.

13. Is there a phone in the office?   Yes, there is.   No, there isn't.

LA FORMA CONCISA CON LOS AUXILIARES

Cuando dos expresiones adversativas se unen por medio de la palabra **but** (o cuando esta palabra se sobreentiende), la segunda expresión constará solamente del sujeto y el auxiliar que corresponda al tiempo empleado.

Si se emplea una forma del verbo **be** en la primera expresión también se empleará una forma del verbo **be** en la segunda expresión.

Si el verbo en la primera expresión va en afirmativo, el auxiliar en la segunda expresión irá en negativo; y si el verbo en la primera expresión va en negativo, el auxiliar en la segunda expresión irá en afirmativo.

Ejemplos:

1. He's Mexican, but we aren't.
   Él es mexicano, pero nosotros no.

2. She doesn't speak Spanish, but her brother does.
   Ella no habla español, pero su hermano sí.

3. We have some money, but they don't.
   Tenemos dinero, pero ellos no.

4. Mary hasn't been to Acapulco, but John has.
   María no conoce Acapulco, pero Juan sí.

5. My father went to the movies, but I didn't.
   Mi papá fue al cine, pero yo no.

6. Bill's brother can't speak Spanish, but his sister can.
   El hermano de Bill no sabe hablar español, pero su hermana sí.

7. I'll come tomorrow, but Sara won't.
   Vendré mañana, pero Sara no.

8. You wouldn't be happier in Mexico, but I would.
   Tú no serías más feliz en México, pero yo sí.

9. He should go, but your friend shouldn't.
   Él debe ir, pero su amigo no.

EXERCISE 8

Fill the blanks with the correct auxiliary and translate.

1. I sleep well at night, but my wife _____ .

175

2. My sister didn't go to the movies, but I _____ .
3. George moved last year, but I _____ .
4. I hadn't ever eaten that before, but he _____ .
5. Mary can come with me, but her sister _____ .
6. She couldn't write well, but her cousin _____ .
7. He's going to study, but his brother _____ .
8. The children won't stay at home, but we _____ .
9. Your sister would like to visit us, but your brother _____ .
10. He often helps, but I _____ .
11. Bob's brother isn't sleepy yet, but we _____ .
12. He says that there were many girls at the party, but there _____ .
13. They think it isn't cold in California, but it _____ .
14. My parents have always lived in Mexico, but I _____ .
15. I wasn't born in the United States, but my brother _____ .
16. We can speak both English and Spanish, but they _____ .
17. She can't ever remember my name, but he always _____ .
18. Your cousin wouldn't like a tie, but we _____ .
19. I don't like Mexico when it rains, but my mother _____ .
20. You have always done your homework, but John _____ .
21. Ed's mother wouldn't feel at home in Mexico, but mine _____ .
22. The teacher forgot, but I _____ .
23. He said it isn't going to rain any more, but it _____ .
24. They won't take their raincoats, but we _____ .
25. The girls like milk, but he _____ .

EXERCISE 9

Translate the following sentences. Change them to the negative, interrogative, and interrogative negative.

1. They kept him from going.
2. You can keep her from singing.
3. He'll keep us from coming.
4. We've kept you from working.
5. He's going to keep it from dying.
6. She'll keep us from talking.
7. The teacher will be able to keep them from playing.
8. His father ought to keep him from spending the money.
9. The girls should keep the children from eating the cake.
10. Mr. Adams kept me from bringing my friends.

EXERCISE 10

Answer the following questions in the affirmative and in the negative.

1. Did he keep you from listening to the music?
2. Will they keep her from getting married?
3. Does she keep you from visiting the United States?
4. Could you keep them from swimming?
5. Have we kept the girls from speaking Spanish?
6. Would Mr. Stone keep John from saving his money?
7. Shouldn't his parents keep him from traveling by plane?
8. Can't you keep the child from spilling the milk?
9. Will you be able to keep your husband from buying a new car?
10. Has the owner of the house been able to keep the thief from stealing the clothes?

EXERCISE 11

Translate into Spanish.

1. Anyone can learn how to speak English if he tries.
2. You'll look good in any color.
3. I haven't been able to keep him from sleeping during the day.
4. We used to make our own clothes, didn't we?
5. He doesn't like to go to the United States during the winter, but I do.
6. At least we can keep him from coming so early.
7. How long should it take to drive from here to Puebla?
8. They can't make him speak English.
9. She'd just translated the letter when we came.
10. You must go home before it gets dark.
11. The teacher began to teach without explaining the new tense to the students.
12. We'll go anywhere you want.
13. My wife gave up movies. She doesn't go any more.
14. On the other hand, I can't see why he won't be able to pay us.
15. I didn't want to dance any more, but she did.

EXERCISE 12

Give the past tense and past participle of the following verbs.

177

walk	ask	believe	change
want	answer	call	correct
watch	arrive (in, at)	clean	clap
worry (about)	add	close	cry
avoid	agree	complete	carry

EXERCISE 13

Give the past tense and past participle of the following verbs.

shine	tell	wake up	bring
spend	think	wear	break
send	take off	wear out	buy
take	understand	bet	begin
teach	write	be able	become

EXERCISE 14

Verb Practice *Expand the following verb practice to include all the tenses studied so far. Use the affirmative, negative, interrogative, and interrogative negative.*

1. The driver explained it to them, didn't he?
2. The driver didn't explain it to them, did he?
3. Did the driver explain it to them?
4. Didn't the driver explain it to them?
5. How many times did the driver explain it to them?

EXERCISE 15

Verb Practice *Make short sentences with forms of the verbs move, lift, own, avoid, bet, get dark, get light, keep (someone) from (doing something). Expand each verb practice to include different tenses, as in the exercise above. Use a different noun or pronoun with each verb. Use the interrogative words when it is possible.*

EXERCISE 16

Verb Practice *Cuando sea posible, desarrolle la siguiente práctica verbal en las formas del presente y pasado progresivo, presente y pasado del* *futuro idiomático, futuro, antepresente, antecopretérito, pospretérito, obligación, presente y pasado de necesidad de los verbos* **want, tell** *y* **ask,** *seguidos de un complemento (nombre o pronombre) más un inifinitivo. Practique usando los infinitivos en negativo. Con cada tiempo use el afirmativo, negativo, interrogativo e interrogativo negativo. Use las palabras interrogativas cuando sea posible. Fíjese en los siguientes ejemplos.*

1. They told me (not) to move.
   Ellos me dijeron que (no) me moviera.
2. They were going to tell me (not) to move.
   Ellos iban a decirme que (no) me moviera.
3. They were telling me (not) to move.
   Ellos estaban diciéndome que (no) me moviera.
4. They had told me (not) to move.
   Ellos me habían dicho que (no) me moviera.
5. They would tell me (not) to move.
   Ellos me dirían que (no) me moviera.
6. They should tell me (not) to move.
   Ellos deberían decirme que (no) me moviera.
7. They had to tell me (not) to move.
   Ellos tuvieron que decirme que (no) me moviera.
8. They wanted to tell me (not) to move.
   Ellos quisieron decirme que (no) me moviera.

1. They told me to move.
2. They didn't tell me to move.
3. Did they tell me to move?
4. Didn't they tell me to move?
5. What did they tell me to move for?

EXERCISE 17

Verb Practice *Make short sentences with forms of the verbs* **explain, lift, bet, pay, take off, get off.** *Expand each verb practice to include different tenses, as in the exercise above. Use a different combination of a nominative and objective noun or pronoun with each verb. Practice using negative infinitives. Use the interrogative words when it is possible.*

EXERCISE 18

Read and translate.

TWO MEN AND SOME ROCKS

A farmer who owned some land that had a lot of rocks on it called the two men who worked for him on the farm and said to them, "I want you to go to the field and move all those big rocks so that I can work there tomorrow."

One of these men had a strong back and a weak mind, and the other one had a weak back and a strong mind. The man who had a strong back was very proud of the fact that he was strong, and he was always showing his friends his strength by lifting and carrying heavy objects.

The friend, on the other hand, had a strong mind instead of a strong back; and he was always using it to avoid heavy work, since he couldn't lift very much with a weak back.

On the way to the field the more intelligent of the two began a conversation with the other one, saying, "What does this farmer think we are? He sends us to the field like slaves to move some heavy rocks that should be work for at least ten men. I'll bet that not even you, as strong as you are, can lift those stones."

"I can lift any stone in that field," replied the stupid man quickly. "Those rocks are nothing. I've carried many rocks much farther than I'll have to carry these."

"I don't believe it," answered the man with the brains. "I don't believe that anyone can carry rocks as big as those in the field."

"When we get to the field, I'll show you," said the man with the strong back.

When the two men got to the field, the smart one sat down in the shade and said to his friend, "Now let me see if you can really lift those stones without any help."

The stupid man took his shirt off and started to work. He lifted the rocks on his back with great difficulty and carried them out of the field one at a time. At last, when it began to get dark, he finished carrying the last stone. Then he proudly said to his friend lying in the shade, "You see, I told you that I was strong enough to carry these rocks. You didn't think I could do it, did you?"

"No," answered the intelligent one getting up, "I didn't think you could do it, but you really are as strong as you say, aren't you?"

EXERCISE 19

Write in English.

1. Han de ser casi las seis. Está amaneciendo en el este.

180

2. Hice grandes esfuerzos para impedir que él dijera todos los nombres.
3. ¿Por qué no quería que él apostara?
4. ¿Crees que él podrá levantar aquella roca pesada?
5. Cualquiera debería poder traducir las oraciones.
6. Me gustaría decirle a él que no tiene razón.
7. Deberías decidir lo que quieres hacer antes de que dejes este empleo.
8. Ellas han tenido que decirle a ella tres veces que no corrija el inglés de otra gente.
9. Las otras alumnas no podrán ir, pero yo sí.
10. Te dijeron que no dejaras que jugaran los niños en la calle, ¿verdad?

EXERCISE 20

Dictation

1. You must clean these vases one at a time.
2. Why don't you let us get on the bus? A few more people won't make any difference.
3. I want to speak to someone—anyone.
4. At least, he should have helped us.
5. The pupils have asked him to explain the lesson again.
6. They can't keep you from getting in, can they?
7. I can't lift these heavy boxes, but my husband can.
8. John is a smart boy.
9. He told me to give you the reddest tie I had.
10. Which of these boys is the most intelligent?

EXERCISE 21

Conversation *Answer the following questions in the affirmative and in the negative.*

1. Do you keep the children from playing in the house?
2. Did you keep the boys from swimming?
3. Will you keep the pupils from talking?
4. Are you going to keep him from going?
5. Have you kept him from getting up?
6. Could you keep him from becoming a doctor?
7. Are you going to keep her from going out?
8. Was she keeping him from having a good time?
9. Do they want to keep him from seeing that movie?

10. Did he want to keep you from listening to the radio?
11. Will I be able to keep her from speaking Spanish?
12. Has he been able to keep them from staying in Acapulco?
13. Would he be able to keep them from stealing?
14. Would she be able to keep him from arriving late?
15. Did you tell your father to keep that man from driving the car?
16. Did you want us to keep them from reading?
17. Do you make him help you?
18. Did you make her leave them alone?
19. Will you make us go early?
20. Would they make him come early?
21. Can he make her do the work?
22. Should she make us pay for the books?
23. Could they make him drive the car?
24. Do you want me to start the lesson?
25. Did you want him to believe you?
26. Will you want her to change the money?
27. Did she tell him to write the letters?
28. Will he tell us how to escape?
29. Do they tell him not to fight?
30. Will he tell her not to go out?

Lección 14

1. **to shoot (at), shot (at), shot (at)** disparar (a); **to shoot, shot, shot** dar (*con un arma*)
2. **to name, named, named** nombrar; ponerle nombre a uno
3. **to hurt, hurt, hurt** lastimar
4. **to hit, hit, hit** pegar
5. **to smell, smelled, smelled** oler
6. **to punish, punished, punished** castigar
7. **certainly** ciertamente; con mucho gusto
8. **calm** tranquilo; calmado **calmly** tranquilamente
9. **brave** valiente
10. **except** menos, excepto
11. **square** cuadrado; plaza **park** parque
12. **distance** distancia; lejanía
13. **half** mitad
14. **order** orden
15. **post** poste
16. **sign** señal; indicación; letrero
17. **shot** disparo, tiro
18. **tyrant** tirano
19. **stream** arroyo
20. **air** aire
21. **arrow** flecha **bow and arrow** arco y flecha
22. **heart** corazón
23. **deer** venado(s)
24. **bear** oso
25. **Europe** Europa

IDIOMS

1. **to stop + (gerund)** dejar de + (infinitivo)

183

He stopped talking. El dejó de hablar.

2. **to get hurt** lastimarse
   He got hurt. El se lastimó.
3. **to hurt your hand, leg, etc.** lastimarse la mano, pierna, etc.
   She hurt her head. Ella se lastimó la cabeza.
4. **to take care of** cuidar de, a; atender a; encargarse de
5. **to go swimming, dancing, riding** ir a nadar, bailar, montar
   I went swimming, dancing, riding. Fui a nadar, bailar, montar.
6. **I was named after my father.** Me pusieron el nombre de mi papá,
   Me llamo como mi papá.
   Who were you named after? ¿Cómo a quién te pusieron?, ¿Cómo
   quién te llamas?
   What did they name him? ¿Cómo le pusieron?
   They named him John. Le pusieron Juan.
7. **such a good shot** tan buen tirador
8. **a pair of shoes** un par de zapatos
   a pair of socks un par de calcetines
   a pair of hose un par de medias
   a pair of stockings un par de medias
   a pair of gloves un par de guantes
9. **all that** todo lo que
10. **if I were you** si yo fuera tú, yo que tú

EXERCISE 1

Translate the following phrases and sentences and practice reading them.

1. instead of explaining
2. besides explaining
3. He likes to dance, but I don't.
4. He wants to dance, but they don't.
5. He wanted to dance, but they didn't.
6. He can dance, but we can't.
7. He could dance, but you couldn't.
8. He'll dance, but I won't.
9. He'd dance, but she wouldn't.
10. He should dance, but you shouldn't.
11. He isn't going to dance, but they are.
12. He wasn't going to dance, but they were.
13. He isn't dancing, but you are.
14. He wasn't dancing, but I was.

184

15. He didn't have to dance, but she did.
16. He hasn't danced, but they have.
17. He won't be able to dance, but we will.
18. It'll be cold.

THE PAST SUBJUNCTIVE
EL PASADO DEL SUBJUNTIVO

Con todos los verbos en inglés se usa el pasado que equivale al pasado del subjuntivo en español.

El pasado del subjuntivo del poder (pudiera) equivale a **could**, la forma pasada del verbo **be able**. Estudie las siguientes oraciones.

1. If I **could** speak English, I would go to the United States.
   Si yo supiera hablar inglés, iría a los Estados Unidos.

2. They would learn Spanish if they **came** to class every day.
   Ellos aprenderían castellano si vinieran a clase todos los días.

3. If we **had** money, we would buy a car.
   Si tuviéramos dinero, compraríamos un coche.

4. He would go to school if he **knew** his lesson.
   Él iría a la escuela si se supiera la lección.

5. If you **ate** more for lunch, you wouldn't be hungry in the afternoon.
   Si comieras más en la comida, no tendrías hambre en la tarde.

TO THE TEACHER

Contemporary grammarians agree that the use of **were** with a singular subject in statements contrary to fact (after the word **if** and after the verb **wish**) has now been replaced by **was** as the past subjunctive of **be**.

In constructions such as **If I were a movie star**, **were** was standard English until three hundred years ago. Since then, **was** has been gradually taking the place of **were** in these constructions; and the preferred form today is **if I was a movie star** and **I wish I was a movie star**.

In present-day English there is only one expression where **were** is preferred with a singular pronoun. This is the expression **if I were you**. (See idioms, Lesson 14.)

185

EXERCISE 2

Verb Practice

1. if I was studying
2. if I wasn't studying
3. if you were studying
4. if you weren't studying
5. if he was studying
6. if he wasn't studying
7. if she was studying
8. if she wasn't studying
9. if we were studying
10. if we weren't studying
11. if you were studying
12. if you weren't studying
13. if they were studying
14. if they weren't studying

EXERCISE 3

Verb Practice *Repeat exercise 2, using forms of the verbs* **work, read, explain, speak, knock (on), push, pull, travel, hide.**

EXERCISE 4

Verb Practice

1. if I ate
2. if I didn't eat
3. if you danced
4. if you didn't dance
5. if he spoke
6. if he didn't speak
7. if she got married
8. if she didn't get married
9. if we jumped
10. if we didn't jump
11. if you paid
12. if you didn't pay
13. if they put on
14. if they didn't put on

EXERCISE 5

Verb Practice *Repeat exercise 4, using forms of the verbs* **be, lend, bet, keep, remember, spend, stay, touch, win.**

PRONOMBRES REFLEXIVOS

Learn the following reflexive pronouns.

I	myself	yo mismo, me
you	yourself	tú mismo, te
you	yourself	Ud. mismo, se

186

he	himself	él mismo, se
she	herself	ella misma, se
it	itself	en sí
we	ourselves	nosotros mismos, nos
you	yourselves	Uds. mismos, se
they	themselves	ellos mismos, se

Se usan los pronombres reflexivos al referirse al sujeto y/o para hacer hincapié sobre el mismo sujeto. Cuando el pronombre reflexivo es complemento, seguirá al verbo. Cuando se usa para énfasis, se puede colocar directamente después del sujeto o al fin de la oración. Estudie las siguientes oraciones.

1. He's talking to himself.   (reflexive)
   Está hablando solo (a sí mismo, para sí).
2. You must help yourself first.   (reflexive)
   Te tienes que ayudar a ti mismo primero.
3. I told you that myself.   (emphatic)
   I myself told you that.   (emphatic)
   Yo mismo le dije eso a Ud.
4. We'll pay them ourselves.   (emphatic)
   We ourselves will pay them.   (emphatic)
   Nosotros mismos les pagaremos.

La preposición **by** seguida de un pronombre reflexivo equivale a **solo** o **sin ayuda** en español. Estudie las siguientes oraciones.

1. They went by themselves.
   Ellos fueron solos.
2. I don't want to sit by myself.
   No quiero estar sentada sola.
3. She can do the work by herself.
   Ella puede hacer el trabajo sola.
4. You'll have to sleep by yourself.
   Tendrás que dormir solo.

EXERCISE 6

Fill the blanks with the correct reflexive pronoun and translate.

1. Those people don't see _____ as we see them.
2. That old man talks to _____ .
3. I won't be able to fix the car by _____ .
4. She was singing to _____ .
5. You saw it _____ .
6. I _____ wrote that letter.
7. She doesn't like to eat by _____ .
8. We _____ will explain what happened.
9. Why can't you do this _____ ?
10. We must help _____ first.
11. Did you go to the movies by _____ ?
12. He _____ stole that money.
13. The city _____ is not very large.
14. They can't learn English by _____ .
15. The trip _____ wasn't very long.

EXERCISE 7

Fill the blanks with the correct auxiliary and translate.

1. I can't help you tomorrow, but he _____ .
2. They didn't study, but we _____ .
3. He won't believe me, but she _____ .
4. They always eat early, but I _____ .
5. She couldn't go, but you _____ .
6. He's here, but his wife _____ .
7. I wanted to help him, but they _____ .
8. We've seen that movie, but she _____ .
9. They'll have to work tomorrow, but we _____ .
10. They're sick, but we _____ .

EL ARTICULO *THE*

Aprenda el uso del artículo the.

1. No use el artículo **the** antes de títulos cuando éstos van seguidos de un apellido.

> President Stone will speak tomorrow.
> Professor White will arrive at eight o'clock.

Use el artículo **the** antes de un título que no es seguido de un apellido.

>**The** president will speak tomorrow.
>**The** professor will arrive at eight o'clock.

2. No use el artículo **the** con las palabras empleadas en sentido general.

>I like coffee.
>Women shouldn't talk so much.

Use el artículo **the** cuando se refiere a algo definido.

>I like **the** coffee from Brazil.
>**The** women at that meeting shouldn't talk so much.

EXERCISE 8

Fill the blanks with the article **the** *when it is required and translate.*

1. I want you to call _____ Dr. Chandler.
2. _____ man is an animal.
3. We'll give it to _____ Mrs. Jones.
4. Do you want me to call _____ doctor?
5. _____ milk is very expensive.
6. _____ milk I bought yesterday isn't good.
7. I'd like to speak to _____ Mr. Stone.
8. Everybody likes _____ bread.
9. Did you like _____ bread I bought yesterday?
10. We saw _____ general yesterday.
11. We didn't see _____ General Gates.
12. _____ charity (la caridad) begins at home.
13. He likes _____ blue suits.
14. He likes _____ blue suit that John has.

LA FORMA CONCISA CON LOS AUXILIARES

El equivalente en inglés de y **tú (no)**, y **él (no)**, y **Juan (no)**, etc. es una pregunta corta en afirmativo o negativo compuesta del sujeto con el auxiliar que corresponda al tiempo empleado.

Si se emplea una forma del verbo **be** en la oración, también se empleará una forma del verbo **be** en la pregunta corta. Estudie las siguientes oraciones.

1. I sleep well at night, **do you**?
   Duermo bien de noche, ¿y **tú**?

2. I'm Mexican, **aren't you**?
   Soy mexicano, ¿y **Ud. no**?

3. We don't have any money, **do they**?
   No tenemos dinero, ¿y **ellos**?

4. Mary has been to Monterrey, **has John**?
   María conoce Monterrey, ¿y **Juan**?

5. Ben's sister can speak Spanish, **can you**?
   La hermana de Ben sabe hablar español, ¿y **Uds.**?

6. We couldn't do the homework, **could they**?
   No pudimos hacer la tarea, ¿y **ellos**?

7. John is going to eat now, **aren't you**?
   Juan va a comer ahora, ¿y **tú no**?

8. We won't wait for Henry, **will you**?
   No esperaremos a Enrique, ¿y **tú**?

EXERCISE 9

Fill the blanks with the correct translation of the Spanish in parenthesis.

1. He wants to visit her, _____ (¿y tú?)
2. We don't want to buy that book, _____ (¿y Roberto?)
3. I'm going to stay late, _____ (¿y él no?)
4. Martha couldn't eat her breakfast, _____ (¿y Juan?)
5. We can go now, _____ (¿y Ud. no?)
6. She's going to leave soon, _____ (¿y nosotros?)
7. They had to buy more bread, _____ (¿y tú?)
8. We wanted to finish our dress tonight, _____ (¿y ella no?)
9. Paul has just finished his homework, _____ (¿y tú no?)
10. My mother is making a cake, _____ (¿y la de Ud. no?)
11. We weren't doing anything, _____ (¿y ellas?)
12. Martin will wash his car tomorrow, _____ (¿y tú no?)
13. They'd like to buy a new house, _____ (¿y a él no?)
14. We wouldn't invite him, _____ (¿y Uds.?)
15. He never used to eat between meals, _____ (¿y ella?)
16. She was going to spend all her money, _____ (¿y Ud.?)
17. Helen has a new dress. _____ (¿y Rosa no?)
18. They can eat in the living room, _____ (¿y yo no?)

19. We went to bed at nine, _____ (¿y tú?)
20. He lives over there, _____ (¿y ellos?)

EXERCISE 10

Translate the following sentences. Change them to the negative, interrogative, and interrogative negative.

1. He wants us to stop talking.
2. It's going to stop raining.
3. The wind stopped blowing about six o'clock.
4. I told them to stop speaking Spanish.
5. She thought he would stop spending his money.
6. He should stop drinking.
7. We'll stop driving so fast.
8. They wanted him to stop playing football.
9. The children have stopped making so much noise.
10. That child can stop crying.

EXERCISE 11

Answer the following questions in the affirmative and in the negative.

1. Did you stop studying English?
2. Is he going to stop pronouncing the words?
3. Have they already stopped eating?
4. Has his finger stopped bleeding yet?
5. Couldn't you stop laughing?
6. Will she be able to stop worrying about us?
7. Did you stop working on Sundays?
8. Will you stop waiting for your teacher every night?
9. Do you want me to stop singing?
10. Did they tell him to stop riding?

EXERCISE 12

Translate into Spanish.

1. Mary used to take care of my children when I went to the movies.
2. Stop talking. I want you to hear what the teacher is saying.
3. Make him stop putting his fingers in his plate.

4. Anyone can stop drinking if he tries hard.
5. Can't you keep him from spending his money?
6. He'll be able to take care of his business himself.
7. I knew you'd get hurt if you didn't stop playing football.
8. She was named after her grandmother.
9. I don't think this pair of shoes will last very long.
10. What do you want me to buy a pair of gloves for?
11. Those soldiers aren't very good shots, are they?
12. They didn't make him take care of the chickens, did they?
13. I can't swim across that river, can you?
14. They told me to keep the dogs from playing in the garden.
15. You're a very lucky young man.

EXERCISE 13

Give the past tense and past participle of the following verbs.

cover	disappear	fix	fill
capture	dance	escape	form
dictate	die	examine	help
drop	drown	explain	hurry
dress	decide	finish	hunt

EXERCISE 14

Give the past tense and past participle of the following verbs.

blow	come back	dig	find
build	cut	drive	fly
bleed	catch	eat	fall(down)
bet	do	feel	feed
come	drink	forget	fight

EXERCISE 15

Verb Practice *Expand the following practice to include all the tenses studied so far. Use the affirmative, negative, interrogative, and interrogative negative when it is possible.*

1. You've shot an animal.
2. You haven't shot an animal.

192

3. Have you shot an animal?
4. Haven't you shot an animal?
5. How many times have you shot?

EXERCISE 16

Verb Practice *Make short sentences with forms of the verbs* name, hurt, hit, smell, punish, get hurt, take care of, cry. *Expand each verb practice to include different tenses, as in the exercise above. Use a different noun or pronoun with each verb. Use the interrogative words when it is possible.*

EXERCISE 17

Verb Practice *Expand the following verb practice to include as many tenses as possible that have been studied so far. Repeat the exercise, using forms of the verbs* want *and* ask *instead of* tell *with as many tenses as possible. Practice using negative infinitives.*

1. They're going to tell him to shoot at the apple.
2. They aren't going to tell him to shoot at the apple.
3. Are they going to tell him to shoot at the apple?
4. Aren't they going to tell him to shoot at the apple?
5. How many times are they going to tell him to shoot at the apple?

EXERCISE 18

Verb Practice *Make short sentences with forms of the verbs* shoot, shoot (at), name, hurt, smell, punish, get hurt, take care of, go dancing. *Expand each verb practice to include different tenses, as in the exercise above. Use a different combination of a nominative and objective noun or pronoun with each verb. Use the interrogative words when it is possible.*

EXERCISE 19

Read and translate.

THE STORY OF WILLIAM TELL

Long ago in a small country in Europe there lived a man named William Tell. William Tell was a hunter who loved the freedom of the streams and woods and the smell of the fresh mountain air; and he spent a lot of his time there, hunting with his bow and arrow, where he shot deer and bears and other animals to feed his family.

After years of practice Tell had become such a good shot with the bow and arrow that he could hit a small animal two or three hundred feet from him.

One day William Tell read an order written by the tyrant of the country that said that a post with the tyrant's hat on it had been placed in the city square, and all the people who passed by the post had to take off their hats as a sign of respect.

So all the people, because they were afraid, took their hats off when they passed by the post in the square—all except one, a brave man named William Tell. "I won't even take off my hat for the tyrant himself, and I certainly won't take it off for a post," said William Tell.

When the tyrant heard this, he got very angry and decided that the hunter should be punished. "They say that you're a very good shot with the bow and arrow," said the tyrant to William Tell. "We're going to find out how good you are. Your small son will be placed at a distance of three hundred feet from you. Then an apple will be put on top of his head. You'll have to hit the apple with your bow and arrow. You'll be given only one shot."

William Tell said nothing. He calmly took two arrows and got ready. The arrow flew through the air and hit the apple. The little boy wasn't hurt.

"Since I told you that you could have only one shot, why did you take two arrows?" the tyrant asked William Tell.

"I was going to shoot you through the heart with the other one if I had killed my son," was the answer.

EXERCISE 20

Write in English.

1. Si yo estuviera en tu lugar, saldría en seguida.
2. Ellos me prestarían el dinero, si lo tuvieran.
3. Los americanos no se dan la mano tanto como los mexicanos.
4. Si lloviera, no iríamos al centro.
5. Pablo no quería ir a Cuernavaca, pero Enrique sí.
6. No vi el juego de futbol, ¿y tú?
7. Si ellos entendieran español, irían a ver aquella película mexicana con nosotros.

194

8. Las lecciones más difíciles están en el segundo libro.
9. Los niños no se enfermarían tan a menudo si no comieran tantos (so much) dulces.
10. No pudimos leer ese letrero, ¿y Ud.?

EXERCISE 21

Dictation

1. I certainly don't want to go if it's raining, do you?
2. Has it stopped raining?
3. Will you take care of my flowers while I'm out of town?
4. He bought a pair of gloves, but she didn't.
5. If I were you, I'd buy a house instead of a car.
6. They told me to do the work myself.
7. We're always afraid that the children will fall and get hurt.
8. We won't be able to buy a television set (aparato) this year, will you?
9. Hose are more expensive now, aren't they?
10. Why don't you name your baby after me?

EXERCISE 22

Conversation *Answer the following questions.*

1. How long does it take to learn how to dance?
2. How long did it take to explain the lesson to you?
3. How long does it take to get to Acapulco?
4. How long did it take you to walk to the movies?
5. How long will it take us to wash these shirts?

Answer the following questions in the affirmative and in the negative.

6. Do you take care of your clothes?
7. Did he take care of his car?
8. Will she take care of her parents?
9. Do you want me to take care of your dog?
10. Were they going to go dancing last Saturday night?
11. Would you like to go dancing at the Patio?
12. Would you like to go swimming?
13. Will you be able to go swimming with me next week?
14. Does she like to go dancing every night?

195

15. Has he stopped reading?
16. Has it stopped snowing?
17. Did it stop raining?
18. Will the wind stop blowing?
19. Do you want me to stop playing?
20. Did he tell them to stop working?
21. Were they going to tell her to stop studying?
22. Did he do the work himself?
23. Did she clean the house by herself?
24. Did they write the book themselves?
25. Was he talking to himself?
26. Did you make that dress yourself?
27. Did you let them help you?
28. Did he help her wash the windows?
29. Can you keep them from playing football?
30. Will you keep her from going out?

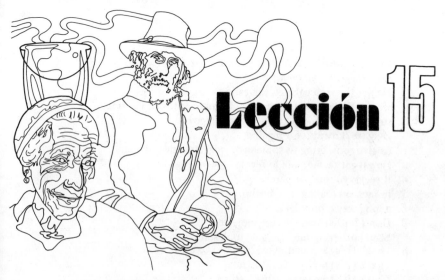

Lección 15

Vocabulary

1. **to bother, bothered, bothered** molestar(se)
2. **to cook, cooked, cooked** cocinar, guisar
3. **to boil, boiled, boiled** hervir
4. **to cost, cost, cost** costar
5. **to throw, threw, thrown** arrojar; tirar; echar
6. **to surprise, surprised, surprised,** sorprender **surprising** sorprendente
7. **widow** viuda
8. **beggar** mendigo
9. **stranger** forastero; extraño
10. **nail** clavo
11. **key** llave
12. **silver** plata **silverware** (*sing.*) cubiertos
13. **pot** olla
14. **fire** fuego; incendio
15. **shelf** estante, repisa
16. **pocket** bolsa (*de ropa*)
17. **ticket** boleto
18. **ice** hielo **iceman** hielero
19. **tea** té
20. **vegetable** legumbre, vegetal
21. **onion** cebolla
22. **tomato** jitomate
23. **salt** sal
24. **pepper** pimienta; pimiento

IDIOMS

1. **to plan + (infinitive)** pensar + (infinitivo)
   I plan to go to New York. Pienso ir a Nueva York.

197

2. **to get through** terminar (de), acabar (de) (*se usa solamente con persona o animal como sujeto*)
   He got through eating. El acabó de comer.
   He got through before ten. El terminó antes de las diez.
3. **to give (something) away** regalar (algo)
   He gave it away. Lo regaló.
   to give something to somebody regalar algo a alguien
   He gave it to me. Me lo regaló.
4. **it seems to me** me parece
5. **in fact** en realidad, de hecho
6. **a long ways** muy lejos
7. **Don't bother me.** No me moleste.
   Stop bothering me. Deja de molestarme.
8. **That's (It's) too bad.** Qué lástima.
   That's (It's) a pity. Qué lástima.
   That's (It's) a shame. Qué lástima.
9. **I'm glad that you came.** Me alegro que haya venido.

EXERCISE 1

Translate the following sentences and practice reading them.

1. Notice this.
2. Let him punish them.
3. Don't let him punish them.
4. What's he shooting for?
5. What's he shooting at?
6. He likes soup, but I don't.
7. She wants to travel, but we don't.
8. They want to rest, but she doesn't.
9. We can't dance, but they can.
10. I can't speak English, but he can.
11. He knows his lesson, do you?
12. They can swim, can you?
13. She can help us, can you?
14. It's been hot.
15. Has it been hot?
16. Hasn't it been hot?
17. Had it been hot?
18. It'd be hot.
19. Would it be hot?
20. Wouldn't it be hot?

198

WOULD HAVE + PAST PARTICIPLE
EL ANTEPOSPRETÉRITO

Se forma el antepospretérito en inglés anteponiendo los auxiliares **would have** al participio.

Se forma la contracción en afirmativo con la partícula **d** agregada al pronombre. La contracción negativa es **wouldn't have**. Fíjese en el ejemplo.

> You would (you'd) have eaten earlier.
> Ud. habría comido más temprano.

EXERCISE 2

Verb Practice

1. He'd have come yesterday.
2. He wouldn't have come yesterday.
3. Would he have come yesterday?
4. Wouldn't he have come yesterday?
5. Why wouldn't he have come yesterday?

EXERCISE 3

Verb Practice *Repeat exercise 2, using past participles of the verbs* **find out, feed, knock (on), keep.** *Use a different noun or pronoun with each verb. Use the interrogative words when it is possible.*

EL USO DEL ANTEPRETÉRITO EN INGLÉS EQUIVALE AL ANTEPRETÉRITO DEL SUBJUNTIVO EN ESPAÑOL

El antepretérito del subjuntivo en español, formado con el pasado del subjuntivo de haber (hubiera) y el participio de un verbo, equivale al antepretérito en inglés. Fíjese en el ejemplo.

> If she **had** come, she would have eaten.
> Si ella hubiera venido, hubiera (habría) comido.

Nótese que en la oración principal en castellano se puede emplear **hubiera** o **habría** mientras que en inglés se debe usar solamente **would have (habría).**

199

EXERCISE 4

Verb Practice

1. if I'd worked
2. if I hadn't worked
3. if you'd worked
4. if you hadn't worked
5. if he'd worked
6. if he hadn't worked
7. if she'd worked
8. if she hadn't worked
9. if we'd worked
10. if we hadn't worked
11. if you'd worked
12. if you hadn't worked
13. if they'd worked
14. if they hadn't worked

EXERCISE 5

Verb Practice *Repeat exercise 4, using forms of the verbs* disappear, dig, bet, hit, hurt, find out, feed, knock (on), keep. *Use noun equivalents in place of some of the pronouns.*

WHOEVER, WHATEVER, WHICHEVER, WHEREVER, WHENEVER

whoever quienquiera que, quien, sea quien sea, cualquiera que
whatever cualquier cosa que, lo que
whichever cualquiera que, el que
wherever dondequiera que, por dondequiera que
whenever siempre que, en cualquier tiempo que sea, cuando sea, cada vez que

Study the following examples:

1. **Whoever** she is, she's beautiful.
   Quienquiera que ella sea, es hermosa.

2. Give the money to **whoever** comes first.
   Dé el dinero a quien venga primero.

3. My mother will buy me **whatever** I want.
   Mi mamá me comprará lo que quiera.

4. **Wherever** you are, I'll find you.
   Dondequiera que estés, te encontraré.

5. Take **whichever** book you want.
   Lleva cualquier libro que quieras.

6. Bring it **whenever** you come.
   Tráigalo cuando Ud. venga.

EXERCISE 6

Read the sentences and translate the words in parentheses.

1. Give the letter to (quien) _____ opens the door.
2. Now that you're rich, you can buy (lo que quiera) _____ you want.
3. I'll find my father (dondequiera) _____ he is.
4. You'll have to take (el que) _____ comes first.
5. (Cada vez que) _____ I see her, I think of my mother.
6. (Sea quien sea)_____ he is, he isn't my brother.
7. Come to see me (cuando) _____ you are in Chicago.
8. My parents will give me (lo que) _____ I ask for.
9. I think Martha is happy (dondequiera) _____ she is.
10. We'll have to take (lo que) _____ they give us.
11. (Quienquiera) _____ he is, he's very polite.
12. I'll do (lo que) _____ he says.
13. He'll write to me (dondequiera) _____ I am.
14. Go with (quien) _____ you want.
15. Visit your family (siempre que) _____ you can.

EXERCISE 7

Fill the blanks with the correct translation of the Spanish in parentheses.

1. He didn't want to sit down, _____ (¿y tú?)
2. They had to be there before six, _____ (¿y él?)
3. The children won't be able to come, _____ (¿y tu papá?)
4. Henry would like two eggs, _____ (¿y a ella?)
5. We used to drink warm milk. _____ (¿y ella no?)
6. I can drive a car, _____ (¿y tú?)
7. He likes to go riding, _____ (¿y a Uds. no?)
8. She could name all the mountains, _____ (¿y María?)
9. I'm going to go to the movies, _____ (¿y tú?)
10. John wants to come to my house on Monday, _____ (¿y Roberto?)

EXERCISE 8

Fill the blanks with the tense of the verb indicated that corresponds to the past subjunctive in Spanish and translate.

201

(have)	1. If I _____ that book, I'd lend it to you.
(be)	2. If that dog _____ mine, I'd feed him better.
(win)	3. He said he'd pay me if he _____.
(listen)	4. They'd be able to hear if they _____ .
(be able)	5. We'd help you if we _____ .
(speak)	6. If she _____ Spanish, you'd understand.
(find out)	7. If you _____ the address, would you tell me?
(know)	8. If you _____ how to speak Spanish, would you go to Mexico?
(be able)	9. He'd tell me where she lives if he _____ find her address.
(go)	10. If you _____ to the market, you'd be able to buy vegetables.
(be)	11. If he _____ sick, he wouldn't go to the office.
(have)	12. Would you go to the movies with me if you _____ time?
(begin)	13. If they _____ now, they'd get through before dinner.
(get up)	14. Henry would work if he _____ earlier.
(own)	15. If we _____ that house, we'd sell it.

LA FORMA CONCISA CON *TOO* y *SO*

El equivalente en inglés de **tú también, él también, Juan también**, etc. es una oración corta compuesta del sujeto, el auxiliar que corresponda al tiempo empleado, y la palabra **too** o **so**. Nótese que las dos formas con **too** y **so** se distinguen por el orden de las palabras.

Si se emplea una forma del verbo **be** en la oración, también se empleará una forma del verbo **be** en la oración corta.

Aprenda a emplear la forma con **too** y a reconocer la otra.

1. They're Mexican, and I am too (*or*) so am I.
   Son mexicanos, y yo también.
2. Robert was sick, and Mary was too (*or*) so was Mary.
   Roberto estuvo enfermo, y María también.
3. She saw that movie, and I did too (*or*) so did I.
   Ella vio esa película, y yo también.
4. My parents have a car, and his do too (*or*) so do his.
   Mis papás tienen coche, y los suyos también.
5. John can come, and they can too (*or*) so can they.
   Juan puede venir, y ellos también.

6. He'll bring money, and Henry will too (*or*) so will Henry.
   Él traerá dinero, y Enrique también.
7. She'd like to go, and he would too (*or*) so would he.
   A ella le gustaría ir, y a él también.
8. We should get up early, and she should too (*or*) so should she.
   Deberíamos levantarnos temprano, y ella también.

EXERCISE 9

Fill the blanks with the correct translation of the Spanish in parentheses.

1. He's hungry, and _____ . (yo también)
2. They're coming, and _____ . (él también)
3. We were looking for Helen, and _____ . (mi papá también)
4. He can come tomorrow, and _____ . (Alice también)
5. Mexico City has many people, and _____ . (New York también)
6. My parents could understand it, and _____ (los tuyos también)
7. They'll be ready by six o'clock, and _____ . (nosotros también)
8. We'll eat downtown this afternoon, and _____ . (Stella también)
9. You should study harder, and _____ . (Ud. también)
10. We used to use his car, and _____ . (ellas también)
11. John and Robert have already eaten, and _____ . (María también)
12. They're always angry at me, and _____ . (su hermana también)
13. We bought a loaf of bread, and _____ . (Pablo también)
14. They should try to eat more, and _____ . (Ud. también)
15. We've told the children a story, and _____ . (mi mamá también)
16. They ran home, and _____ . (el perro también)
17. Her saint's day was yesterday, and _____ (el mío también)
18. Her father will wake up at nine, and _____ . (su mamá también)
19. They used to get up later, and _____ . (él también)
20. We caught two rabbits, and _____ . (Juan también)
21. John learns very quickly, and _____ . (María también)
22. They've eaten two apples, and _____ . (nosotros también)
23. She got off on Madero, and _____ . (el muchacho también)
24. I ought to get off the bus, and _____ . (tú también)
25. John's sister got on the bus, and _____ . (Juan también)

LA FORMA CONCISA CON *EITHER* y *NEITHER*

El equivalente en inglés de **ni tú tampoco, ni él tampoco, ni Juan tampoco,** etc. es una oración corta en negativo compuesta del sujeto, el auxiliar que corresponda al tiempo empleado, y la palabra **either** o **neither**. Nótese que las dos formas con **either** y **neither** se distinguen por el orden de las palabras.

Con **either** se empleará un verbo en negativo, y con **neither** un verbo en afirmativo.

Si se emplea una forma del verbo **be** en la oración, también se empleará una forma del verbo **be** en la oración corta.

Aprenda a emplear la forma con **either** y a reconocer la otra.

1. They aren't Mexican, and I'm not either (*or*) neither am I.
   No son mexicanos, ni yo tampoco.
2. Robert wasn't sick, and Mary wasn't either (*or*) neither was Mary.
   Roberto no estuvo enfermo, ni María tampoco.
3. She didn't see that movie, and I didn't either (*or*) neither did I.
   Ella no vio esa película, ni yo tampoco.
4. My parents don't have a car, and his don't either (*or*) neither do his.
   Mis papás no tienen coche, ni los suyos tampoco.
5. John can't come, and they can't either (*or*) neither can they.
   Juan no puede venir, ni ellos tampoco.
6. He won't bring any money, and Henry won't either (*or*) neither will Henry.
   No traerá dinero, ni Enrique tampoco.
7. She wouldn't like to go, and he wouldn't either (*or*) neither would he.
   A ella no le gustaría ir, ni a él tampoco.
8. We shouldn't get up early, and she shouldn't either (*or*) neither should she.
   No deberíamos levantarnos temprano, ni ella tampoco.

EXERCISE 10

Change the sentences in exercise 9 to the negative. Fill the blanks with the negative forms of the Spanish in parentheses.

EXERCISE 11

Translate the following sentences. Change them to the negative, interrogative, and interrogative negative.

1. They plan to go to the United States in September.
2. We planned to finish before morning.

204

3. He'll plan to see you next week.
4. She's planned to buy a new coat this winter.
5. I should plan to buy a house.
6. You'd plan to sell your car if you needed the money.
7. James was planning to visit me in October.
8. I planned to invite him to the party.
9. The Masons are planning to have dinner with us on Sunday.
10. We plan to make the dresses ourselves.

EXERCISE 12

Answer the following questions in the affirmative and in the negative.

1. Do you plan to sell your car?
2. Did he plan to go out of town on Saturday?
3. Will they plan to capture the thief?
4. Have they planned to drive to Cuernavaca?
5. Should I plan to examine the house?
6. Would you plan to build an office?
7. Does the teacher plan to explain the lesson?
8. Is Miss Russel planning to correct the sentences?
9. Was Henry planning to be a doctor?
10. Did she plan to get married in June?

EXERCISE 13

Translate into Spanish.

1. Will you get through before it gets dark?
2. We don't have any old clothes to give away.
3. Make him stop bothering me.
4. It seems to me that you should have kept the boys in the class from bothering the girls.
5. If you had taken care of your cold, you wouldn't be sick now.
6. It's a long ways from here to the market.
7. If you had a headache, would you go to work?
8. John always used to have an earache after going swimming.
9. I plan to be able to stop working when I'm sixty years old.
10. This suit doesn't fit me any more. I'm going to give it away.
11. Don't bother him when he's busy.
12. I plan to go to the movies if I get through before five-thirty.

13. It's a shame that he spent all his brother's money.
14. It's too bad that he didn't take care of his eyes.
15. I'll get you whatever you want.

EXERCISE 14

Give the past tense and past participle of the following verbs.

invite	live	laugh (at)	move
jump	like	listen (to)	need
kill	learn	love	notice
kiss	look (at)	last	name
knock (on)	look (for)	lift	open

EXERCISE 15

Give the past tense and past participle of the following verbs.

find out	go out	get here,	get away
give	go to sleep	there, (to)	get off
give up	go to bed	get sleepy	get old
go	get	get rich	get ready
go back	get up	get thirsty	get wet
			get married

EXERCISE 16

Verb Practice *Expand the following verb practice to include all the tenses studied so far, including the use of the past tense for the Spanish past subjunctive and the use of the past perfect for the Spanish past perfect subjunctive. Be sure to include forms of the verbs* **want, tell, ask,** *followed by an objective noun or pronoun.*

1. They'll bother us.
2. They won't bother us.
3. Will they bother us?
4. Won't they bother us?
5. Why won't they bother us?

EXERCISE 17

Verb Practice *Make short sentences with forms of the verbs* **cook, boil, cost, throw, surprise, get through, give (something) away.** *Expand each verb practice to include different tenses, as in the exercise above. Use a different noun or pronoun with each verb. Use the interrogative words when it is possible.*

206

Read and translate.

NAIL SOUP

A poor traveler, tired and hungry, stopped one evening, as it was getting dark, at the door of a poor widow's house to see if he could get something to eat.

In answer to his knock the woman opened the door.

"Excuse me for bothering you," began the traveler, "but I've walked a long ways today, and I'm very tired and hungry. Would it be possible to eat a meal here and rest a while?"

"There's nothing in the house to eat," answered the woman. "As you can see, I'm a poor widow with no husband to take care of me. I could hardly find enough food for my dinner today, and I certainly have nothing to give to beggars. I think that I'll have to go to bed without my supper."

"That's too bad," said the stranger. "It's a pity that with so much food in the world there isn't enough for us. However, I know how to make a soup that is very cheap. In fact, it costs nothing. It's called nail soup."

"Nail soup?" asked the woman surprised.

"Yes, nail soup. All I need is a nail and a little water. The water, of course, costs nothing; and I have a nail with me," said the traveler as he took one out of his pocket.

"If you'll let me use your fire to cook the soup," added the traveler, "I'll be glad to invite you to eat with me."

The woman opened the door and let the stranger in the kitchen. She watched him as he took a large pot from the wall, filled it half full of water, and set it over the fire. Then he took a nail out of his pocket, washed it carefully, and dropped it into the soup.

"How long will it take the soup to cook?" asked the woman.

"It won't take very long," replied the stranger. "As soon as the water boils, it'll be ready to eat."

"Really?" said the woman. "And will it be good?"

"Yes," answered the traveler, "it'll be good soup; however, it'd be better if I had a little piece of meat to throw in the water with the nail."

"I'll see if I can find a little piece of meat," said the poor widow. "It seems to me that there was a little piece left."

She went to a shelf in the kitchen and came back with a fine piece of meat.

207

"Thank you," said the stranger, as he dropped the meat into the pot. "Now if I had an onion—a very small one would be all right—and a few potatoes—."

"I believe I have a small onion left, and I'll see if there are any potatoes. Oh, yes, and here are some beans and some corn and a tomato."

"Thank you," said the traveler as he threw the vegetables into the pot. "Now if I had a little butter and some salt and pepper and a few more vegetables—."

"Oh, there's plenty of butter," said the woman, "and salt too, and there are more vegetables in the garden."

"All we need now," said the stranger, "is some milk and about a cup of cream."

Soon the pot was boiling over the fire.

"The soup is ready to eat," said the stranger.

"It smells very good," said the woman as she set the table.

When supper was over and the stranger got ready to leave, the widow said to him, "Thank you for inviting me to have supper with you. Your nail soup was fine."

"It's surprising what one can do with a nail, isn't it?" said the stranger as he went out of the door.

EXERCISE 19

Write in English.

1. ¿Por qué le diste a ese conejo?
2. Ha hecho mucho frío este invierno.
3. ¿Sabe cocinar la hija del Sr. Mathew?
4. Pensamos estudiar español, ¿y tú?
5. Él no cree que hará demasiado frío para nadar. Ni yo tampoco.
6. Eres muy afortunado de que esos niños dejaran de molestarte.
7. Él no sabe manejar un coche, pero yo sí.
8. Si yo estuviera en tu lugar, iría; y ellos también.
9. Elena compraría aquella falda si no costara tanto.
10. Si hubiera desayunado Ud. esta mañana, ahora no tendría tanta hambre.

EXERCISE 20

Dictation

1. Let's put all the pots on this shelf.

2. The iceman knocked on my door at six-fifteen this morning.
3. I told you to buy two tickets for me, didn't I?
4. My mother doesn't like tomato soup, and I don't either.
5. Don't give those books away. You'll need them some day.
6. You shouldn't let strangers in your house.
7. They don't have a key to this door. Do you?
8. A thief got in my house last night and stole all the silver.
9. I don't want you to give any more money to beggars.
10. It's too bad that your horse didn't win the race.

EXERCISE 21

Conversation *Answer the following questions in the affirmative and in the negative. Notice that the infinitive without* **to** *is used after* **let, make, help.**

1. Did she let the stranger come in the house?
2. Did she let him make any soup?
3. Will you help me move this heavy chair?
4. Will they help me find my book?
5. Do you make the children play in the house?
6. Does he make his wife work?

Answer the following questions in the affirmative and in the negative.

7. Does he want you to come early?
8. Did she want you to get married?
9. Did you tell them to clean the house?
10. Will you tell her to help you?
11. If you had money, would you buy a car?
12. If the suit cost $20.00 (dollars), would you buy it?
13. If he was rich, would he work?
14. Would you go with me if you had time?
15. Would he marry her if he loved her?
16. Would you work if you needed money?
17. If he had had a car, would he have gone to the United States?
18. If you had worn your coat, would you have been cold?
19. If he had sold his house, would he have paid you?
20. If they had taken the train, would they have arrived on time?
21. Would she have washed the clothes if they had been dirty?
22. Would John have learned English if he had tried hard?
23. Would he have worn a coat if it had been cold?

Answer the following questions in the affirmative and in the negative, using the necessary pronoun as a subject and repeating the auxiliary used in the sentence.

24. I don't like peaches, do you?
25. We don't have to get up early. Do they?
26. They work six days a week. Does he?
27. He can speak Spanish. Can she?
28. We live in the city, do you?
29. I got mad. Didn't you?
30. They've worked every day this week. Has he?

Answer the following questions in the affirmative and in the negative.

31. Do you plan to go to Acapulco during your vacation?
32. Did you plan to buy a new dress for the party?
33. Do you plan to help us on Saturday?
34. Are you planning to see him again?

Lección 16

1. **to realize, realized, realized** darse cuenta; realizar
2. **to test, tested, tested** probar (*no del sentido del gusto*)
3. **to fail, failed, failed** fallar; fracasar; reprobar
4. **to choose, chose, chosen** escoger
5. **to follow, followed, followed** seguir
6. **to fool, fooled, fooled** engañar; bromear
7. **wise** sabio
   wisdom sabiduría
8. **power** poder
   powerful poderoso
9. **handsome** guapo
10. **straight** derecho, recto
11. **humble** humilde
12. **artificial** artificial
13. **human** humano
14. **nature** naturaleza
15. **universe** universo
16. **jewel** joya
    jewelry (*sing.*) alhajas, joyas
17. **diamond** diamante
18. **toy** juguete
19. **bouquet** ramillete
20. **dew** rocío
21. **bee** abeja
22. **queen** reina
23. **sister-in-law** cuñada
24. **brother-in-law** cuñado

IDIOMS

1. **to get rid of** deshacerse de; quitársele a uno

211

I want to get rid of my old car. Me quiero deshacer de mi viejo coche.

I can't get rid of my cold. No se me quita el catarro.

2. **to look alike** parecerse
   They look alike. Ellos se parecen.
3. **to go shopping** ir de compras
4. **How far—?** ¿Qué tan lejos—?
   How far is it to New York? ¿Qué tan lejos queda Nueva York?
5. **Walk straight ahead.** Camine derecho.
6. **at midnight** a medianoche
7. **soft drink** refresco
8. **(hard) liquor** bebida alcohólica
9. **Whose book is this?** ¿De quién es este libro?
   It's mine. Es mío.

EXERCISE 1

Translate the following phrases and sentences and practice reading them.

1. instead of boiling
2. before boiling
3. in spite of boiling
4. besides boiling
5. What are you boiling the water for?
6. What did you boil the water for?
7. What are they shooting at?
8. What did they shoot at?
9. Who are you going to go with?
10. Who did you go with?
11. Who will you go with?
12. I don't have to stay, and he doesn't either.
13. He has to stay, and I do too.
14. We don't have to take care of the children, and you don't either.
15. You have to take care of the children, and we do too.
16. He doesn't want to go, but I do.
17. I want to go, but he doesn't.
18. It must be cold in December.
19. It probably isn't cold in December.
20. Is it cold in December?

Learn the following words.

may puede (ser) que
might puede (ser) que

POSIBILIDAD CON *MAY* y *MIGHT*

Se usan los auxiliares **may** y **might** para expresar posibilidad. No hay diferencia alguna en el significado y el uso de estos dos auxiliares; por tanto son intercambiables, menos cuando se usan con un verbo en el pasado, donde se prefiere **might**. Puesto que son auxiliares, irán seguidos del infinitivo sin la partícula **to**. Las formas negativas de éstos son **may not** y **might not**. No hay contracción en el negativo. Estudie las siguientes oraciones:

1. He may(might) come tomorrow.
   Puede que él venga mañana.

2. We may(might) not work on Monday.
   Puede que no trabajemos el lunes.

3. It may(might) rain soon.
   Puede que llueva pronto.

4. She may have eaten.
   Puede que haya comido.

5. He said that John migth come.
   Dijo que puede que venga Juan.

EXERCISE 2

Verb Practice

1. I may go at four o'clock.
2. I may not go at four o'clock.
3. You might go with them.
4. You might not go with them.
5. He may go in the morning.
6. He may not go in the morning.
7. She might go without us.
8. She might not go without us.
9. We may go after eating.
10. We may not go after eating.
11. You might go tomorrow.
12. You might not go tomorrow.
13. They may have gone by plane.
14. They may not have gone by plane.

EXERCISE 3

Verb Practice *Make short sentences with forms of the verbs* sleep, drink, eat, play, be, sell, love, forget, remember, *using both auxiliaries* may *and* might *with each verb form.*

PREGUNTAS INDIRECTAS

Se llama **pregunta indirecta** la oración subordinada que empieza con las palabras interrogativas **which, when, where, what, why, how, how much, how many, whose (de quién).**

Recuerde que la pregunta indirecta no es interrogativa; así es que el orden de las palabras es el mismo que el de, las oraciones **afirmativas** y **negativas.** Estudie las siguientes oraciones.

1. **Where is he?** (*pregunta directa*)
   I don't know **where he is.** (*pregunta indirecta*)

2. **What time is it?** (*pregunta directa*)
   Do you know **what time it is?** (*pregunta indirecta*)

3. **Whose is it?** (*pregunta directa*)
   Have they found out **whose it is?** (*pregunta indirecta*)

4. **Why didn't she come?** (*pregunta directa*)
   I don't know **why she didn't come.** (*pregunta indirecta*)

EXERCISE 4

Translate the following sentences.

1. ¿Sabes dónde está (*cosa*)?
2. No sé quién es ese señor.
3. ¿No sabe él qué hora es?
4. No recuerdo por qué no vino él.
5. Ellos nos van a preguntar qué comimos.
6. ¿No te puede decir Enrique dónde están los muchachos?
7. Mi esposa no sabe por qué él no va a terminar.
8. ¿Sabes dónde está la Ciudad de México?
9. ¿Saben los muchachos cuántos se comió ella?
10. Ellos averiguarán por qué lo hicimos.

EXERCISE 5

*Answer the following questions in the affirmative and in the negative,
using* Yes, I know (knew)—; No, I don't (didn't) know—.

1. Do you know who those boys are?
2. Did you know when we arrived?
3. Do you know where the market is?
4. Did you know where we were?
5. Do you know what time it is?
6. Do you know what we mean?
7. Did you know where I lived?
8. Did you know who my teacher was?
9. Do you know how we found out?
10. Did they know why I went home?
11. Do you know whose it is?

LA FORMA CONCISA CON LA PARTICULA *TO*

En vez de repetir un verbo que se ha expresado anteriormente, se
usa una forma concisa que consiste en el empleo de la partícula **to** del
verbo implícito.

Esta forma concisa se emplea mucho después de verbos tales como
want, like, need, have.

Ejemplo: He doesn't study because he doesn't like **to.**
Él no estudia porque no le gusta.

EXERCISE 6

Translate the following sentences and practice reading them.

1. He told me to help him, but I didn't want **to.**
2. John isn't going to study, but he needs **to.**
3. We didn't work yesterday because we didn't have **to.**
4. Why doesn't she dance? Doesn't she like **to?**
5. The Smiths went to the movies because they wanted **to.**
6. I don't want to go. Do I have **to?**

215

7. They study every day because they like **to**.
8. I went to see the doctor because I needed **to**.
9. I'll spend this money if I want **to**.
10. You can go downtown with us. Would you like **to**?

EXERCISE 7

Translate into English, using the short form with **to**.

1. A él le gustaría estudiar más inglés, pero no creo que lo necesite.
2. Podemos trabajar todo el sábado, pero no tenemos que hacerlo.
3. Que vaya con nosotros si él quiere.
4. Puedes ir con nosotros. ¿Quieres?
5. Ella siempre nos ayuda en la noche, pero no creo que le guste.
6. Puedes trabajar el domingo si quieres, pero no lo necesitas.
7. Fui a la escuela hoy porque el profesor me dijo que tenía que ir.
8. El doctor le dijo a mi papá que podía tomar si quería.
9. Sus papás nunca han viajado. ¿Les gustaría?
10. Mi hermana sabe hablar inglés, pero no le gusta.

EXERCISE 8

Fill the blanks with the correct translation of the Spanish in parentheses.

1. I won't be able to go to the meeting. _____ . (Ni el señor Foster tampoco.)
2. We should tell the workers the truth, and _____ . (ellos también)
3. Martin would go to Betty's party if he knew her better, and _____ (Bill también)
4. Mrs. Wood has been in Mexico many times, and _____ . (su hijo también)
5. He didn't test the car before he bought it. _____ . (Ni su amigo tampoco.)
6. I don't want you to go downtown by yourself at night. _____ . (Ni su mamá tampoco.)
7. My father couldn't fix the stove. _____ . (Ni mi hermano tampoco.)

8. My husband would like to visit Paris in the spring, and _____ . (a mí también)
9. Her teacher didn't tell her not to get married. _____ . (Ni su familia tampoco.)
10. My sister has told you to bring the clothes on Tuesday, and _____ . (mi esposa también)

EXÉRCISE 9

Fill the blanks with the correct form of the verb indicated and translate.

(want)	1. If I had _____ that coat, would you have bought it for me?
(wait)	2. If she had _____ five minutes more, would he have come?
(sing)	3. Would you have listened if she had _____ that song?
(have)	4. He'd have gone if he'd _____ time.
(go)	5. If he had _____ with me, they'd have punished him.
(tell)	6. If they had _____ me the truth, I'd have believed them.
(cost)	7. Would you have bought the hat if it had _____ twenty dollars?
(work)	8. If he had _____ all his life, he'd have money now.
(call)	9. She wouldn't be sick now if she'd _____ the doctor sooner.
(be)	10. If you had _____ old enough, would you have gone to school?

EXERCISE 10

Translate the following sentences. Change them to the negative, interrogative, and interrogative negative.

1. I want you to get rid of that dirty cat.
2. He got rid of his small house.
3. She can get rid of her cold.
4. They'll get rid of the chickens that don't lay eggs.
5. Mr. Forest should get rid of all those old papers.

217

6. You have to get rid of your old radio before buying a new one.
7. Mr. Jones ought to get rid of the flowers.
8. We must get rid of all this food before we leave.
9. I know how to get rid of a headache.
10. The teacher told him to get rid of his books.

EXERCISE 11

Answer the following questions in the affirmative and in the negative.

1. Did you get rid of that mouse in the kitchen?
2. Does she get rid of her old clothes?
3. Will she be able to get rid of her car?
4. Did he get rid of his stomach-ache?
5. Are you going to get rid of all your tickets?
6. Is he getting rid of his farm?
7. Did you tell me to get rid of my old letters?
8. Should they get rid of that fruit?
9. Haven't you got rid of your earache yet?
10. Was she going to get rid of her business?

EXERCISE 12

Translate into Spanish.

1. I didn't want to go, but I had to.
2. We want to get rid of everything we don't need before we leave.
3. Those two boys look so much alike I thought they must be brothers.
4. She wanted me to go shopping with her, but I told her I didn't want to.
5. Go straight ahead until you get to the market. Then turn to the right.
6. You can't buy hard liquor in some places in the United States.
7. The party was over before midnight.
8. Would you like coffee, tea, or a soft drink with your meal?
9. How can I get rid of this toothache?
10. Why don't you make him stop giving away those tickets?
11. Can't you make Ruth go shopping with me?
12. We plan to keep her from getting married until she's nineteen.
13. I want to get rid of my car because it's so expensive.
14. If your stomach-ache isn't better in the morning, the doctor should be called.
15. It seems to me that you should have come to class once in a while.

218

EXERCISE 13

Give the past tense and past participle of the following verbs.

own	practice	pull	rest
pass	pronounce	punish	remember
pick out	play	reply	return
pick up	prefer	reach	realize
place	push	rain	shout (at)

EXERCISE 14

Give the past tense and past participle of the following verbs.

get drunk	get in	get dark	hang
get sick	get out	get hurt	hide
get scared	get lost	get rid of	hurt
get better	get tired	have	hit
get worse	get light	hear	keep

EXERCISE 15

Verb Practice *Expand the following verb practice to include different tenses.*

1. They'd realize that you're right.
2. They wouldn't realize that you're right.
3. Would they realize that you're right?
4. Wouldn't they realize that you're right?
5. Why wouldn't they realize that you're right?

EXERCISE 16

Verb Practice *Make short sentences with forms of the verbs* **test, fail, choose, follow, fool, look alike, go shopping, get rid of.** *Expand each verb practice to include different tenses, as in the exercise above. Use a different noun or pronoun with each verb. Use the interrogative words when it is possible.*

EXERCISE 17

Read and translate.

THE WISDOM OF SOLOMON

Long ago there was a very wise and powerful king named Solomon and a very beautiful queen called the Queen of Sheba (Saba). The Queen of Sheba heard of the wisdom of Solomon, and she traveled from her own country to his to ask him questions.

When they met, it was like the meeting of the sun and the moon because she was as beautiful as he was handsome. He was followed by the most handsome men of his country, and she was followed by the most beautiful women of her country. These beautiful and handsome young men and women were like the stars around the sun and moon.

The Queen of Sheba brought a huge treasure with her of gold and silver and jewels—rich presents that shone as bright as the sun. She brought a bird made of gold that could fly and sing and many things that you could not believe had been made by human hands.

"Powerful Solomon, wisest of all men," said the Queen of Sheba, "I am only a queen from a small and humble country, but I have brought you some small toys to play with."

As she spoke, one of her slaves placed two beautiful bouquets that looked exactly alike on the table.

"One of these bouquets," explained the queen, "was made by nature; and the other was made by human hands. If you can tell me which bouquet is real and which is artificial, all the treasure that I have brought with me will be yours."

Now King Solomon knew that this was not a game. The Queen of Sheba was testing his wisdom. If he failed, he would be laughed at by all the people of his country; and they would no longer believe that he was the wisest man in the world.

King Solomon looked at the bouquets. They were so much alike! "One has dew on it. That must be the real one," thought King Solomon to himself. Then he noticed that the other bouquet also had dew on it. He saw a dead leaf on one and was about (estuvo a punto) to choose that one when he saw that the other one also had a dead leaf on it in the same place.

Then King Solomon heard the bees in the garden outside the window, and he had an idea.

"Open the window," he told the slave.

The slave opened the window, and the bees came into the room. The bees went straight as an arrow to the real bouquet of flowers. Diamonds, jewels, and gold couldn't fool them. The Queen of Sheba then realized that Solomon was really wise.

If you want to understand the strange things of the universe, you must let nature be your teacher.

EXERCISE 18

Write in English.

1. ¿Sabe Ud. cómo se llama ese muchacho?
2. Nunca he viajado en avión, pero me gustaría.
3. El siempre está bromeando.
4. Estos son los árboles más rectos que he visto.
5. No siempre podemos entender la naturaleza humana.
6. ¿Sabe ella quién es la reina de Inglaterra?
7. He tenido este catarro dos semanas, y no se me puede quitar.
8. ¿Me pueden decir qué hora es?
9. Puede que Ud. engañe a mi hermano, pero a mí no me puede engañar.
10. Puede que ella consiga a alguien que sepa cuidar a los niños.

EXERCISE 19

Dictation

1. Do your brothers look alike?
2. If you'll follow me, I'll show you where the market is.
3. Did you know who I was?
4. I don't know how you got rid of all that money so fast.
5. She went shopping and bought some toys for the children's birthday.
6. It might rain today if the wind doesn't stop blowing.
7. If it wasn't so cold, I might go with you.
8. He may know where the money is.
9. We couldn't buy the jewels ourselves, and he couldn't either.
10. The most beautiful diamonds were found in Africa.

EXERCISE 20

Conversation *Answer the following questions.*

1. How far is it from here to the market?
2. How far is it from here to the movies?

3. How far is it to Acapulco?
4. How far is it to your house?
5. How far is it to the mountains?

Answer the following questions, using the necessary pronoun as a subject and repeating the auxiliary in the sentence.

6. That man is handsome, isn't he?
7. Diamonds are expensive, aren't they?
8. I don't wear jewelry. Does she?
9. We don't want to come tomorrow, do you?

Answer the following questions in the affirmative and in the negative.

10. Do you know where he is?
11. Do you know where he went?
12. Do you know what time it is?
13. Did you know where they were?
14. Do you know who he lives with?
15. Did you tell her where you live?
16. Do you know who I am?
17. Do you know how he came?
18. Did you know who I was?
19. Did you know how much it cost?
20. Does he know what this is?
21. Did he know whose it was?
22. Will you tell me where they are?
23. Will you tell me how they went?
24. Can you tell me when pay day is?
25. Did you go before eating?
26. Did he leave without saying good-bye?
27. Will she come in spite of being sick?
28. Will you tell Mary instead of telling John?
29. Is she going to study instead of resting?
30. Will you help me before going shopping?

Lección 17

1. **to smoke, smoked, smoked** fumar; humear
2. **to count, counted, counted** contar
3. **to bury, buried, buried** enterrar
4. **to discover, discovered, discovered** descubrir
5. **to breathe, breathed, breathed** respirar
6. **to prepare, prepared, prepared** preparar
7. **recently** recientemente
8. **slim** delgado
9. **interest** interés
10. **amount** cantidad
11. **advice** consejo(s)
12. **bottom** fondo; parte inferior
13. **wood** madera
14. **bank** banco
15. **furniture** (*sing.*) muebles

    a piece of furniture un mueble
16. **dishes** trastos; platos
17. **mail** correo; correspondencia
    mailman cartero
18. **relative** pariente
19. **nephew** sobrino
20. **niece** sobrina
21. **New Year's** el día de año nuevo
    New Year's Day el día de año nuevo
    New Year's Eve la víspera de año nuevo
22. **Easter Sunday** domingo de resurrección
    Easter Week semana de Pascua
    Holy Week semana santa
23. **Halloween** víspera de Todos los Santos

223

24. **Thanksgiving** (*U.S.A.*) día de acción de gracias **Thanksgiving Day** (*U.S.A.*) día de acción de gracias 25. **Christmas** Navidad	**Christmas Day** día de Navidad **Christmas Eve** víspera de Navidad, Nochebuena

IDIOMS

1. **to be worth** valer
   How much is it worth? ¿Cuánto vale?
   It's worth one hundred dollars. Vale cien dólares.
   to be worth it valer la pena
   It isn't worth it. No vale la pena.
   He isn't worth it. No vale la pena.
   to be worth + (gerund) valer la pena + (infinitivo)
   It's worth reading. Vale la pena leerse.
   It isn't worth seeing. No vale la pena verse.
2. **to run away** huir, fugarse
3. **to change your mind** cambiar de idea
4. **to draw interest, drew interest, drawn interest** ganar intereses
5. **Whose fault is it?** ¿Quién tiene la culpa?
   It's my fault. Tengo la culpa, La culpa es mía.
   It was my fault. Tuve la culpa, La culpa fue mía.
6. **without fail** sin falta
7. **I hope so.** Espero que sí.
   I hope not. Espero que no.
8. **after all** después de todo
9. **Be careful.** Tenga cuidado.
10. **to dig (something) up** desenterrar algo

EXERCISE 1

Translate the following sentences and practice reading them.

1. I may sleep this afternoon.
2. I may not sleep this afternoon.
3. I might sleep in this room.
4. I might not sleep in this room.
5. I'm going to go, but they aren't.
6. I went, but they didn't.

7. I've gone, but they haven't.
8. I'll go, but they won't.
9. I work every day, do you?
10. I worked yesterday, did you?
11. I'm going to work tomorrow, are you?
12. I've worked every day, have you?
13. I'll work tomorrow, will you?
14. I can go, and he can too.
15. I can't go, and he can't either.
16. I want to go, and he does too.
17. I don't want to go, and he doesn't either.
18. I'll be hungry before noon.
19. I won't be hungry before noon.
20. I might be hungry before noon.

Learn the following words.

maybe tal vez, quizá
perhaps tal vez, quizá

POSIBILIDAD CON *MAYBE* y *PERHAPS*

Aun cuando **maybe** y **perhaps** no son auxiliares, tienen el mismo significado que **may** y **might** y se utilizan también para expresar posibilidad. Por lo tanto, **maybe** y **perhaps** se colocan distintamente en la oración que los auxiliares. Generalmente se colocan al principio de la oración.

Maybe y **perhaps** irán seguidos por el futuro en inglés cuando la oración en español implique este mismo tiempo. Estudie las siguientes oraciones.

1. Maybe he's sick. (*or*) Perhaps he's sick.
   Tal vez él esté enfermo.
   Quizá él esté enfermo.

2. Maybe he didn't go. (*or*) Perhaps he didn't go.
   Tal vez él no fue.
   Quizá él no fue.

3. Maybe she hasn't left. (*or*) Perhaps she hasn't left.
   Tal vez ella no haya salido.
   Quizá ella no haya salido.

4. Maybe they'll work. (or) Perhaps they'll work
   tomorrow.   tomorrow.
   Tal vez ellos trabajen mañana.
   Quizá ellos trabajen mañana.

EXERCISE 2

Verb Practice

1. Maybe I'll go in the morning.
2. Maybe I won't go in the morning.
3. Perhaps I'll go in the morning.
4. Perhaps I won't go in the morning.
5. Maybe he went yesterday.
6. Maybe he didn't go yesterday.
7. Perhaps he has already gone.
8. Perhaps he hasn't gone yet.
9. Maybe I'd go with them.
10. Maybe I wouldn't go with them.
11. Perhaps I should go too.
12. Perhaps I shouldn't go either.
13. Maybe I'm going to go with you.
14. Maybe I'm not going to go with you.
15. Perhaps I can go early.
16. Perhaps I can't go early.
17. Maybe he could go.
18. Maybe he couldn't go either.

EXERCISE 3

Verb Practice *Make short sentences with forms of the verbs* decide, boil, cook, appear, agree, follow, find out, name, realize. *Expand each verb practice to include different tenses, as in the exercise above. Use a different noun or pronoun with each verb. Use the interrogative words when it is possible.*

EXERCISE 4

Translate the following sentences. Change them to possibility (affirmative and negative) four different ways, using may, might, maybe, perhaps. *Translate each time. Remember to use the future after* maybe *and* perhaps *when the future is implied.*

226

1. John sleeps in that big bed.
2. The teacher explains each lesson.
3. He's dictated the sentences to the class.
4. She looks good in green.
5. They play football on Saturday.
6. His wife chooses his ties.
7. They've written to him.
8. They give it to me themselves.
9. He's kept his money in the bank.
10. She's in school.

EXERCISE 5

Translate the following sentences. Change them to the negative, interrogative, and interrogative negative.

1. You know what time it is.
2. He remembers where I live.
3. They can tell you when she left.
4. She wants to tell us who she is.
5. We know who they are.
6. You remember what his name is.
7. They always ask me where it is.
8. I know where we are.
9. They remember where you were.
10. She knows who he is.

EXERCISE 6

Fill the blanks with the correct translation of the Spanish in parentheses.

1. I can't stay. _____ . (Ni él tampoco.)
2. I can stay, and _____ . (él también)
3. He doesn't have to work tomorrow. _____ . (Ni yo tampoco.)
4. He has to work tomorrow, and _____ . (yo también)
5. They won't be at the party. _____ . (Ni nosotros tampoco.)
6. They'll be at the party, and _____ . (nosotros también)
7. You didn't go to the movies. _____ . (Ni él tampoco.)
8. You went to the movies, and _____ . (ella también)
9. We don't want to speak Spanish. _____ . (Ni él tampoco.)
10. We want to speak Spanish, and _____ . (él también)

227

EXERCISE 7

Translate the following sentences. Change them to the negative, interrogative, and interrogative negative.

1. This furniture is worth a lot of money.
2. My house was worth a great deal.
3. His car is worth a thousand dollars.
4. My clothes are worth more than yours.
5. It'll be worth something in a few years.
6. She's worth it.
7. That movie was worth seeing.
8. Television is worth watching.
9. Those vegetables are worth buying.
10. This lesson is worth studying.

EXERCISE 8

Answer the following questions, using It's worth about—.

1. How much is a large diamond worth?
2. How much is a new car worth?
3. How much is this book worth?
4. How much is a peso worth in American money?
5. How much is a dollar worth in Mexican money?
6. How much is this land worth?

Answer the following questions in the affirmative and in the negative.

7. Is Acapulco worth visiting?
8. Are those tomatoes worth buying?
9. Are these old papers worth keeping?
10. Are these old clothes worth saving?

EXERCISE 9

Translate into Spanish.

1. These old letters aren't worth anything.
2. I planned to study English last year, but then I decided it wasn't worth it.
3. Women have a right to change their minds.

228

4. You said you'd be there at ten o'clock.
5. If we don't get there on time, it'll be your fault.
6. How far is Monterrey from Mexico City?
7. My money isn't drawing any interest at all. Is yours?
8. Be careful. A car is coming.
9. We've decided to spend Christmas Day with the Martins after all.
10. Won't you be able to keep him from running away?
11. I'll take care of the children on New Year's Eve, but you'll have to take care of them on New Year's Day.
12. They plan to go to Acapulco during Easter Week.
13. Why don't you stop giving away your money?
14. We must get rid of this old furniture before our relatives come.
15. I've changed my mind about going shopping with you.

EXERCISE 10

Give the past tense and past participle of the following verbs.

tie	turn off	seem	spill
turn	try	smell	save
touch	translate	surprise	stay
test	turn over	talk	smile (at)
use	travel	turn on	satisfy

EXERCISE 11

Give the past tense and past participle of the following verbs.

leave	lend	pay	see
lie (down)	make	read	speak
lose	meet	run	sit (down)
let	put	ride	sleep
lay eggs	put on	say	sell

EXERCISE 12

Verb Practice *Expand the following verb practice to include different tenses.*

1. My brother-in-law would smoke, wouldn't he?
2. My brother-in-law wouldn't smoke, would he?

3. Would my brother-in-law smoke?
4. Wouldn't my brother-in-law smoke?
5. When would my brother-in-law smoke?

EXERCISE 13

Verb Practice *Make short sentences with forms of the verbs* bury, discover, breathe, count, prepare, run away, change your mind, draw interest, dig (something) up. *Expand each verb practice to include different tenses, as in the exercise above. Use the interrogative words when it is possible.*

EXERCISE 14

Read and translate.

THE BLIND MAN WHO COULD SEE

A blind man who had a little money decided to bury it in the garden behind his house, where he thought it would be safe from thieves. He dug up the money once in a while to count it and to add his savings to it.

One day a neighbor who used to watch the blind man at work in his garden realized that he was burying money there; so the neighbor went into the garden one night, dug up the money, and took it home with him.

When the blind man discovered that his money had been stolen, he thought, perhaps, that his neighbor might be the thief; and he began to think of a way to get the money back (recobrar el dinero).

The blind man went to his neighbor and said to him, "I've saved a little money, but it isn't drawing any interest. Recently a relative of mine let me a large amount of money, and I want to ask your advice about what I should do with it. Should I keep all the money here with me, or should I take all that I have saved and put it in a safe place? I was planning to put it in a bank, where it would draw a little interest."

"A bank would be the worst place you could put it," answered the neighbor. "You'd be in danger of losing everything you have. My advice would be for you to keep your money here with you."

"Maybe you're right," said the blind man. "I'll do as you say."

As soon as the blind man left, the neighbor hurried to the garden to bury the money in the place where he had found it because he didn't want the blind man to find out that the money had been gone. Then he

230

went back to his house to wait until the blind man had buried all the money together so he could dig it up and have it all.

As soon as the blind man was sure that the money had been returned, he went into the garden and dug it up. Then he went to his neighbor and said to him, "I've changed my mind and have decided to put my money in the bank after all, now that I have it together again. Don't you think that blind men can sometimes see better than those who have eyes?"

EXERCISE 15

Write in English.

1. Cuando llegué a casa, descubrí que se me había olvidado la llave y no pude entrar.
2. ¿Ha llegado ya la correspondencia? No, todavía no.
3. Habrá una fiesta la víspera de Todos los Santos, el treinta y uno de octubre.
4. Avíseme Ud. si cambia de idea.
5. Tengo catarro y apenas puedo respirar.
6. ¿Te dijo el doctor que dejaras de fumar?
7. ¿Qué tan lejos puedes tirar esta piedra?
8. Todos mis amigos van a nadar pasado mañana, pero yo no quiero.
9. ¿No recuerdas cómo me llamo?
10. Tal vez se sientan mejor mañana.

EXERCISE 16

Dictation

1. You don't have to listen to my advice if you don't want to.
2. Wood is more expensive now than it was last year.
3. I'm going to put my money in the bank so it'll draw interest.
4. She's slimmer now than she was before she got sick.
5. They aren't going to prepare a Christmas dinner, and I'm not either.
6. It isn't my fault if you can't make any more money.
7. These two dresses look alike.
8. I don't know who the tallest boy in the class is.
9. Instead of going to the movies, I'm going shopping.
10. Maybe he forgot to pay you.

EXERCISE 17

Conversation *Answer the following questions.*

1. How far is it from Mexico City to Acapulco?
2. How far is it from the hotel to the bank?
3. How far is it from my house to your house?
4. How far is it from New York to Europe by ship?

Answer the following questions in the affirmative and in the negative.

5. Do you know how far it is from dowtown to your house?
6. Do you know how far it is from New York to Chicago?
7. Do you know how far it is from the market to my house?
8. Do you know how far it is from here to school?

Answer the following questions in the affirmative and in the negative, using the necessary pronoun and repeating the auxiliary.

9. It's late, isn't it?
10. He came early, didn't he?
11. She changed her mind, didn't she?
12. You've met him, haven't you?

Answer the following questions, using ago.

13. How long ago did you meet your husband?
14. How long ago did you live in the United States?
15. How long ago did you study English?
16. How long ago did you go to Europe?
17. How long ago did you get married?
18. How long ago did you see him?
19. How long ago did you buy your car?
20. How long ago did you sell your house?

Answer the following questions in the affirmative and in the negative.

21. Is that movie worth seeing?
22. Is this furniture worth selling?
23. Is that book worth reading?
24. Is it worth it?
25. Is it worth anything?
26. Is the bathing suit worth buying?
27. Do you know who that man is?

232

28. Do you know what that man's name is?
29. Do you know who the richest man in the world is?
30. Do you know what my sister's name is?
31. Do you know where my brother is?
32. Do you know where my husband went?
33. Do you know who my wife went with?
34. Do you know where we are?
35. Do you know what time it is?

Lección 18

Vocabulary

1. **to express, expressed, expressed** expresar
2. **to repeat, repeated, repeated** repetir
3. **to suffer, suffered, suffered** sufrir
4. **to draw, drew, drawn** dibujar
5. **to rent, rented, rented** alquilar, rentar
6. **to burn, burned, burned** quemar
7. **fortunate** afortunado
   fortunately afortunadamente
   unfortunately desgraciadamente
8. **constant** constante
   constantly constantemente
9. **quiet** callado
10. **conceited** (*adj.*) creído, vano
11. **brokenhearted** (*adj.*) con el corazón roto
12. **talkative** locuaz, parlanchín
13. **pale** pálido
14. **delicate** delicado
15. **bill** cuenta; billete; pico
16. **hill** colina
17. **person** persona
18. **goddess** diosa
19. **chocolate** chocolate
20. **lip** labio
21. **tongue** lengua
22. **storm** tempestad
23. **insect** bicho, insecto
24. **army** ejército
25. **navy** marina

IDIOMS

1. **would rather + (infinitive without to) than**
   preferir + (infinitivo) que

234

John would rather play than study. Juan prefiere jugar que estudiar.

2. **to die down** acabarse poco a poco; calmarse
3. **to take (something) away (from)** quitar (algo) (a); llevarse (algo)
   He took the book away from her. Le quitó el libro a ella.
   They took the furniture away. Se llevaron los muebles.
4. **to fall in love (with)** enamorarse (de)
   to be in love (with) estar enamorado (de)
5. **to insist on + (gerund)** empeñarse (insistir) en + (infinitivo)
   He insisted on going. Se empeñó en ir.
6. **It doesn't do any good.** No sirve de nada.
   It didn't do any good. No sirvió de nada.
7. **from then on** desde entonces
8. **over and over** una y otra vez
   He said it over and over. Él lo dijo una y otra vez.
9. **on purpose** a propósito, adrede
10. **How often?** ¿Qué tan a menudo? ¿Cada cuándo?
    How often do you go? ¿Qué tan a menudo (cada cuándo) va Ud.?
11. **once a week** una vez a la semana
    twice a week dos veces a la semana
    three times a week tres veces a la semana

EXERCISE 1

Translate the following sentences and practice reading them.

1. Maybe they live on this street.
2. Maybe they don't live on this street.
3. They might live at this number.
4. They might not live at this number.
5. Perhaps they live in that apartment.
6. Perhaps they don't live in that apartment.
7. He smokes, but she doesn't.
8. She doesn't smoke, but he does.
9. We'll have time, but they won't.
10. They won't have time, but we will.
11. I smoke, do you?
12. I used to smoke, did you?
13. I like to smoke, do you?
14. I smoke, and he does too.
15. I don't smoke, and he doesn't either.

16. We're smoking, and she is too.
17. We aren't smoking, and she isn't either.
18. I've been hungry since noon.
19. I'd been hungry all morning.
20. He should be hungry by this time.

TO HOPE y TO EXPECT

Study the following infinitives and sentences.

> **to hope** esperar (*de tener esperanza*), ojalá

1. I hope my son will be a doctor.
   Espero que mi hijo sea doctor. (*tengo la esperanza*)
   Ojalá mi hijo sea doctor.

2. We hope you get better before the party.
   Esperamos que se mejore antes de la fiesta. (*tenemos la esperanza*)

3. John hopes to get rich in two years.
   Juan espera hacerse rico en dos años. (*tiene la esperanza*)

> **to expect** esperar (*de contar con, de estar casi seguro o de exigir*)
> Expect is often followed by an objective noun or pronoun and an infinitive with **to**.

1. I didn't expect so many people at the party.
   No esperaba a tanta gente en la fiesta. (*no contaba con tanta gente*)

2. You're early. We didn't expect you so soon.
   Llegó temprano. No lo esperábamos tan pronto. (*no contábamos con que llegara tan temprano*)

3. He expects to buy a new car next year.
   Espera comprar un coche nuevo el año que viene. (*casi está seguro*)

4. I expect you to do your homework every day.
   Espero que hagas la tarea todos los días. (*exijo que la haga*)

EXERCISE 2

Fill the blanks with forms of the verbs **hope** *or* **expect,** *as required, and translate.*

1. We're paying you well; therefore we'll _____ good work.
2. He's already late. I _____ him ten minutes ago.

236

3. We _____ you can visit us at Christmas time.
4. I _____ you have a happy New Year.
5. They _____ me to get up early and help them.
6. He _____ her to do her work.
7. I _____ it stops raining before the party.
8. They _____ a letter from her today.
9. The children _____ their dog doesn't die.
10. We _____ to go to the movies tonight. I _____ it doesn't rain.

EXERCISE 3

Translate the following sentences. Change them to the negative, interrogative, and interrogative negative.

1. We expected you on Wednesday.
2. They should expect her to do better work.
3. I expect you to wash the windows every day.
4. He'll expect too much.
5. You can expect an expensive present this year.
6. She has expected money from her family.
7. We're expecting a long vacation this month.
8. They were expecting her to come yesterday.
9. He expects to make more money next year.
10. They'd expect you to take them if it was raining.

LA EXPRESIÓN DE DESEO CON *HOPE*

Study the following sentences. Notice the use of the verb hope.

1. I hope you have a nice vacation.
   Que pase felices vacaciones.

2. I hope you'll be very happy.
   Que seas muy feliz.

3. I hope you get well soon.
   Que se mejore Ud. pronto.

4. I hope it won't rain tomorrow.
   Ojalá no llueva mañana.

5. I hope you have a happy birthday.
   Que tengas un feliz cumpleaños.

6. I hope you didn't get hurt.
   Ojalá no te hayas lastimado.

Translate the following sentences.

1. I hope he doesn't get sick.
2. I hope you have many children.
3. I hope it rains soon.
4. I hope the news will be better tomorrow.
5. I hope he tells the truth.

WISH COMPARADO CON *HOPE*

Ojalá + Presente del Subj. = I Hope + Pres. or Future

Ojalá él esté aquí.	I hope he's here.
Ojalá él venga.	I hope he comes (will come).
Ojalá él coma.	I hope he eats (will eat).

Nota: En los ejemplos anteriores se emplea el presente cuando se refiere al presente, y el presente o futuro cuando se refiere al futuro.

Ojalá + Pasado del Subj. = I wish + Would + Inf. (sin *to*)

Ojalá él viniera.	I wish he'd come.
Ojalá no lloviera.	I wish it wouldn't rain.

Excepciones: Cuando hay una forma del verbo **be, have, can, feel** o **know** se emplea el pasado en vez de **would** con el infinitivo.

Ojalá yo fuera rico.	I wish I was rich.
Ojalá él estuviera aquí.	I wish he was here.
Ojalá él tuviera dinero.	I wish he had money.
Ojalá él pudiera venir.	I wish he could come.
Ojalá él hubiera venido.	I wish he had (he'd) come.
Ojalá él supiera la lección.	I wish he knew the lesson.
Ojalá él no se sintiera enfermo.	I wish he didn't feel sick.

LA EXPRESION DE DESEO CON *WISH*

Las formas del verbo **wish** (gustaría, quisiera, desearía) sirven para expresar deseo en inglés cuando el deseo es contrario a la realidad. En general el sujeto de estas formas será el pronombre **I**. Estudie las siguientes oraciones y fíjese en las traducciones.

1. I wish it would rain.
   Ojalá(que) lloviera.
   (*no está lloviendo*)

2. Don't you wish it would rain?
   ¿No te gustaría (no quisieras) que lloviera?
   (*no está lloviendo*)

3. I wish I was thinner.
   Ojalá (que) fuera más delgada.
   (*no soy más delgada*)

4. Don't you wish you were thinner?
   ¿No te gustaría (no quisieras) ser más delgada?
   (*no eres más delgada*)

5. I wish I could swim well.
   Ojalá (que) supiera nadar bien.
   (*no sé nadar bien*)

6. Don't you wish you could swim well?
   ¿No te gustaría (no quisieras) saber nadar bien?
   (*no sabes nadar bien*)

EXERCISE 5

Answer the following questions in the affirmative.

1. Don't you wish the wind would stop blowing?
2. Do you wish they'd stop singing?
3. Don't you wish they'd study more?
4. Don't you wish she'd come tomorrow?
5. Don't you wish you could ride a horse?
6. Do you wish you could swim?
7. Do you wish you could speak Spanish?
8. Don't you wish you were younger?
9. Do you wish you were in Mexico?
10. Do you wish you were older?
11. Don't you wish we were at home?
12. Don't you wish it was true?

EXERCISE 6

Translate the following sentences. Change them to possibility (affirm-

ative and negative) four different ways, using may, might, maybe, perhaps. *Translate each time. Remember to use the future after* maybe *and*
perhaps *when the future is implied.*

1. They speak English in that store.
2. We eat early on Sunday.
3. He's gone home for dinner.
4. She stays with her cousin during the summer.
5. They live in Mexico City.
6. They've eaten everything.
7. We have fun in the park.
8. He's sick.
9. They go to the zoo every day.
10. She's studied English in the United States.

EXERCISE 7

*Translate the following sentences. Change them to the negative, inter-
rogative, and interrogative negative.*

1. He'd rather go to the movies than to a posada.
2. They'd rather live in Mexico than in the United States.
3. You'd rather work on Saturday than on Sunday.
4. She'd rather study English than Spanish.
5. John would rather marry Alice than Jane.
6. The children would rather visit their grandfather than their uncle.
7. My mother would rather travel by train than by plane.
8. Mrs. Rogers would rather teach Spanish than English.
9. My husband would rather eat than sleep.
10. The neighbors would rather have a new car than a vacation.

EXERCISE 8

Answer the following questions.

1. Would you rather play canasta or read?
2. Would you rather go to Cuernavaca or Taxco?
3. Would you rather have cake or fruit?
4. Would you rather have milk or water?
5. Would you rather have tea or coffee?
6. Would you rather come on Tuesday or on Thursday?
7. Would you rather live in Chicago or New York?

240

8. Would you rather speak English or Spanish?
9. Would you rather study Spanish or English?
10. Would you rather be early or late?

EXERCISE 9

Translate the following sentences. Change them to the negative, interrogative, and interrogative negative.

1. The wind died down before midnight.
2. The noise died down after a while.
3. The fire died down the next day.
4. The storm died down on Monday.
5. The wind will die down soon.
6. The noise will die down in a few hours.
7. The fire will die down before morning.
8. The storm will die down about noon.
9. The wind has died down.
10. The noise has died down.
11. The fire has died down.
12. The storm has died down.

EXERCISE 10

Translate into Spanish.

1. Would you rather be rich or poor?
2. The fire died down before dinner was over.
3. We couldn't make the payments on the television, so they came over and took it away.
4. He fell in love with a woman much older than he.
5. I'm going to insist on correct pronunciation.
6. The teachers tell them to study, but it doesn't do any good.
7. It rained every day from then on.
8. You'll have to repeat these verbs over and over if you expect to learn them well.
9. I hope you haven't been sick.
10. They pushed that old man into the water on purpose.
11. How long ago did you see your oldest son?
12. Take care of the dog and don't let him run away.
13. I planned to go shopping this morning, but I can't go until the storm dies down.

241

14. What did you give those shirts away for?
15. I wish you'd stop bothering me.

EXERCISE 11

Give the past tense and participle of the following verbs.

visit	want	answer	avoid
work	watch	arrive (in, at)	believe
wash	worry (about)	add	bother
wait (for)	wish	agree	boil
walk	ask	appear	bury

EXERCISE 12

Give the past tense and past participle of the following verbs.

stand up	take	take care of	wake up
set	teach	throw	wear
sing	tell	take (some-	win
swim	think (about)	thing) away	wear out
shoot	take off	understand	be
		write	be able

EXERCISE 13

Verb Practice *Expand the following verb practice to include different tenses.*
1. This wood should burn better.
2. This wood shouldn't burn better.
3. Should this wood burn better?
4. Shouldn't this wood burn better?
5. Why shouldn't this wood burn better?

EXERCISE 14

Verb Practice *Make short sentences with forms of the verbs* repeat, suffer, draw, express, rent, take (something) away, insist on, fall in love (with), be in love (with). *Expand each verb practice to include different tenses, as in the exercise above. Use a different noun or pronoun with each verb. Use the interrogative words when it is possible.*

242

Read and translate.

THE STORY OF ECHO

Echo was a very talkative person who lived in the woods and hills, where she often went hunting with her friend Diana, goddess of the hunt.

As the two walked through the woods and hunted together, Echo talked constantly. She was never quiet a minute. When she could think of nothing else to say, she repeated the songs of the birds and the noises that the animals made.

At last another goddess got so tired of listening to so much talk, perhaps because she never got a chance to say anything herself, that she took away Echo's voice except for the purpose of reply (menos para la facultad de repetir).

The loss of her voice made Echo very sad, because she had fallen in love with a conceited young man who always liked to hear nice things about himself; and Echo found it impossible to express her love for him except by repeating everything he said. And what he said, unfortunately, didn't always express her feelings for him.

After a while Echo's lover also began to get tired of hearing her repeat everything he said. He told her to stop talking, but it didn't do any good. Instead, he only heard his own words repeated again and again. Finally he shouted at her, "I'd rather die than be your lover!"

Poor Echo was brokenhearted, but she could only repeat over and over, "I'd rather die than be your lover. I'd rather die than be your lover."

From then on she lived in the caves and in the mountains and suffered for her lost lover until she became so thin and pale that finally there was nothing left of her but her voice.

And wherever you go, you can hear her repeating stupidly everything she hears, because, like a woman, Echo still insists on having the last word.

EXERCISE 16

Write in English.

1. Espero que hayas traído bastante comida para todos.

2. Ellos dijeron que preferían tomar café que chocolate.
3. Espero a Juan a las ocho. Espero que venga.
4. Creo que lo hizo a propósito.
5. Puede ser que se acabe el ruido poco a poco.
6. El me dijo que dejara de trabajar a medianoche, pero yo no quería.
7. ¿Quién se llevó mis libros?
8. Ojalá que siempre estés tan feliz como estás ahora.
9. Puede que el Sr. Adams sepa dónde está Enrique.
10. ¿Sabes dónde está la montaña más alta del mundo?

EXERCISE 17

Dictation

1. I told him to stop working so hard, but I don't think it did any good.
2. He's a very conceited person.
3. Maybe he was sick. He looks so pale.
4. We rented a house in Acapulco, where we'll spend our vacation.
5. Unfortunately, there may not be enough presents for all the children.
6. Tell them not to burn those newspapers until I read them.
7. How long ago did you put your money in the bank?
8. How far is it from here to Europe?
9. I'd rather be a doctor than a teacher.
10. We didn't expect a present from the pupils.

EXERCISE 18

Conversation *Answer the following questions.*

1. How often do you go to class?
2. How often do you go to the movies?
3. How often do you go to the United States?
4. How often do you get a vacation?
5. How often do you see your parents?
6. How often do you have a party?
7. How often do you write to him?
8. How often do you go out of town?
9. How long ago did you buy your car?
10. How long ago did you sell your house?
11. How long ago did you pay your bill?

12. How long ago did you meet him?
13. How far is it from here to the movies?
14. How far is it from here to the market?
15. How far is it from here to Taxco?

Answer the following questions in the affirmative and in the negative.

16. Does the fire die down every night?
17. Did the wind die down yesterday?
18. Will the storm die down before the party?
19. Has the noise died down?
20. Is the wind going to die down?
21. Is the fire dying down?
22. Do you wish you were a movie star?
23. Do you wish you were in Acapulco?
24. Do you wish you were twenty years old?
25. Do you wish you were a child again?
26. Did he insist on leaving?
27. Did she insist on coming?
28. Did they insist on talking?
29. Did he insist on helping you?

Answer the following questions.

30. Would you rather be old or young?
31. Would you rather be rich or poor?
32. Would you rather be here or at home?
33. Would you rather be rich or beautiful?
34. Would you rather be a teacher or a doctor?

Lección 19

1. **to cross, crossed, crossed** cruzar, atravesar
2. **to freeze, froze, frozen** helar; congelar(se)
3. **to paint, painted, painted** pintar
4. **to attack, attacked, attacked** atacar
5. **to wrap, wrapped, wrapped** envolver
6. **to sound, sounded, sounded** oírse
7. **special** especial **especially** sobre todo
8. **although** aunque **though** aunque
9. **marvelous** maravilloso
10. **courage** valor
11. **patience** paciencia
12. **sympathy** compasión; simpatía

13. **part** parte
14. **group** grupo
15. **jail** cárcel **prison** prisión **prisoner** prisionero
16. **canoe** canoa **boat** bote; barco **row boat** bote de remos
17. **history** historia
18. **sled** trineo
19. **blanket** cobija, frazada
20. **sheet** sábana; hoja (*de papel*)
21. **pillow** almohada; cojín
22. **berry** mora
23. **church** iglesia
24. **savage** salvaje
25. **Indian** indio
26. **French** (*adj.*) francés **France** Francia

IDIOMS

1. **to pay attention to** hacer caso a; poner atención a
   Don't pay any attention to him. No le haga caso.
2. **to stand in line** hacer cola, pararse en fila
3. **to go on + (gerund)** seguir + (gerundio)
   He went on eating. Siguió comiendo.
4. **to make a mistake** equivocarse; tener o cometer un error
5. **to wrap (something) up** envolver (algo)
6. **by the time** a la hora, para cuando
   It was raining by the time we left. A la hora que salimos estaba lloviendo.
7. **Shut up.** Cállate la boca.
   Be quiet. Cállate.
8. **Keep quiet.** Cállate.
   I kept quiet. Me callé.
9. **How long has it been since you saw him?**
   ¿Cuánto tiempo hace que lo vio?
   ¿Cuánto tiempo hace que no lo ves (que no lo has visto)?
   It's been about two months. Hace como dos meses.
   It's been two months since I saw him.
   Hace dos meses que no lo veo (que no lo he visto, que lo vi).

EXERCISE 1

Translate the following phrases and sentences and practice reading them.

1. He might live in a hotel.
2. He might not live in a hotel.
3. Maybe he lives in Cuernavaca.
4. Maybe he doesn't live in Cuernavaca.
5. He may live with the Smith family.
6. He may not live with the Smith family.
7. before choosing
8. after choosing
9. without choosing
10. besides choosing
11. instead of choosing
12. in spite of choosing
13. Choose this one.
14. Don't choose that one.

15. Let's choose this one.
16. I can win, and he can too.
17. I can't win, and he can't either.
18. Perhaps they aren't in Acapulco.
19. Maybe they aren't in Acapulco.
20. They might be in Cuernavaca.

THE PRESENT PERFECT PROGRESSIVE
EL PROGRESIVO DEL ANTEPRESENTE

La forma progresiva del antepresente se construye con el tiempo presente del verbo **have** y el participio del verbo **be (been)** seguido por el gerundio. Estudie las siguientes frases.

She's been coming every day.
Ella ha estado viniendo todos los días.

She hasn't been coming every day.
Ella no ha estado viniendo todos los días.

Has she been coming every day?
¿Ha estado viniendo ella todos los días?

Hasn't she been coming every day?
¿No ha estado ella viniendo todos los días?

LA FORMA PROGRESIVA DEL ANTEPRESENTE
CON UN ELEMENTO DE TIEMPO

Con la forma progresiva del antepresente también se emplean las palabras **for** y **since** para expresar complementos de tiempo. Se emplea la palabra **for** (hace, desde hace) para especificar el plazo de tiempo y **since** (desde, desde que) para indicar cuándo comenzó la acción. Compare el inglés con el castellano.

How long has he been studying English?
¿Cuánto tiempo hace que él estudia (está estudiando) inglés?
¿Cuánto tiempo lleva él estudiando inglés?
¿Cuánto tiempo tiene él estudiando (de estudiar) inglés?
¿Cuánto tiempo ha estado estudiando inglés?

248

He's been studying English for six months.
Hace seis meses que él estudia (está estudiando) inglés.
Lleva seis meses estudiando (de estudiar) inglés.
Tiene seis meses estudiando (de estudiar) inglés.

He's been studying English since January.
Lleva estudiando inglés desde enero.
Tiene estudiando (de estudiar) inglés desde enero.
Ha estado estudiando inglés desde enero.

He's been studying English since he came to Mexico.
El estudia (está estudiando, lleva estudiando, tiene estudiando) inglés desde que llegó a México.
El ha estado estudiando inglés desde que llegó a México.

EXERCISE 2

Verb Practice

1. She's been working in the bank for two years.
2. She hasn't been working in the bank for two years.
3. Has she been working in the bank for two years?
4. Hasn't she been working in the bank for two years?
5. Why has she been working in the bank for two years?

EXERCISE 3

Verb Practice *Make short sentences with forms of the verbs* live, play, smoke, read, ride, dance, examine, talk, eat. *Expand each verb practice to include different tenses, as in the exercise above. Practice ending the sentences with phrases beginning with both* for *and* since. *Use a different noun or pronoun with each verb. Use the interrogative words when it is possible.*

EXERCISE 4

Translate the following sentences. Change them to the present perfect progressive.

1. It's snowed all day.
2. We've saved our money since we got married.
3. They've traveled for two years.

4. She's cleaned the silver every day for a week.
5. He's taken care of the store since he was seventeen.
6. I've played basketball since I was ten.
7. The sun has shone since noon.
8. The wind has blown for two days.
9. We've listened to the radio all day.
10. They've waited for me since five o'clock.

THE PAST PERFECT PROGRESSIVE
EL PROGRESIVO DEL ANTECOPRETÉRITO

La forma progresiva del antecopretérito se construye con el tiempo pasado del verbo **have (had)** y el participio del verbo **be (been)** seguido por un gerundio. Estudie las siguientes frases.

She'd been coming every day.
Ella había estado viniendo todos los días.

She hadn't been coming every day.
Ella no había estado viniendo todos los días.

Had she been coming every day?
¿Había ella estado viniendo todos los días?

Hadn't she been coming every day?
¿No había ella estado viniendo todos los días?

LA FORMA PROGRESIVA DEL ANTECOPRETÉRITO
CON UN ELEMENTO DE TIEMPO

Con la forma progresiva del antecopretérito también se emplean las palabras **for** y **since** para expresar complementos de tiempo. Se emplea **for** (hace, desde hace) para especificar el plazo de tiempo y **since** (desde, desde que) para indicar cuándo empezó la acción. Compare el inglés con el castellano.

How long had he been studying English?
¿Cuánto tiempo hacía que él estudiaba (estaba estudiando) inglés?
¿Cuánto tiempo llevaba él estudiando inglés?
¿Cuánto tiempo tenía él estudiando (de estudiar) inglés?
¿Cuánto tiempo había estado estudiando inglés?

250

He'd been studying English for six months.
Hacía seis meses que él estudiaba (estaba estudiando) inglés.
Llevaba seis meses estudiando inglés.
Tenía seis meses estudiando (de estudiar) inglés.
Había estado estudiando inglés seis meses.

He'd been studying English since January.
Llevaba estudiando inglés desde enero.
Tenía estudiando (de estudiar) inglés desde enero.
Había estado estudiando inglés desde enero.

He'd been studying English since he came to Mexico.
El estudiaba (estaba estudiando, llevaba estudiando, tenía estudian-do) inglés desde que llegó a México.
El había estado estudiando inglés desde que llegó a México.

EXERCISE 5

Verb Practice

1. They'd been talking to me since ten-thirty.
2. They hadn't been talking to me since ten-thirty.
3. Had they been talking to me since ten-thirty?
4. Hadn't they been talking to me since ten-thirty?
5. Why had they been talking to me since ten-thirty?

EXERCISE 6

Verb Practice *Make short sentences with forms of the verbs* write, speak, steal, swim, dress, rest, dig, save, hide. *Expand each verb practice to include different tenses, as in the exercise above. Practice ending the sentences with phrases beginning with both* for *and* since. *Use a different noun or pronoun with each verb. Use the interrogative words when it is possible.*

EXERCISE 7

Change the sentences in exercise 4 to the past perfect progressive and translate.

EXERCISE 8

Translate the following sentences.

1. I hope I see you at the party.
2. I hope it stops raining.
3. I hope it isn't cold tomorrow.
4. I hope we can finish the book this year.
5. I hope you have a nice time.
6. ¡Que pase felices vacaciones!
7. ¡Que Ud. tenga muchos niños!
8. ¡Que la tormenta termine pronto!
9. ¡Que Ud. tenga un cumpleaños muy feliz!
10. ¡Que Ud. se mejore pronto!

EXERCISE 9

Translate the following sentences. Change the second verb of the sentence to the negative and translate again.

1. I wish you'd listen to your parents.
2. I wish you'd stay in Mexico until Christmas.
3. I wish you'd hurry.
4. I wish you'd wear your new skirt.
5. I wish you'd put on your coat.
6. I wish you'd pick up these papers.
7. I wish you'd come back tomorrow.
8. I wish you'd go to the movies.
9. I wish you'd swim in the lake.
10. I wish you'd ask your father.

EXERCISE 10

Translate the following sentences. Change them to the negative, interrogative, and interrogative negative.

1. They pay attention to the teacher.
2. They paid attention to the movie.
3. She'll pay attention to me.
4. You've paid attention to everything I said.
5. He wants me to pay attention to the lesson.
6. They told her to pay attention to her parents.
7. The boys paid attention to what he said.
8. Children like to pay attention to their brothers and sisters.
9. We'll be able to pay attention to him.
10. They should pay attention when he talks.

EXERCISE 11

Answer the following questions in the affirmative and in the negative.

1. Do you want me to pay attention to you?
2. Did you tell them to pay attention to the teacher?
3. Are you going to pay attention to what he says?
4. Were you paying attention when Mr. Wilson spoke?
5. Are you paying attention now?
6. Would you pay attention if I told you a story?
7. Should you pay attention to your mother?
8. Have you been paying attention?
9. Do you always pay attention to your lesson?
10. Did they make you pay attention?

EXERCISE 12

Translate into Spanish.

1. Stop talking and pay attention to what I'm saying.
2. I won't go to the movies on Sunday if I have to stand in line.
3. They went on talking after the teacher came into the room.
4. How many mistakes did you make in your homework?
5. I'm so tired and thirsty that I don't think I can walk any farther.
6. By the time we got to the party all the food had been eaten.
7. I wish you'd shut up and let me think.
8. How often do you have a cold?
9. Helen took care of Margaret's baby while she stood in line.
10. When the boys found out that they were going to be punished, they ran away.
11. I'd rather work all day than go shopping at Christmas time.
12. That store plans to give away two radios on Christmas Eve.
13. If you stopped talking maybe you'd be able to pay attention to what I'm telling you.
14. That stove isn't worth anything. Why don't you get rid of it?
15. The noise died down as soon as I went into the room.

EXERCISE 13

Give the past tense and past participle of the following verbs.

breathe	close	carry	drop
burn	complete	cover	dictate
cross	change	capture	dress
call	correct	cook	disappear
clean	clap	count	dance

EXERCISE 14

Give the past tense and past participle of the following verbs.

bring	blow	come back	dig
buy	build	cut	drive
begin	bleed	catch	draw
become	bet	do	eat
break	come	drink	freeze

EXERCISE 15

Verb Practice *Expand the following verb practice to include different tenses.*

1. That bus will be able to cross the street at the next corner.
2. That bus won't be able to cross the street at the next corner.
3. Will that bus be able to cross the street at the next corner?
4. Won't that bus be able to cross the street at the next corner?
5. Why won't that bus be able to cross the street at the next corner?

EXERCISE 16

Verb Practice *Make short sentences with forms of the verbs* **paint, freeze, attack, wrap, wrap (something) up, sound, stand in line, go on, make a mistake.** *Expand each verb practice to include different tenses, as in the exercise above. Use a different noun or pronoun with each verb. Use the interrogative words when it is possible.*

EXERCISE 17

Read and translate.

THE LITTLE RED SHOES

In 1674 a little girl named Sally Coleman lived in Hatfield, Massachusetts. One day in the fall of that year little Sally was the proudest child in the whole colony because she was the owner of a pair of new shoes. She was especially proud of these shoes because they were as red as the berries that grew in the woods near the town. Sally liked her shoes so much that she kept them near her bed at night when she went to sleep.

Then one night a group of Indians attacked the town. Houses were burned, men and women were killed, and many others were taken away by the Indians.

As Sally left the house, she picked up her red shoes and took them with her; and as she walked through the snow, she was glad that she had remembered to take her red shoes.

Sally's courage and patience during the long, cold trip that followed won the sympathy of an Indian named Painted Arrow; and although sick and weak prisoners were left behind to die of cold or hunger, this savage friend often carried Sally in his arms when she was too tired to walk any farther. When they had to cross rivers, he swam in the cold water beside Sally's canoe to keep it from turning over; and whenever he was lucky with his bow and arrow, he always gave her part of his bear meat.

As the prisoners went on toward Canada, they found the water of Lake Champlain frozen solid. Painted Arrow wrapped Sally in his own blanket and some animal skins and, after building a sled, pulled her to the other side of the lake.

Three months of travel still hadn't worn out the little red shoes; and while Sally was a captive of the Indians, Painted Arrow fixed them with deerskin. Later, after Sally was sold to the French as a slave, ribbon from France was put around the edges of the little shoes.

By the time Sally was returned to her people in June, 1678, the little shoes had traveled six hundred miles; and if you visit the Old South Church in Boston, you can still see them there, the little red shoes with such an interesting history.

EXERCISE 18

Write in English.

1. ¿Cuánto tiempo hace que vives en la misma casa? Hace más de (than) once años.
2. Llevo todo el día envolviendo regalos de Navidad.

3. No podremos pintar la casa hasta que deje de llover.
4. Aunque sabíamos que haría frío en Chicago, no llevamos nuestros abrigos (de invierno).
5. No deje de hablar solamente porque cometió un error.
6. ¿Fuiste al centro la Nochebuena? No, no quería.
7. El agua del lago ha estado congelada todo el invierno.
8. Los niños habían estado jugando desde temprano en la mañana.
9. Quizá las veamos la víspera del Año Nuevo.
10. Puede ser que haga demasiado frío para salir sin abrigo.

EXERCISE 19

Dictation

1. She's been studying English for three years.
2. It's been raining all day.
3. I wish you wouldn't cross the street until the cars stop.
4. It'll be time to eat by the time we finish.
5. Next time I hope you pay attention to me.
6. Do you know where the largest market in Mexico is?
7. You'll get hurt if you aren't careful.
8. We returned the books when we got through with them.
9. I plan to stop working in another year or two.
10. How long ago did you buy that suit?

EXERCISE 20

Conversation *Answer the following questions in the affirmative and in the negative.*

1. Do you know where we are?
2. Do you know who he is?
3. Do you know where they are?
4. Do you know what time it is?
5. Do you know what his name is?
6. Did you know where we were?
7. Did you know who he was?
8. Did you know what time it was?

Answer the following questions.

9. How long has it been since he sold his car?
10. How long has it been since you had a vacation?

11. How long has it been since you read a good book?
12. How long has it been since you saw that movie?
13. How long has it been since you were in the United States?
14. How long has it been since you ate downtown?
15. How long had it been since he saw his mother?
16. How long had it been since he ate French food?
17. How long have you been studying French?
18. How long have they been waiting for us?
19. How long had John been waiting when it began to rain?

Answer the following questions in the affirmative and in the negative.

20. Have you been working all day?
21. Have you been eating Mexican food?
22. Have you been listening to the radio?
23. Have you been watching television?
24. Has he been studying Spanish?
25. Has he been living in France?
26. Have they been making a cake?
27. Have they been smoking?
28. Have they been making a lot of money?
29. Have they been paying attention?
30. Have they been standing in line?

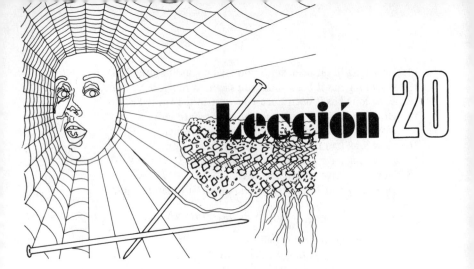

Lección 20

Vocabulary

1. **to sew, sewed, sewed** coser
2. **to weave, wove, woven** tejer (*en telar*)
   to knit, knitted, knitted tejer (*con agujas*)
3. **to admire, admired, admired** admirar
4. **to include, included, included** incluir
5. **to join, joined, joined** juntar; hacerse socio de
6. **to tear, tore, torn** rasgar, romper
7. **immediately** inmediatamente
8. **wonderful** maravilloso
9. **natural** natural
10. **jealous** celoso
11. **guilt** culpa
    guilty culpable
12. **warning** amonestación, advertencia
13. **art** arte
14. **center** centro
15. **cloth** tela, género
    material tela, género
16. **needle** aguja
17. **thread** hilo
18. **contest** competencia, concurso
19. **heaven** cielo
20. **spider** araña
21. **spider web** telaraña
    cobweb telaraña
22. **fly** mosca
23. **butterfly** mariposa
24. **worm** gusano
25. **earth** tierra; suelo

IDIOMS

1. **to make fun of** burlarse de

2. **to go with** acompañar a
   I went downtown with my mother. Acompañé a mi mamá al centro.
3. **to throw (something) away** tirar o botar (algo)
   Throw it away. Tíralo.
4. **to take a bath** bañarse (*en tina*)
   to take a shower bañarse (*en regadera*)
5. **to be guilty** ser culpable
6. **shades of color** matices de color
7. **a bad cold** un catarro fuerte
   a bad cough una tos fuerte
   a sore throat un dolor de garganta

EXERCISE 1

Translate the following sentences and practice reading them.

1. They may sing later.
2. They may not sing later.
3. They might sing some more.
4. They might not sing any more.
5. Maybe they'll sing that song again.
6. Maybe they won't sing that song again.
7. Cross here.
8. Don't cross here.
9. Let's cross here.
10. Let's not cross here.
11. Let him cross there.
12. Don't let him cross there.
13. Let her cross too.
14. Don't let her cross either.
15. Let them cross there.
16. Don't let them cross there.
17. What are you thinking about?
18. What are you talking about?
19. Who are you going to go with?
20. Who did you go with?

Learn these words.

SUPPLEMENTARY VOCABULARY

1. **addition** adición   2. **additional** adicional

3. **agreement** acuerdo
4. **agreeable** agradable
5. **attack** ataque
6. **admiration** admiración
7. **admirable** admirable
8. **annoying** molesto
9. **bet** apuesta
10. **bother** molestia
11. **breath** aliento
12. **breathing** respiración
13. **cook** cocinero
14. **cooking** cocina
   (*arte de cocinar*)
15. **cost** costo, precio
16. **costly** caro
17. **choice** selección
18. **cross** cruz
19. **crossing** crucero
20. **discovery** descubrimiento
21. **drawing** dibujo
22. **examination** examen,
   prueba
23. **explanation** explicación
24. **expression** expresión
25. **expectation** expectación
26. **failure** fracaso
27. **drunkard** (*noun*) borracho
28. **drunk** (*adj.*) borracho

29. **insult** insulto
30. **insulting** insultante
31. **knitting** tejido
32. **notice** aviso
33. **noticeable** notable
34. **name** nombre
35. **punishment** castigo
36. **preparation** preparación
37. **painter** pintor
38. **paint** pintura (*el líquido*)
39. **painting** pintura (*el arte*)
40. **realization** realización
41. **repetition** repetición
42. **rent** renta
43. **smile** sonrisa
44. **smiling** sonriente
45. **satisfaction** satisfacción
46. **satisfactory** satisfactorio
47. **smell** olor
48. **surprise** sorpresa
49. **smoke** humo
50. **sound** sonido
51. **sewing** costura
52. **wish** deseo
53. **weave** tejido (*de telas*)
54. **weaving** el acto de tejer
55. **weaver** tejedor

EXERCISE 2

Translate the following sentences.

1. Have they reached an agreement?
2. Was the attack made by the Indians?
3. I have a lot of admiration for that person.
4. The bet he won was not large.
5. Students who always talk are annoying.
6. I knew by his breathing that he was asleep.
7. My mother is a good cook.
8. Everybody likes Mexican cooking.

260

9. You made a good choice when you chose that teacher.
10. There's a cross on the church.
11. I'll get off when the bus comes to the crossing.
12. The discovery of America was made by a man named Columbus
13. Do you study drawing at school?
14. The examination was very difficult.
15. Did you understand the explanation?
16. That man is a complete failure.
17. Her father was a drunkard.
18. Did you read the notice on the wall?
19. Her Spanish accent is very noticeable.
20. There's a lot of smoke in this room.
21. We listened, but we couldn't hear a sound.
22. This dress has a very fine weave.
23. Weaving is done by the women and children.
24. He spoke to me in a very insulting way.

EXERCISE 3

Translate the following sentences. Change them to the negative, interrogative, and interrogative negative.

1. I've been admiring your new dress.
2. Alice has been sewing for two hours.
3. We've been examining the new dishes.
4. She's been expecting you.
5. The girls have been knitting sweaters.
6. They've been preparing the fish for dinner.
7. The pupils have been repeating the verbs.
8. Carl has been smoking too much.
9. Jane has been feeling bad all week.
10. You've been talking to the teacher.

EXERCISE 4

Translate the following sentences. Change them to the negative, interrogative, and interrogative negative.

1. They've been living in Mexico for a year.
2. Charles had been sleeping for three hours when his father woke him up.

3. I've been waiting for you for more than an hour.
4. She's been studying English a long time.
5. Her husband had been working in Mexico for four months when he was sent to Europe.
6. My mother has been washing since eight o'clock this morning.
7. He's been feeling well all day.
8. They've been writing since early this morning.
9. My brother has been waiting for more than an hour.
10. Mary had been reading the newspaper for an hour when her mother came home.

EXERCISE 5

Translate the following sentences. Change them to the negative, interrogative, and interrogative negative.

1. The boys made fun of that old man.
2. The children are making fun of that beggar.
3. Bill makes fun of the way I speak English.
4. The girls made fun of the dresses worn in 1925.
5. My wife makes fun of my old car.
6. He's making fun of me.
7. They'll make fun of your funny hat.
8. They like to make fun of American movies.
9. She made fun of the book he wrote.
10. They're making fun of him.

EXERCISE 6

Translate the following sentences. Change them to the negative, interrogative, and interrogative negative.

1. He takes a bath every morning.
2. They took a bath in cold water.
3. We took a bath in the sea.
4. She's taken two baths today.
5. I'll take a bath before I go to the movies.
6. You're going to take a shower now.
7. They were going to take a shower early.
8. He's taking a shower in hot water.
9. She'd take a shower if she had time.
10. They should take a shower every day.

262

EXERCISE 7

Translate into Spanish.

1. Aren't you ashamed to make fun of my paintings?
2. I have to go with him so he won't get lost.
3. If those papers aren't any good, throw them away.
4. Do you want to take a shower before you go to the movies?
5. He has a bad cold and a sore throat.
6. He turned off the water while I was taking a shower.
7. I told him to get rid of that dog.
8. We've just painted the bedroom.
9. You should pay attention to what he says.
10. Diamonds are worth a lot of money.
11. I'd rather stay at home than go to that party.
12. The wind died down as soon as the storm was over.
13. I won't go to the football game if I have to stand in line to buy a ticket.
14. I won't have time to go with you tomorrow.
15. Helen Wood knows how to knit beautiful socks.

EXERCISE 8

Give the past tense and past participle of the following verbs.

die	examine	fix	help
drown	explain	form	hurry
decide	express	fail	hunt
discover	expect	follow	hope
escape	finish	fool	insult

EXERCISE 9

Give the past tense and past participle of the following verbs.

feel	go	go to bed	get hurt
fly	go back	go shopping	get dark
fall	go with	give	get light
feed	go on	get	get better
fight	go to sleep	get mad (at)	get worse

EXERCISE 10

Verb Practice *Expand the following verb practice to include different tenses.*

1. Mrs. White's daughter is sewing, isn't she?
2. Mrs. White's daughter isn't sewing, is she?
3. Is Mrs. White's daughter sewing?
4. Isn't Mrs. White's daughter sewing?
5. Why isn't Mrs. White's daughter sewing?

EXERCISE 11

Verb Practice *Make short sentences with forms of the verbs* weave, knit, admire, include, join, tear, go with, throw (something) away, take a bath, take a shower, make fun of. *Expand each verb practice to include different tenses, as in the exercise above. Use a different noun or pronoun with each verb. Use the interrogative words when it is possible.*

EXERCISE 12

Read and translate.

THE CONTEST

Minerva, the goddess of the art of weaving, heard about a girl named Arachne, who could weave so well that everyone around her stopped whatever they were doing to watch her work and admire the beautiful things she made.

The delicate colors of the beautiful threads formed pictures which were so natural that the people thought the goddess Minerva herself must have taught her how to weave. But Arachne said that she was not a pupil of the goddess.

"I can weave better than Minerva," said Arachne, "and if she wants to have a contest with me, let her come; and I'll show her whose work is more beautiful."

When Minerva heard this, she got very angry. Arachne's words were an insult, so Minerva went to Arachne and told her that the contest would begin immediately.

Each began her work at once. The weavers' fingers flew over the cloth and among the beautiful threads, joining the delicate shades of color in such a way that the eye could not see where the colors changed.

Minerva wove things of the powers in heaven and in the sea and on the earth. The center of her cloth was wonderful to look at, and in each corner she formed pictures showing the punishment of those who had made the gods angry. This was meant as a warning for Arachne to give up the contest.

But Arachne did not stop. She filled her cloth with pictures showing the mistakes of the gods. Minerva could not keep from admiring her work; but because she thought the things Arachne had woven were an insult or, perhaps, because she was a little jealous of Arachne's fine weaving, she hit the cloth with her needle and tore it to pieces. In this way she made Arachne realize her guilt for insulting the gods.

"Live, guilty woman," said Minerva, as she changed Arachne into a spider, "and so that you can remember the lesson that I have taught you, you will forever weave spider webs in which you will hang for all future time."

EXERCISE 13

Write in English.

1. ¿Cómo rasgó su falda?
2. Hacía veinte minutos que te estábamos esperando cuando empezó a llover.
3. No se burle de cómo él habla inglés.
4. ¿Cuánto tiempo hace (desde) que leyó este libro?
5. ¿Cuánto tiempo se tarda Ud. en tejer un par de calcetines?
6. Oscurece temprano en enero.
7. ¿Para qué dejó Ud. de fumar? ¿Ya no le gusta?
8. ¿Recuerda Ud. dónde dejé mi bolsa?
9. Tal vez llueva antes de que lleguemos a casa.
10. Mi hermano fuma desde que cumplió los quince años.

EXERCISE 14

Dictation

1. Would you rather have fried eggs or scrambled eggs?
2. Do you know where he was born?
3. It doesn't make any difference what he thinks.
4. He likes chocolate cake better than anything else.
5. If you have a cold, don't take a shower in cold water.

6. Let's stop working for a few minutes and have some coffee.
7. Don't throw those things away. You might need them some day.
8. All the clouds have disappeared.
9. Do you think that I can rent a house for a thousand pesos?
10. I have a bad cough.

EXERCISE 15

Conversation *Answer the following questions in the affirmative and in the negative.*

1. Are you making fun of me?
2. Were you making fun of their car?
3. Did you make fun of her hat?
4. Did you go with your mother?
5. Will you go with me?
6. Are you going with your friends?
7. Do you have to go with your father?
8. Did you throw away those letters?
9. Are you going to throw away those old clothes?
10. Will you throw away these old books?
11. Do you take a shower every morning?
12. Did you take a shower in cold water?
13. Would you take a shower if you had a cold?
14. Do you know what time it is?
15. Do you know where the market is?
16. Do you know how old I am?
17. Do you know how far we walked?
18. Do you know when my birthday is?
19. Do you know where we are?
20. Do you know who I am?

Answer the following questions.

21. How far is it from here downtown?
22. How far is it from my house to your house?
23. How far is it from here to Texas?
24. How long ago did you learn how to drive?
25. How long ago did you paint the house?
26. How long ago did you live in Monterrey?
27. How long ago did you get married?
28. How long ago did you give a party?

266

29. How often do you go out of town?
30. How often do you go to the movies?
31. How long has it been since I saw you?
32. How long has it been since Mr. Smith died?
33. How long has it been raining?
34. How long has he been studying?
35. How long have they been waiting?

Vocabulario inglés-español

A

(to) add agregar; sumar
 added
 added
 addition adición
 additional adicional
 address dirección
 admirable admirable
(to) admire admirar
 admired
 admired
 admiration admiración
 advantage ventaja
 advice consejo(s)
 afraid: to be afraid of
  tener miedo a (de)
 Africa África
 against contra
 age edad
(to) agree estar de acuerdo
 agreed
 agreed
 agreeable agradable
 agreement acuerdo
 air aire

alone solo
along por; a lo largo de
already ya
also también
although aunque
amount cantidad
annoying molesto
ant hormiga
any alguno(s); cualquier(a)
 not ... any no ...
 ninguno(s)
anybody alguien; cualquiera
 not ... anybody no ...
 nadie
any longer ya no
any more ya no
anyone alguien; cualquiera
 not ... anyone no ...
 nadie
any place alguna parte;
 en cualquier parte
 not ... any place no ...
 ninguna parte
anything algo; cualquier cosa

not ... anything no ... nada
anywhere alguna parte; en
   cualquier parte;
   not ... anywhere no ...
   ninguna parte
(to) appear aparecer
   appeared
   appeared
arm brazo
army ejército
(to) arrive (in, at) llegar (a)
   arrived (in, at)
   arrived (in, at)
   arrival llegada

arrow flecha
art arte
artificial artificial
ashamed apenado
   avergonzado
at all en absoluto
(to) attack atacar
   attacked
   attacked
(to) avoid evitar, eludir,
   esquivar, rehuir
   avoided
   avoided

B

back espalda; de atrás
bank banco
baseball béisbol
basketball basquetbol
bathing suit traje de baño
beans frijoles
bear oso
beauty belleza
(to) be able poder
   could pudo, podía
   been able podido
(to) be born nacer
   was, were born
   been born
(to) be in love (with)
   estar enamorado (de)
   was, were in love (with)
   been in love (with)
(to) be over acabarse
   was, were over
   been over
(to) be worth valer
   was, were worth
   been worth

(to) be worth it valer la pena
   was, were worth it
   been worth it
(to) be worth + (gerund)
   valer la pena + (inf.)
   was, were worth +
   (gerund)
   been worth + (gerund)
bee abeja
beggar mendigo
behind atrás de, detrás de
belief creencia
(to) believe creer
   believed
   believed
bell campana; cascabel
belt cinturón
berry mora
beside al lado de
besides además (de)
bet apuesta
(to) bet apostar
   bet
   bet

better mejor
bill cuenta; pico; billete
bird pájaro
birth nacimiento
blanket cobija, frazada
(to) bleed sangrar
    bled
    bled.
blind ciego
blindness ceguera
block cuadra, manzana
blood sangre
bloody sangriento
(to) blow soplar
    blew
    blown
boat barco; bote
body cuerpo
(to) boil hervir
    boiled
    boiled
bone hueso
both ambos; both–and
    tanto–como
bother molestia
(to) bother molestar(se)
    bothered
    bothered
bottom fondo; parte
    inferior
bouquet ramillete
bow arco
box caja
brain cerebro
brains sesos

brave valiente
(to) break romper
    broke
    broken
breast pecho; seno
breath aliento
(to) breathe respirar
    breathed
    breathed
breathing respiración
bridge puente
bright brillante
(to) bring traer
    brought
    brought
brokenhearted (*adj.*) con
    el corazón roto
brother-in-law cuñado
brown color café
bucket cubeta
(to) build construir
    built
    built
building edificio
(to) burn quemar
    burned
    burned
bus camión
business (*sing.*) negocio(s)
busy ocupado
butterfly mariposa
(to) buy comprar
    bought
    bought

C

calm tranquilo; calmado
calmly tranquilamente
camel camello

Canada Canadá
canoe canoa
captive cautivo

capture captura
(to) capture capturar
    captured
    captured
    careful cuidadoso
    carefully con cuidado
(to) carry cargar, llevar
    (*cargando*)
    carried
    carried
    cat gato
(to) catch atrapar; coger
    caught
    caught
    cave cueva
    center centro
    certainly ciertamente; con
      mucho gusto
    chain cadena
    chair silla
    chance oportunidad
    change cambio
(to) change your mind
      cambiar de idea
    changed your mind
    changed your mind
    charity caridad
    cheap barato; corriente
    cheese queso
    chocolate chocolate
    choice selección
(to) choose escoger
    chose
    chosen
    Christmas Navidad
    Christmas Day día de
      Navidad
    Christmas Eve Noche-
      buena, víspera de
      Navidad
    church iglesia

(to) clap aplaudir
    clapped
    clapped
    class clase
    closet closet
    cloth tela; manta; género
    clothes (*plural*) ropa
    cloud nube
    cloudy nublado
    coat abrigo
    cobweb telaraña
    cold frío; catarro;
      I'm cold tengo frío:
      I have a cold
      tengo catarro;
      It's cold hace frío
(to) come venir
    came
    come
(to) come back regresar
      (*de allá para acá*)
    came back
    come back
    complete completo
    completely completamente
    completion terminación
    conceited (*adj.*) creído,
      vanidoso
    constant constante
    constantly constantemente
    contest concurso,
      competencia
    cook cocinero
(to) cook cocinar, guisar
    cooked
    cooked
    cooking cocina (*arte de
      cocinar*)
    corn maíz; elote
    corner esquina; rincón
    correct correcto

(to) correct corregir
    corrected
    corrected
    correctly correctamente
cost costo, precio
(to) cost costar
    cost
    cost
    costly caro
    cough tos
(to) count contar
    counted
    counted
    courage valor
    cover tapa, tapadera

(to) cover cubrir, tapar
    covered
    covered
    crazy loco, demente
    crooked torcido, chueco
    cross cruz
(to) cross cruzar, atravesar
    crossed
    crossed
    crossing crucero
    cruel cruel
(to) cry llorar
    cried
    cried

D

dance baile
(to) dance bailar
    danced
    danced
    dancer bailarín
    danger peligro
    dangerous peligroso
    dark oscuro
    day día; the day after
        tomorrow pasado
        mañana; the day
        before yesterday
        anteayer
    dead (*adj.*) muerto
    death muerte
(to) decide decidir
    decided
    decided
    decision decisión
    decreasing scale escala
        descendente
    deer venado(s)

degree grado
delicate delicado
dew rocío
diamond diamante
dictation dictado
dictator dictador
(to) die morirse; secarse
    (*plantas*)
    died
    died
(to) die down acabarse poco a
    poco; calmarse
    died down
    died down
    different (from)
        diferente (de, a)
    difficult difícil
(to) dig excavar, cavar
    dug
    dug
(to) dig (something) up
    desenterrar (algo)

dug (something) up
dug (something) up
(to) disappear desaparecer
disappeared
disappeared
disappearance desaparición
(to) discover descubrir
discovered
discovered
discovery descubrimiento
dishes trastos; platos
distance distancia; lejanía
(to) do hacer
did
done
donkey burro
downtown en el (al) centro
(to) draw dibujar
drew
drawn
drawing dibujo
(to) draw interest ganar
intereses

drew interest
drawn interest
dream sueño
(to) dress vestir(se)
dressed
dressed
(to) drive manejar
(*un vehículo*); arrear;
ir en coche
drove
driven
driver chofer, el que
maneja
(to) drop caérsele a uno
dropped
dropped
(to) drown ahogar(se)
drowned
drowned
drunk (*adj.*) borracho
drunkard (*sust.*) borracho
during durante
dying (*adj.*) moribundo

E

earth tierra; suelo
easily fácilmente
east este
Easter Sunday
domingo de
resurrección
Easter Week semana santa
edge orilla; borde
either tampoco; o
elephant elefante
elevator elevador
else: what else qué más;
who else quién más
empty vacío

enemy enemigo
enough bastante (*de
alcanzar*)
(to) escape escaparse
escaped
escaped
especially sobre todo
Europe Europa
even hasta; a mano;
not even ni siquiera
even if aunque,
aun cuando
even though aunque
ever alguna vez, a veces

not ever nunca, jamás
exact exacto, preciso
exactly exactamente,
    precisamente
examination examen,
    prueba
(to) examine examinar
    examined
    examined
except excepto, menos
excitement emoción;
    excitación
(to) expect esperar (*de contar
*   *con, de estar casi*
*   seguro o de exigir*)

    expected
    expected
expectation expectación
expensive caro; costoso
(to) explain explicar
    explained
    explained
explanation explicación
(to) express expresar
    expressed
    expressed
expression expresión

F

face cara
fact hecho
(to) fail fallar; reprobar;
    fracasar
    failed
    failed
failure fracaso
fall caída
(to) fall (down) caer(se)
    fell (down)
    fallen (down)
(to) fall in love (with)
    enamorarse (de)
    fell in love (with)
    fallen in love (with)
fan abanico; ventilador
far lejos
far from lejos de
farther más lejos
    (*comparativo*)
farthest más lejos
    (*superlativo*)

fat gordo; gordura
fault culpa
favorite predilecto,
    favorito
feather pluma
(to) feed dar de comer
    fed
    fed
(to) feel at home sentirse como
    en su propia casa;
    estar a gusto
    felt at home
    felt at home
feeling sentimiento
feet pies
fight pelea, pleito
(to) fight pelear, luchar
    fought
    fought
fighter luchador; boxeador
finally por fin
(to) find encontrar

found
found
(to) find out averiguar,
  enterarse
found out
found out
finger dedo
fire fuego; incendio
fish pez, peces;
  pescado(s)
flat plano
flier aviador
flight vuelo
fly mosca
(to) fly volar
flew
flown
flying volador
(to) follow seguir
followed
followed
fool (*sust.*) tonto
(to) fool engañar; bromear
fooled
fooled
foolish (*adj.*) tonto
foot pie
football fútbol

forever para siempre
(to) forget olvidar(se)
forgot
forgotten
form forma, esqueleto
formation formación
fortunate afortunado
fortunately afortunada-
  mente
fortune fortuna
France Francia
free gratis; libre
freedom libertad
(to) freeze helar; congelar(se)
froze
frozen
French (*adj.*) francés
fresh fresco
fruit fruta
full lleno; satisfecho
funny divertido, chistoso;
  raro
furniture (*sing.*) muebles;
  a piece of furniture
  un mueble
future tense tiempo
  futuro

G

game juego
gate reja, portal
(to) get conseguir
got
got
(to) get angry (mad) (at)
  enojarse (con)
got angry (mad) (at)
got angry (mad) (at)
(to) get away escaparse

got away
got away
(to) get better mejorarse
got better
got better
(to) get dark oscurecer,
  anochecer
got dark
got dark
(to) get drunk emborracharse

got drunk
got drunk
(to) get here, there (to)
    llegar (a)
got here, there (to)
got here, there (to)
(to) get hurt lastimarse
got hurt
got hurt
(to) get in subir (a); meterse
got in
got in
(to) get light amanecer
got light
got light
(to) get lost perderse
got lost
got lost
(to) get off bajarse (de)
got off
got off
(to) get married casarse
got married
got married
(to) get old envejecerse
got old
got old
(to) get on subir (a);
    montar (a, en)
got on
got on
(to) get out (of) bajarse (de)
    (*un coche*); salirse
    (de)
got out (of)
got out (of)
(to) get ready alistarse,
    prepararse
got ready
got ready
(to) get rich enriquecerse,
    hacerse rico

got rich
got rich
(to) get rid of deshacerse de;
    quitársele a uno
got rid of
got rid of
(to) get scared asustarse
got scared
got scared
(to) get sick enfermarse
got sick
got sick
(to) get sleepy darle a uno
    sueño
got sleepy
got sleepy
(to) get through terminar,
    acabar
got through
got through
(to) get tired cansarse
got tired
got tired
(to) get thirsty darle a uno sed
got thirsty
got thirsty
(to) get wet mojarse
got wet
got wet
(to) get worse empeorarse
got worse
got worse
(to) give dar
gave
given
(to) give (something) away
    regalar (algo)
gave (something) away
given (something) away
(to) give something to somebody
    regalar algo a alguien
gave something to

somebody
given something to
somebody
(to) give up darse por vencido;
dejar; renunciar
gave up
given up
glad contento, feliz
glove guante
God Dios
goddess diosa
(to) go ir(se)
went
gone
(to) go back regresar (de acá
para allá)
went back
gone back
(to) go dancing ir a bailar
went dancing
gone dancing
(to) go on seguir, continuar
went on
gone on
(to) go on + (ger.)
seguir + (ger.)
went on + (ger.)
gone on + (ger.)

(to) go riding ir a montar
went riding
gone riding
(to) go shopping ir de
compras
went shopping
gone shopping
(to) go swimming ir a nadar
went swimming
gone swimming
(to) go with acompañar a
went with
gone with
grain grano
grasshopper chapulín
grateful agradecido
great gran; a great deal (of)
mucho
ground tierra, suelo
group grupo
(to) grow crecer; cultivar
grew
grown
growth crecimiento
guide guía
guilt culpa
guilty culpable

H

hair pelo; vello
half mitad
Halloween víspera de
Todos los Santos
hand mano
handkerchief pañuelo
handsome guapo
(to) hang colgar
hung
hung

happiness felicidad
hard duro; fuerte
hardly apenas
(to) have a good time
divertirse
had a good time
had a good time
(to) have fun divertirse
had fun
'had fun

278

(to) have just + (past. part.)
       acabar de + (inf.)
       had just + (past. part.)
  head cabeza
  heart corazón
  heaven cielo
  heavy pesado
  help ayuda
(to) help ayudar
  helped
  helped
  helper ayudante
  helpful útil; comedido
  her su(s) de ellas; la (*pron. obj.*)
  hers el suyo (de ella)
  herself ella misma; se
(to) hide esconder(se); ocultar(se)
  hid
  hidden
  high (*de cosas*) alto
  highway carretera
  hill colina
  him lo, le (*pron. obj.*)
  himself él mismo, se
  his su(s) de él; el suyo (de él)
  history historia
(to) hit pegar
  hit
  hit
  hog cochino o puerco grande
  hole agujero

Holy Week semana santa
homework tarea (*de escuela*)
honesty honradez
(to) hope esperar (*de tener esperanza*), ojalá
  hoped
  hoped
  horse caballo
  hose medias
  hot caliente
  however sin embargo
  huge gigantesco, enorme
  human humano
  hundred: one hundred cien(to)
  humble humilde
  hump joroba
  hungry: to be hungry tener hambre
  hunt caza
(to) hunt cazar
  hunted
  hunted
  hunter cazador
(to) hurry apresurarse
  hurried
  hurried
(to) hurt lastimar
  hurt
  hurt
(to) hurt you hand, leg, etc. lastimarse (la mano, pierna, etc.)
  hurt your hand, leg, etc.
  hurt your hand, leg, etc.

I

ice hielo

iceman hielero

279

immediately inmediata-
mente
important importante
impossible imposible
impression impresión
in en, dentro de
(to) include incluir
included
included
increasing scale escala
ascendente
in fact de hecho, en
realidad
in front of delante de,
enfrente de
Indian indio
insane loco
insect bicho, insecto

inside adentro (de)
(to) insist (on) empeñarse,
insistir (en)
insisted (on)
insisted (on)
instead of en vez de
insult insulto
(to) insult insultar
insulted
insulted
insulting insultante
intelligent inteligente
interest interés
invitation invitación
it lo, la (*neutro*)
its su (*neutro*)
itself en sí

J

jail cárcel
jealous: to be jealous
tener celos
jewel joya, alhaja
jewelry (*sing.*) joyas,
alhajas
job empleo, trabajo

(to) join juntar; hacerse
socio de
joined
joined
judgment criterio
just solamente; **just then**
en este momento

K

(to) keep conservar; quedarse
con; guardar
kept
kept
(to) keep (someone) from impedir
(a alguien) que
kept (someone) from
kept (someone) from

key llave
killer asesino
kind clase; amable,
bondadoso
kindness bondad,
amabilidad
king rey
kiss beso

280

(to) kiss besar
    kissed
    kissed
(to) knit tejer (*con agujas*)
    knitted
    knitted

knitting tejido
(to) knock (on) toca (*la puerta*)
    knocked (on)
    knocked (on)
knowledge conoci-
    miento(s)

L

lake lago
land tierra, terreno
large grande (*de
    tamaño*)
last último, pasado;
    last name apellido;
    last night anoche;
    last week la semana
    pasada
(to) last durar
    lasted
    lasted
lazy perezoso, flojo
leaf hoja (*de árbol*)
least menos (*superlativo*)
(to) leave dejar; salir,
    marcharse
    left
    left
leaves hojas
left izquierdo; **to have left**
    quedarle a uno; **there's**
    —left queda—; **there**
    are—left quedan—
leg pierna
(to) lend prestar
    lent
    lent
less menos (*comparativo*)
(to) let dejar, permitir
    let
    let

(to) lie (down) recostarse;
    echarse
    lay (down)
    lain (down)
life vida
(to) lift alzar, levantar
    lifted
    lifted
light claro; liviano, ligero
like como, parecido a
lion león
lip labio
(to) listen (to) escuchar
    listened (to)
    listened (to)
listener el que escucha,
    oyente
loan préstamo
(to) look (at)
    looked (at)
    looked (at)
(to) look alike parecerse
    looked alike
    looked alike
(to) look for buscar
    looked for
    looked for
(to) look + (adj.) verse,
    parecer (*con adjetivo*)
    looked + (adj.)
    looked + (adj.)
(to) look like + (noun)

281

parecer; parecerse a
(*con sust.*)
looked like + (noun)
Looked like + (noun)
(to) lose perder
lost
lost
loser (*noun*) perdedor
losing (*adj.*) perdedor
loss pérdida
lot: a lot of (of) mucho,
muchos

lots: lots (of) mucho,
muchos
loud fuerte; recio (*de
sonido*); chillante
(*de color*)
love amor
lover amante
low (*de cosas*) bajo
luck suerte
lucky afortunado

M

mail correo;
correspondencia
mailman cartero
(to) make hacer
made
made
(to) make a living ganarse
la vida
made a living
made a living
(to) make a mistake
equivocarse; tener o
cometer un error
made a mistake
made a mistake
(to) make fun of burlarse de
made fun of
made fun of
(to) make money ganar dinero
made money
made money
mark marca
market mercado
marriage casamiento;
matrimonio

(to) marry casarse con
married
married
marvelous maravilloso
master amo
material tela, género
maybe puede (ser) que
meal comida
(to) mean querer decir,
significar
meant
meant
meaning significado
(to) meet encontrar personas
(*por casualidad*);
conocer personas (*por
primera vez*)
met
met
meeting junta, mitin;
encuentro
mice ratones
midnight medianoche
might poder
mind mente

mine el mío, la mía, los
míos, las mías
mistake error, falta,
equivocación
moon luna
mountain montaña
mouse ratón
(to) move mover(se); cambiarse
de casa

moved
moved
movies cine; películas
music música
my mi(s)
myself yo mismo, me

N

nail clavo
name nombre
(to) name nombrar; ponerle
nombre a uno
named
named
natural natural
nature naturaleza
navy marina
necessary necesario
necessarily necesariamente
necessity necesidad
neck cuello; pescuezo
needle aguja
neighbor vecino
neither—nor ni—ni
nephew sobrino
net red
nevertheless sin embargo
news (*sing.*) noticias
newspaper periódico
New Year's el día de año
nuevo
New Year's Day el día de
año nuevo
New Year's Eve la víspera
de año nuevo

next próximo; next week
la semana próxima
next to junto a
niece sobrina
night noche; at night de
noche
no no; ningún(o)
nobody nadie, ninguna
persona
noise ruido
noisy ruidoso; escandaloso
none ninguno
noon mediodía
no one nadie, ninguna
persona
north norte
nose nariz
not even ni siquiera
nothing nada
notice aviso
(to) notice fijarse en
noticed
noticed
noticeable notable,
perceptible
nut nuez

283

O

object objeto;
    complemento
on en, sobre, encima de
onion cebolla
on purpose a propósito;
    adrede
opportunity oportunidad,
    ocasión
orange naranja
orchard huerto
order orden
our nuestro(a, os, as)
ours el nuestro, la nuestra,
    los nuestros, las
    nuestras
ourselves nosotros
    mismos, nos

out afuera
out of afuera de
outside afuera, afuera de
over sobre, por,
    directamente
    encima de
overcoat abrigo de
    invierno
over here para acá, hacia
    acá, por acá
over there para allá, hacia
    allá, por allá
own propio
(to) own poseer, tener
    owned
    owned
owner dueño

P

paint pintura (*el líquido*)
(to) paint pintar
    painted
    painted
painter pintor
painting pintura (*el arte*)
pair par
pale pálido
paper papel; periódico
park parque
part parte
party fiesta; partido
pasture campos para pastar
patience paciencia
paw pata (*de animal*)
pay sueldo, salario
(to) pay pagar
    paid
    paid

(to) pay attention (to)
    poner atención a;
    hacer caso a
    paid attention (to)
    paid attention (to)
pay day día de pago
payment pago; abono
peace paz
peach durazno
pepper pimienta; pimiento
perhaps quizá, tal vez
person persona
phone teléfono
piece pedazo
pig cochino o puerco
    pequeño
pillow almohada; cojín
pink color de rosa
plan plan

284

(to) plan + (inf.)
      pensar + (inf.)
    planned + (inf.)
    planned + (inf.)
  plane avión
(to) play jugar
  played
  played
  player jugador
  playful juguetón
  plenty suficiente, bastante
    (de sobrar)
  pocket bolsa (de ropa)
  pole poste; pértiga
  polite cortés
  possible posible
  post poste
  pot olla
  power poder
  powerful poderoso
(to) prefer preferir
  preferred
  preferred
  preference preferencia
  preparation preparación
(to) prepare preparar
  prepared
  prepared

present presente
president presidente
pretty lindo, bonito
prison prisión
prisoner prisionero
pronunciation pronun-
    ciación
proud orgulloso
proudly orgullosamente
(to) pull jalar, tirar de
  pulled
  pulled
(to) punish castigar
  punished
  punished
  punishment castigo
  pupil alumno
  purpose propósito
  purse bolsa (de mujer)
(to) push empujar
  pushed
  pushed
(to) put poner
  put
  put
(to) put on ponerse
  put on
  put on

Q

queen reina
quick rápido

quickly rápidamente
quiet callado

R

(to) rain llover
  rained
  rained
  raincoat impermeable

rainy lluvioso
rather: would rather
    preferir
(to) read leer

read
read
real verdadero
(to) realize darse cuenta;
　　　　realizar
　　realized
　　realized
　　realization realización
　　really verdaderamente
　　　　en serio; de veras
　　recently recientemente
　　record player tocadiscos
　　relative pariente
　　remains restos
(to) remember recordar,
　　　　acordarse (de)
　　remembered
　　remembered
　　rent renta
(to) rent alquilar, rentar
　　rented
　　rented
(to) repeat repetir
　　repeated
　　repeated
　　repetition repetición
(to) reply contestar
　　replied
　　replied
　　respect respeto
　　rest resto; descanso

(to) rest descansar
　　rested
　　rested
(to) return regresar
　　returned
　　returned
　　ribbon listón
(to) ride montar; andar o ir
　　　　(*en vehículo*)
　　rode
　　ridden
　　rider jinete
　　right derecho; correcto;
　　　　cierto
　　river río
　　road camino
(to) rob robar
　　robbed
　　robbed
　　roof techo; azotea
　　rope soga, cuerda, reata
　　round redondo
　　row boat bote de remos
(to) run correr
　　ran
　　run
(to) run away huir, fugarse
　　ran away
　　run away
　　runner corredor

S

safe seguro; a salvo
sale venta; barata
saleslady vendedora
salesman vendedor
salt sal
satisfaction satisfacción

satisfactory satisfactorio
(to) satisfy satisfacer,
　　　　complacer
　　satisfied
　　satisfied
　　savage salvaje

(to) save salvar; ahorrar; guardar
    saved
    saved
    savings ahorros
(to) say decir
    said
    said
    sea mar
    season estación;
        temporada
    seat asiento
(to) see ver
    saw
    seen
(to) seem parecer
    seemed
    seemed
(to) send mandar, enviar
    sent
    sent
(to) set poner
    set
    set
    several varios
(to) sew coser
    sewed
    sewed
    sewing costura
    shade sombra; matiz
(to) shake sacudir, mover;
        temblar
    shook
    shaken
(to) shake hands (with)
        dar la mano (a),
        saludar (a)
    shook hands with
    shaken hands with
    sharp agudo, filoso
    sheet sábana; hoja (*de papel*)
    shelf repisa, estante

    shelter albergue
(to) shine brillar
    shone
    shone
    ship barco
    shirt camisa
(to) shoot dar (*con un arma*)
    shot
    shot
(to) shoot (at) disparar (a)
    shot (at)
    shot (at)
    shot disparo, tiro
    shoulder hombro
    shout grito
(to) shout (at) gritar
    shouted (at)
    shouted (at)
    side lado
    sign señal, indicación;
        letrero
    sitting sentado
    silly (*adj.*) zonzo, tonto,
        bobo
    silver plata
    silverware (*sing.*)
        cubiertos
    simple sencillo
    since desde que; puesto
        que, ya que
(to) sing cantar
    sang
    sung
    singer cantante
    sister-in-law cuñada
(to) sit (down) sentarse
    sat (down)
    sat (down)
    skin piel; cutis
    skirt falda
    sky cielo, firmamento

slave esclavo
sled trineo
(to) sleep dormir
 slept
 slept
 sleepy: to be sleepy
  tener sueño
slim delgado
smart listo, inteligente
smell olor
(to) smell oler
 smelled
 smelled
smile sonrisa
(to) smile (at) sonreir
 smiled (at)
 smiled (at)
 smiling sonriente
smoke humo
(to) smoke fumar; humear
 smoked
 smoked
snake víbora, serpiente
snow nieve
(to) snow nevar
 snowed
 snowed
sock calcetín
soft suave, blando
softly suavemente;
  quedito
soil tierra
  (para sembrar)
soldier soldado
some alguno(s)
somebody alguien,
  alguna persona
something algo, alguna
  cosa
song canción
sore adolorido,

lastimado
so tan; so many tantos;
 so much tanto
so far hasta ahora
so (that) para que
sound sonido
(to) sound oírse
 sounded
 sounded
sour agrio, ácido
south sur
(to) speak hablar, platicar
 spoke
 spoken
speaker orador
special (adj.) especial
speech discurso
(to) spend gastar (dinero);
  pasar (tiempo)
 spent
 spent
spider araña
spider web telaraña
(to) spill derramar(se); tirar
  (líquido)
 spilled
 spilled
spring primavera
square cuadrado; plaza
(to) stand in line hacer cola,
  pararse en fila
 stood in line
 stood in line
(to) stand up ponerse de pie
 stood up
 stood up
star estrella
station estación (de
  ferrocarril)
(to) stay quedarse; alojarse
 stayed

stayed
(to) steal robar
stole
stolen
still todavía
stocking media
stomach-ache dolor de
estómago
(to) stop detenerse
stopped
stopped
storm tempestad
story cuento
straight derecho, recto
strange raro; curioso
stranger forastero;
extraño
stream arroyo
strength (*sing.*) fuerzas
student alumno
stupid estúpido
such (a) tal, semejante

such as tal(es) como
(to) suffer sufrir
suffered
suffered
summer verano
sun sol
sunny: it's sunny
hace sol, hay sol
surprise sorpresa
(to) surprise sorprender
surprised
surprised
surprising sorprendente
sweet dulce
(to) swim nadar
swam
swum
swimmer nadador
swimming natación
sympathy compasión;
simpatía

T

`tail rabo, cola
(to) take llevar, tomar
took
taken
(to) take a bath bañarse
(*en tina*)
took a bath
taken a bath
(to) take a shower bañarse
(*en regadera*)
took a shower
taken a shower
(to) take care of cuidar de, a;
atender a; encargarse
de

took care of
taken care of
(to) take off quitarse
took off
taken off
(to) take (something) away
(from) quitar
(algo) a; llevarse
(algo)
took (something) away
(from)
taken (something)
away (from)
talk plática
talkative locuaz, parlanchín

tea té
(to) teach enseñar
    taught
    taught
    teacher profesor
(to) tear rasgar, romper
    tore
    torn
    eeth dientes
(to) tell decir, contar
    told
    told
    test prueba, examen
(to) test probar (*no del sentido de gusto*)
    tested
    tested
    telephone` teléfono
    than que
    Thanksgiving (*U.S.A.*) día de acción de gracias
    Thanksgiving Day (*U.S.A.*) día de acción de gracias
    that que; ese(a); aquel(la); eso; aquello
    that one ése(a); aquél(la)
    their su(s) de ellos o ellas
    theirs el suyo (de ellos o de ellas)
    them los, las (*pron. obj.*)
    themselves ellos mismos, ellas mismas, se
    there are hay (*plural*)
    therefore así es que, por lo tanto
    there is hay (*sing.*)
    these estos(as); éstos(as)
    thick espeso; grueso
    thief ladrón

thieves ladrones
thin delgado
(to) think (of, about) pensar (en o de)
    thought (of, about)
    thought (of, about)
    thirsty: to be thirsty tener sed
    this este(a); esto
    this one éste(a)
    thorn púa; espina
    those esos(as), aquellos(as); ésos(as), aquéllos(as)
    though aunque
    thought pensamiento
    thoughtful atento; considerado
    thoughtless desatento; desconsiderado
    thousand: one thousand mil
    thread hilo
    throat garganta; sore throat dolor de garganta
    through por, a través de
(to) throw arrojar; tirar; echar
    threw
    thrown
(to) throw (something) away botar o tirar (algo)
    threw (something) away
    thrown (something) away
    ticket boleto
    tie corbata
(to) tie amarrar
    tied

tied

(to) tie (someone or something) up amarrar (a alguien o algo)

tied (someone or something) up

tied (someone or something) up

tight apretado, ajustado

to a; hasta

toe dedo del pie

together junto(s)

tomato jitomate

tongue lengua

tonight esta noche

too también; demasiado

too many demasiados

too much demasiado

tooth diente

(to) touch tocar, palpar

touched

touched

town pueblo

toy juguete

train tren

translation traducción

(to) travel viajar

traveled

traveled

traveler (*noun*) viajero

traveling (*adj.*) viajero

treasure tesoro

trip viaje

true verdadero

trunk trompa (*de elefante*); baúl

truth verdad

(to) try hard hacer lo posible (por), esforzarse (por)

tried hard

tried hard

(to) turn dar vuelta, voltear, doblar

turned

turned

(to) turn around voltear(se), darse vuelta

turned around

turned around

(to) turn off apagar, cerrar, parar

turned off

turned off

(to) turn on poner, encender, prender, abrir

turned on

turned on

(to) turn over voltear(se), volcar(se); remover

turned over

turned over

U

ugly feo

under debajo de, abajo

unfortunately desgraciadamente

unhappy infeliz

universe universo

until hasta; hasta que

use uso

used + (inf.) acostumbraba + (inf.)

useful útil

useless inútil

V

vacation vacaciones; **on
vacation** de
vacaciones
vegetable legumbre,
vegetal

visit visita
visitor visita, visitante
voice voz

W

(to) wait (for) esperar
waited (for)
waited (for)
(to) wake up despertar(se)
woke up
woke up
warm caliente; **I'm warm**
tengo calor; **it's warm**
hace calor
warning amonestación,
advertencia
watch reloj (*de mano o de
bolsillo*)
(to) watch observar; vigilar
watched
watched
(to) wear llevar puesto, usar
wore
worn
(to) wear out acabarse
wore out
worn out
(to) wear (something) out
acabársele a uno (algo)
wore (something) out
worn (something) out
weather tiempo
(*atmosférico*)
weave tejido (*de telas*)
(to) weave tejer (*en telar*)

wove
woven
weaver tejedor
weaving el acto de tejer
week end fin de semana
west oeste
whatever lo que
cualquier cosa que,
wheat trigo
whenever siempre que, en
cualquier tiempo que
sea, cuando sea, cada
vez que
wherever dondequiera
que, por dondequiera
que
which ¿cuál?; que
whichever el que,
cualquiera que
who ¿quién(es)?;
quien(es)
whoever quienquiera
que; quien, sea
quien sea
whole entero
whose ¿de quién?; de
quien, cuyo
wide ancho, amplio
widow viuda
(to) win ganar

won

won

wind viento

windy: it's windy
    hace aire

wing ala

winner (*sust.*) ganador

winning (*adj.*) ganador

winter invierno

wisdom sabiduría

wise sabio

wish deseo

(to) wish desear, querer

    wished

    wished

with con

without sin

wolf lobo

wolves lobos

wonderful maravilloso

wood madera

worker trabajador;
    obrero

world mundo

(to) worry (about)
    preocuparse (por)

    worried (about)

    worried (about)

worse peor (*comparativo*)

worst peor (*superlativo*)

(to) wrap envolver

    wrapped

    wrapped

(to) wrap (something) up
    envolver (algo)

    wrapped (something) up

    wrapped (something) up

writer escritor

wrong equivocado

XYZ

yard patio; espacio que
    rodea una casa

yellow amarillo

yet ya (*interrogativo*)
    not yet todavía no

your su(s) de Ud. o Uds.

yours el tuyo, la tuya, los
    tuyos, las tuyas; el

suyo, la suya, los
suyos, las suyas (de
Ud. o de Uds.)

yourself Ud. mismo, se;
    tú mismo, te

yourselves Uds. mismos; se

zoo zoológico

La publicación de esta obra la realizó
Editorial Trillas, S. A. de C. V.

División Administrativa, Av. Río Churubusco 385,
Col. Pedro María Anaya, C. P. 03340, México, D. F.
Tel. 56884233, FAX 56041364

División Comercial, Calz. de la Viga 1132, C. P. 09439
México, D. F. Tel. 56330995, FAX 56330870

Se imprimió en
Litográfica Ingramex, S. A. de C. V.
AO 75 XW